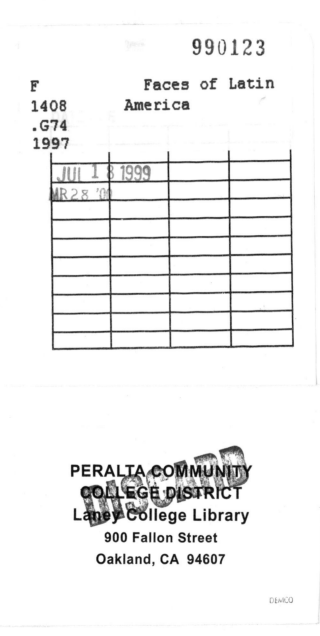

FACES OF
LATIN
AMERICA

LATIN AMERICA BUREAU

FACES OF LATIN AMERICA

Duncan Green

For Catherine, Calum and Finlay

LATIN AMERICA BUREAU

The Latin America Bureau is an independent research and publishing organisation. It works to broaden public understanding of issues of human rights and social and economic justice in Latin America and the Caribbean.

First published in 1991 by the Latin America Bureau (Research and Action) Ltd, 1 Amwell Street, London EC1R 1UL
Second edition, 1997

© Duncan Green 1991, 1997

A CIP catalogue record for this book is available from the British Library

ISBN: 1 899365 10 9

Written by Duncan Green
Edited by James Ferguson

Cover photographs: main picture, Alain Keler/Sygma; soldiers, Randy Taylor/Sygma; Kayapó child, Susan Cunningham; Guatemalan women, Mike Goldwater/Network; Diego Maradona, David Canon/Allsport

Cover design: Andy Dark
Trade distribution in the UK: Central Books, 99 Wallis Road, London E9 5LN
Distribution in North America: Monthly Review Press, 122 West 27th Street, New York, NY 10001

Printed and bound by Russell Press, Nottingham NG7 3HJ

Contents

Chapter 7: No Fit State: The State and Politics   **109**

Authoritarian and democratic traditions since independence.
Caudillos and caciques. Populism. The PRI. Military rule.
Democracy in the 1990s.

Chapter 8: Men at Arms: The Military   **127**

The army and politics. The Cold War and national security
doctrine. Military rule. End of the Cold War and the return to
democracy. Military in the 1990s.

Chapter 9: The Left: Guerrillas, Social Movements and the Struggle for Change   **145**

Urban and rural guerrilla movements. Social movements, the
role of church and women's groups. The left and electoral
politics after the Cold War.

Chapter 10: Women's Work: Gender and Politics   **165**

Machismo. The family. Gays. Women at work. Impact of
adjustment. Women and politics. Social movements.

Chapter 11: Race Against Time: Indigenous Peoples   **183**

Pre-Columbian civilisation and the conquest. Modern
highland and lowland Indians. Rebellion and resistance.

Chapter 12: Thy Kingdom Come: The Church   **201**

The traditional Catholic Church and the rise of liberation
theology. Life in the Base Christian Communities. The rise
of African and Protestant Evangelical churches.

List of tables and figures

Acronyms and Glossary of Spanish and Portuguese words

ARENA	*Alianza Republicana Nacionalista*
	Nationalist Republican Alliance (El Salvador)
CEB	*Comunidad Eclesial de Base*
	Base Christian Community
CLAI	Latin America Council of Churches
DEA	Drug Enforcement Agency
ELN	*Ejército de Liberación Nacional*
	National Liberation Army (Colombia)
ESG	*Escola Superior de Guerra*
	Higher War School
EZLN	*Ejército Zapatista de Liberación Nacional*
	Zapatista Army of National Liberation
FMLN	*Frente Farabundo Martí para la Liberación Nacional*
	Farabundo Martí National Liberation Front (El Salvador)
FPL	*Fuerzas Populares de Liberación – Farabundo Martí*
	Popular Liberation Forces (El Salvador)
FSLN	*Frente Sandinista de Liberación Nacional*
	Sandinista National Liberation Front
IMF	International Monetary Fund
M-19	*Movimiento 19 de Abril*
	19 April Movement (Colombia)
Mercosur	*Mercado Común del Sur*
	Southern Cone Common Market
MRTA	*Movimiento Revolucionario Túpac Amaru*
	Túpac Amaru Revolutionary Movement (Peru)
MST	*Movimento dos Trabalhadores Rurais Sem Terra*
	Landless Workers' Movement (Brazil)
NAFTA	North American Free Trade Agreement
NGOs	Non-governmental Organisations
OPEC	Organisation of Petroleum Exporting Countries
PDVSA	*Petróleos de Venezuela S.A.*
	Venezuelan state oil company
PRD	*Partido de la Revolución Democrática*
	Party of the Democratic Revolution (Mexico)
PRI	*Partido Revolucionario Institucional*
	Institutional Revolutionary Party (Mexico)
PT	*Partido dos Trabalhadores*
	Workers' Party (Brazil)
Sendero Luminoso (Shining Path)	*Partido Comunista del Peru – por el Sendero Luminoso de José Carlos Mariátegui*
	Communist Party of Peru – for the Shining Path of José Carlos Mariátegui

URNG	*Unidad Revolucionaria Nacional Guatemalteca*
	Guatemalan National Revolutionary Unity
WBT	Wycliffe Bible translators, also known as the Summer Institute of Linguistics (US)

altiplano	high plateau region, Bolivia
cacique	local political boss
candomblé	religion of African origin, Brazil
campesino	peasant
capoeira	traditional Brazilian slave dance combining both dance and ritualised martial arts
caudillo	leader, political boss
chicha	corn beer
comedores	communal kitchens
compañeros	comrades
conscientización	education and organisation to counteract injustice
Contras	Nicaraguan counter-revolutionaries
criollo	Latin-American-born descendant of Spanish settlers
descamisados	the 'shirtless ones', the dispossessed of Argentina
ejidos	communally-owned Indian lands, Mexico
empate	rural confrontation, Brazil
encomenderos	landowners and beneficiaries of the encomienda
encomienda	forced labour system
favela	shanty town, Brazil
fazenda	large estate, Brazil
foco	small nucleus of guerrilla fighters
foquismo	theory of guerrilla warfare based on focos
garimpeiros	gold-prospectors, Brazil
gaucho	Argentine cowboy
gringo	uncomplimentary name for North American/European
hacienda	large traditional farms
huaynu	traditional Andean musical form
justicialismo	Peronism
ladinos	Spanish-speaking people of mixed Indian and Spanish descent
macho	male, masculine, tough
malocas	communal houses
maquila	manufacturing assembly industry
maquiladora	maquila factory
marianismo	female equivalent of machismo
mestizo	people of mixed Spanish and Indian descent
mita	forced labour system
nahual	animist spirit
orixá	candomblé deity
Pai de santo	candomblé priest
pampas	Argentine grasslands
tamales	maize cakes, El Salvador
telenovela	soap opera
tío	'uncle', god of the underworld, Bolivia
toma	land invasion
tortillas	maize pancakes

**Latin America
and the Caribbean**

Peters Projection

Latin America in Figures

Country	1	2	3	4	5	6
Argentina	30 (1)	34.2	8110	72	24	4
Bolivia	111 (17)	7.2	770	60	74	17
Brazil	58 (9)	159.1	2970	67	57	17
Chile	33 (4)	14.0	3520	72	15	5
Colombia	49 (8)	36.3	1670	70	37	9
Costa Rica	31 (2)	3.3	2400	77	13	5
Cuba*	79 (12)	10.9	-	75	12	5
Dominican Republic	87 (14)	7.6	1330	70	41	18
Ecuador	64 (10)	11.2	1280	69	49	10
El Salvador	115 (20)	5.6	1360	67	44	29
Guatemala	112 (18)	10.3	1200	65	48	44
Guyana*	103 (16)	0.8	350	65	47	2
Haiti	145 (22)	7.0	230	57	85	55
Honduras	114 (19)	5.8	600	66	42	27
Mexico	48 (7)	88.5	4180	71	35	10
Nicaragua	117 (21)	4.2	340	67	50	34
Panama	43 (5)	2.6	2580	73	25	9
Paraguay	85 (13)	4.8	1580	68	38	8
Peru	91 (15)	23.2	2110	65	64	11
Suriname*	75 (11)	0.4	1180	71	27	8
Uruguay	32 (3)	3.2	4660	73	20	3
Venezuela	44 (6)	21.2	2760	71	23	9
Latin America and the Caribbean		470.9	3340	68	41	13

Columns and Sources
1. Human Development Index, world ranking, based on a composite index of social and economic indicators. Latin American ranking in brackets. UNDP Human Development Report 1996
2. Population, millions, 1994, World Bank, *World Development Report 1996*
3. Gross National Product per capita, US dollars, 1994, World Bank, *World Development Report 1996*
4. Life expectancy at birth, 1994, World Bank, *World Development Report 1996*
5. Infant mortality per thousand live births, UNDP *Human Development Report 1996*
6. Illiteracy as a percentage of population over 15, World Bank, *World Development Report 1996*

* Countries absent from *World Development Report 1996*, figures from *Human Development Report,* 1996

Introduction

Carnival in Rio; Inca ruins and condors; witty Zapatista *comandantes* in Mexico; Colombian cocaine barons in plush, purpose-built prisons; sleek, best-selling novelists on the TV; glue-sniffing street children; death squads and disappearances; snapshots of a continent that fail to add up to a sense of place and people.

Latin America has been portrayed to the outside world through stereotype and myth since *El Dorado*, the mirage of a golden king in a golden city, first excited the Spanish *conquistadores'* greed. Back in Europe, idealised accounts of the Inca and Mayan civilisations inspired Thomas More's *Utopia*. The West has both plundered and been dazzled by Latin America ever since.

This book tries to fill in some of the missing pieces, to make sense of the jumbled images that pour from television, newspaper, novel and tourist brochure. It is about Latin Americans, not just generals and presidents, but the millions of faces of the shanty towns, small farms, mountains and rainforests, factories and plantations. It explores the processes which have shaped their lives, the jobs they do, where they live, and how they see and want to change their world. Through the lives of its inhabitants, the book attempts to capture the everyday ebullience and dynamism of Latin America, a world away from the cynicism and corruption of much of its formal political life.

Far from being the passive victims of circumstance, ordinary Latin Americans possess depths of courage and creativity, enabling them to confront with humour and grace a seemingly endless array of problems: how to feed and educate their families, find a home, improve their neighbourhood. In recent years, many such attempts at self-help have been led by women, struggling to free themselves from the stifling values of *machismo*. The indigenous peoples of Latin America have also belied their reputation for passivity by fighting vigorously to defend their ways of life.

They face a dispiriting number of obstacles. Internationally, Latin America is a region in decline, still largely dependent on the export of its raw materials, with an ever-diminishing slice of world trade. The debt crisis of the 1980s has given way to the harsh world of the 1990s, when economic growth does not create jobs, and the gulf between rich and poor grows ever wider. At home, the rural poor must struggle for a plot of land on which to feed their families in an environment devastated by deforestation, soil erosion, and unregulated mining and industrial development. Landless peasants flock to the shanty towns that encircle the region's cities, where they must improvise both a house and a means of earning a living if they are to survive. Although currently content to remain in their barracks, the military, which has rarely proved a friend of the poor, retain enormous power.

Faces of Latin America was first published in 1991, in the run-up to the 500th anniversary of Christopher Columbus' first voyage to the Americas. Much has happened since then: civil wars have ended in Central America; an unprecedented period of elected government has held sway; neoliberal economics has steamrollered across the continent at vast human cost. This second edition includes a considerable amount of new material covering developments up to 1997, and adds a new chapter on the history and nature of the Latin American state.

I would like to thank the following for their help and advice in producing this new edition: Andy Atkins, Phillip Berryman, Isabel Danel, James Ferguson, John King, Lorenzo Meyer, Robyn Morales, Liz Morrell, James Painter, Andrew Paxman, Renee Pendergrass, George Philip, Jan Rocha, Fred Rosen, Rachel Sieder and William Rowe, as well as the numerous lecturers on both sides of the Atlantic who responded to a questionnaire on how best to update the first edition. Most of all I would like to thank the thousands of Latin American men, women and children who over the years have devoted hours of their time talking to a nosy gringo with a notebook and too many questions.

The quincentenary briefly aroused great passion on both sides of the Atlantic, as people took stock of Latin America's scarred history. Since then, the Columbus media circus has moved on. In North America and Europe, Latin America still surfaces sporadically in the news, but is largely confined to the financial pages, where it is lauded as a land of economic dynamism and opportunity for the foreign investor. Yet such optimism rings hollow in the forgotten shanty towns and peasant villages of the continent. If this book has one principal purpose, it is to celebrate the vigour, hope and inspiration of Latin America's people, and to urge its readers not to turn their backs on them.

Duncan Green, February 1997

Indian woman examines tin ore, looking for higher grade deposits, Potosí, Bolivia

Chronology

1493	Columbus introduces sugar-cane in Hispaniola
1545	Silver discovered in Cerro Rico, Potosí
1690s	Brazilian gold rush begins in Minas Gerais
1808-26	Latin American independence: Britain takes over from Spain as the major trade partner and foreign power
1922	Venezuela strikes oil
1930s	Great Depression – collapse of commodity prices
1938	Nationalisation of Mexican oil industry
Early 80s	Beginning of cocaine boom
1982	Start of debt crisis, leading to renewed emphasis on commodity exports
1993	Head of the Medellín cartel Pablo Escobar killed in a shoot-out with Colombian police
1995	Total area sown with coca reaches record height

The Curse of Wealth   1

The Commodity Trade

'The Indians have suffered, and continue to suffer, the curse of their own wealth. That is the drama of all Latin America.'
Eduardo Galeano, *Open Veins of Latin America*, 1973

Fourteen thousand feet up on the Bolivian plateau, Cerro Rico ('Rich Hill') looms high over the bleak mining town of Potosí. A giant rust-red spoil heap, it tells the story of Bolivia's cruel past and impoverished present. For two centuries after the Spanish conquistadores marched into the Andes and defeated the Inca empire, a stream of silver ore flowed down the slopes of Cerro Rico, through the furnaces and mints of Potosí and over the sea to Spain. Hundreds of thousands of press-ganged Indian labourers died bringing out the ore.

The silver rush made 17th-century Potosí into the largest city in the Hispanic world and earned Cerro Rico a place on the Bolivian national flag, but today only some fine colonial churches recall the days when the streets were literally paved with silver. For the Corpus Christi procession of 1658 the authorities ordered that the cobbles be removed in the centre of the city and be replaced with solid silver bars.

Boomtown Potosí was a chaotic, brawling city of 160,000 people, including, according to a census in 1601, 800 professional gamblers and 120 prostitutes. Today, some Latin Americans still describe immense wealth with the phrase 'worth a Potosí', first coined by Cervantes in *Don Quixote*. But behind the splendour of the churches and the antics of the Spaniards lay the grim reality of the *mita*, the Spanish-imposed system by which each Indian community had to send a portion of its able-bodied men to work in the mines, working shifts of up to 36 hours, only to be swindled of what little wages they were due.

Cerro Rico is now an anthill of 5,000 tunnels, where self-employed miners scratch a perilous living from what the Spanish left behind. 'In the old days the veins were a yard thick. Now they're half an inch,' says Marco Mamani, a young Indian miner. 'It's like a tree – the Spaniards took the trunk and left us the little branches.' For many years, Potosí has been the poorest region of the poorest country in South America.

Potosí's path from poverty to riches and back to even greater poverty is an extreme example of the process which has dominated Latin American development, the commodity trade. Although the exact definition varies, commodities are the raw materials which drive the world's economy. They include natural resources, such as oil and copper, and agricultural products like wheat or coffee. Europe's insatiable appetite for commodities was the driving force behind the centuries of colonial expansion which left the largest part of what is now called the Third World under the rule of competing European powers.

Ever since the conquest, Latin America has produced commodities for export – coffee, tin, oil, sugar – and used the proceeds to import manufactured products from industrialised nations in Europe, and later from the US and Japan. The richer nations used their power to keep commodity prices low, playing one desperate producer country off against another and when necessary using their military and technological might to reinforce their supremacy. In human terms the unequal struggle between commodity producers and industrialised powers has condemned millions of the Third World's people to lives of suffering and want. Only in the 20th century have the larger countries like Brazil and Mexico developed large-scale industry, and even then much of it has been under foreign control.

TABLE 1: MAJOR WORLD COMMODITIES

Commodity	Latin America and Caribbean's share of world production (%)	Value of annual world trade
Oil (1994)	12.6	$338 bn
Cocaine (1990)	100	$17 bn
Copper (1995)	34.0	$16.1 bn
Coffee (1994)	53.8	$11.9 bn
Sugar (1994)	31.0	$10.0 bn
Cotton (1994)	5.4	$7.3 bn
Soybeans (1994)	33.3	$7.2 bn
Bananas (1994)	63.4	$4.1bn

Sources: FAO Production Yearbook 1994, International Petroleum Encyclopaedia 1996, World Metal Statistics Yearbook 1996, The Economist

Within Latin America commodities have chiefly enriched those engaged in exporting them abroad. Export crops such as cotton or sugar are more profitable when grown on large plantations, so the expansion of cash crops led to a concentration of land ownership and wealth in the hands of a few very powerful individuals. Mining interests were historically controlled by entrepreneurs like Simón Patiño, Bolivia's greatest tin baron, who rose from poverty to become one of the ten wealthiest men on earth. From the luxury of his European home, Patiño could make or break Bolivia's governments, acting as an absentee landlord towards an entire country.

Migrant cotton pickers, Bolivia

The fabulous wealth of a few commodity exporters failed to 'trickle down' to the poor majority, since it was either invested abroad or used to import luxury goods. Farmers could make more money growing crops for export than by growing food to sell at home. The commodity barons felt no need to create a domestic market by redistributing wealth more evenly, since this would have meant giving up some of their privileges. The source of their wealth and power lay overseas; all they required at home was cheap and docile labour. When the workforce in their mines or plantations demanded better wages or living conditions, the commodity magnates were quite prepared to use the most extreme violence to prevent them winning. In El Salvador during the 1980s, the heads of the coffee-growing families were believed to run the 'death squads' that killed tens of thousands of peasant activists and trade unionists.

White Gold

The European colonists pursued different commodities depending on the soil, climate, mineral deposits and accessibility of each region. On his second voyage to the Americas in 1493, Christopher Columbus brought sugar-cane to Hispaniola (now the Dominican Republic) and it flourished. Sugar

subsequently fuelled Brazil's first and greatest commodity boom. Per acre the 'white gold' produces four times the food energy of potatoes and ten times that of wheat, and sugar was in great demand to feed Europe's new industrial working class. Brazil's sugar boom was centred in the Northeast, around Salvador de Bahia.

Sugar is a capital-intensive crop, requiring substantial investment to part-process the cane immediately after cutting, before it can be shipped off to foreign refineries. In Brazil, the Dutch West Indies Company initially financed the sugar industry. The monotonous cane fields rapidly spread across the Northeast, squeezing out food crops such as beans and maize, so that even in the best years of the sugar boom, there was chronic malnutrition. Today in the Northeast little has changed: on the ten metre strip of ground between the road and the barbed wire fences of the sugar estates, landless peasants hack at the soil with handtools, planting food crops. The verges belong to the state and therefore are the only places which the peasants can squat and farm, safe from the depredations of the sugar barons. Every few miles, behind the fences, the opulent whitewashed house of a sugar grower shines among the green cane-fields.

The Dutch later expanded into the Caribbean, which was nearer to the European market. In Brazil, the soil was already losing its fertility through overuse. By the 18th century, the Caribbean had completely eclipsed northeast Brazil: Haiti's exports to Europe at that time exceeded those of all

thirteen American colonies put together. As production rose, prices fell, and Brazil's Northeast became one of the most deprived areas of the continent. Refugees fled its famine- and drought-stricken lands and headed for the next commodity boom – the gold-rush in the south.

An elusive El Dorado. poor miners haul gold-rich soil at the open-cast gold mine, Serra Pelada, Brazil.

Sugar also left its mark on Brazil's racial composition. The plantations were worked by African slaves, victims of a deadly but lucrative trade dominated by British slavers. Today the people are largely a blend of black African and white European immigrant stock, with an unmistakable 'pigmentocracy'. Although the Brazilian government denies claims of racism, most black people are poor, most rich people are white.

Following the OPEC price rises of the 1970s, Brazilian sugar has had a revival as the government has struggled to overcome its dependence on imported oil by trying to replace petrol with 'gasohol' – sugar-based alcohol. The sugar plantations briefly resumed their march across the Northeast, driving out new generations of peasant farmers and forcing them to take jobs as poorly-paid plantation labourers. However, the gasohol boom depended on oil prices, and when prices fell in the 1990s, many sugar plantations went bankrupt. Now landless peasants are starting to invade the newly-idle sugar lands.

Boom and Bust

Gold was discovered in the Brazilian state of Minas Gerais in the 1690s, and came on stream just as Portugal signed a trade agreement with Britain. Brazil's gold duly underwrote British industrialisation, and the accumulated gold reserves later paid for Britain's war against Napoleon.

Hides drying ready for export, Argentina. Exports of wool, hides and beef made Argentina into a major world power by the early 20th century.

Although Brazil's boom-bust cycles have been the most spectacular, they have occurred at regular intervals all over the continent right up to the present day. In El Salvador the indigo industry collapsed following the discovery of synthetic dyes in 19th-century Germany. In the northern deserts of Chile, the nitrate fields which had provided fertilisers for Europe's agriculture, and over which Chile had fought a war with Peru and Bolivia, became worthless overnight in 1909 when a German chemist discovered how to make artificial fertilisers. In the 1980s, the bottom fell out of the Caribbean's sugar market as US manufacturers switched to maize-based sweeteners and the Europeans increased their production of sugar beet.

Some commodities have produced better long term results than others. Demand for temperate climate products such as meat and grain is more steady than that for tropical products such as coffee and sugar, whose prices therefore swing more wildly. In Argentina, the cattle and grain trades laid the basis for significant economic development making it perhaps the tenth largest world power in 1914. In Brazil, the coffee boom which gave the country between fifty and seventy per cent of the world market between 1850 and 1950 made São Paulo into the economic boilerhouse of the most powerful nation in Latin America.

The commodity trade has shaped both European and Latin American history. The flow of gold and silver through Spain and Portugal to the manufacturing nations of Holland, France and Britain financed the early stages of their development as world industrial powers. After most Latin American nations won their independence in the early 19th century, Britain rapidly became the dominant economic influence. In 1824 the British Foreign Minister George Canning wrote to a friend, 'the deed is done, the nail is

Take his whole equipment – examine everything about him – and what is there not of raw hide that is not British? If his wife has a gown, ten to one it is made in Manchester; the camp-kettle in which he cooks his food, the earthenware he eats from, the knife, his poncho, spurs, bit, are all imported from England.

Description of pampas *gaucho* (cowboy) by British consul in La Plata. Sir Woodbine Parish, *Buenos Ayres and the Provinces of the Rio de la Plata,* London, 1839

In all of Brazil's haciendas the master and his slaves dress in the products of free labour, and nine-tenths of them are British. Britain supplies all the capital needed for the internal improvements in Brazil and manufactures all the utensils in common use, from the spade on up, and nearly all the luxury and practical items from the pin to the costliest clothing...Great Britain supplies Brazil with its steam and sailing ships, and paves and repairs its streets, lights its cities with gas, builds its railways, exploits its mines, is its banker, puts up its telegraph wires, carries its mail, builds its furniture, motors, wagons...

James Watson Webb, US Ambassador in Rio, c.1865

driven, Spanish America is free; and if we do not mismanage our affairs sadly, she is English.'

The first fifty years after independence were a time of political and economic chaos, but from the 1870s onwards, a new commodity boom took off, lasting until the great depression of the 1930s. Beef and grain from the Argentine pampas; Chilean copper, Brazilian coffee, Central American bananas, Peruvian silver and Cuban sugar led the way in a continental export boom which made thousands of fortunes, many of them British. British investment in Latin America, concentrated in railways and telecommunications, went up nine-fold from 1870 to 1913, by which time it represented two-thirds of all foreign investment in the region.

When necessary, the British government used its political clout to give its businesses a helping hand. In 1879 when Chile embarked on the War of the Pacific against Peru and Bolivia, the then US Secretary of State, James Blaine, commented, 'one shouldn't speak of a Chilean/Peruvian war, but rather of an English war against Peru with Chile as an instrument.' Britain's reward lay in the hostile deserts which Chile seized from Peru, where British capital bought up the world's greatest deposits of nitrates, used as fertilisers in agriculture.

By the early 20th century, Britain had been overtaken by the US as the major continental power. Washington's hemispheric ambitions began with the Monroe Doctrine of 1823, which declared that 'the American continents, by the free and independent condition which they have assumed and maintained, are henceforth not to be considered as subject for colonisation by the European powers.' The US steadily expanded its economic strength and political influence throughout the 19th century and came of age after its decisive defeat of Spain in the Cuban-Spanish war of 1898. The victory marked a symbolic changing of the guard, ushering in the 'American century' in Latin America.

Since the 1960s, European and Asian countries such as Japan and Germany have risen to become major economic influences, but they do not yet dispute US political dominance in the region.

Rise of the Multinationals

Up to the late 19th century, European and US businesses used their capital and control over transport, processing and marketing to ensure they obtained a low price from local growers of agricultural commodities. However, by the end of the century increasingly powerful US companies had decided to take over production as well in order to achieve 'vertical integration' - control over each stage of production, transport and marketing in their chosen product. The pioneers were the banana companies like United Fruit and Standard Fruit which acquired so much power over domestic politics in countries like Honduras, that these countries became pejoratively known as 'banana republics'. In the 1920s, one banana baron boasted of his company's control over local politicians, observing that 'in Honduras a mule costs more than a deputy.' Since then the multinational companies have steadily extended their grip to most key areas of Latin America's economy, including virtually all mineral extraction, the most dynamic areas of industry and many agricultural commodities.

Multinationals' heavy-handed behaviour led to a backlash in the shape of trade union mobilisation and occasional government attempts to nationalise their holdings. This prompted a rethink, and agricultural multinationals increasingly prefer to concentrate on the transport and marketing of a product, which are the most profitable areas.

Unilever is one of the largest food manufacturers in the world, and is a giant among multinational companies. Its annual turnover in 1996 was US$49 billion, giving this one company an economy comparable in size to that of Chile, the sixth largest in Latin America. Founded in the early years of the century by an amalgamation of British and Dutch companies, its operations now span the globe, employing some 300,000 people world-wide.

Like many of the largest multinationals, Unilever is less well known than the brand names of some of its products, including Flora margarine, Birds Eye and Walls frozen foods, Liptons teas, Persil washing powder and Calvin Klein perfumes. It operates throughout Latin America, from soap factories in Brazil to salmon farms in the south of Chile.

Multinational companies such as General Foods (coffee), Amstar (sugar) and Cargill (grain) make up an informal coalition with western banks and commodity brokers which exerts a powerful grip on the world market in each product. Their sheer size also places them in a strong bargaining position with third world governments which are competing for sources of jobs and investment.

Black Gold

Petroleum is the greatest commodity of all. As a fuel and source of plastics and chemicals, it drives world industry. Latin America contains major world oil exporters, such as Mexico and Venezuela, and many other less fortunate countries condemned to dependence on oil imports. Over the last seventy years, control over oil has become a politically explosive issue. In 1938, Mexico became the first Latin American country to nationalise its oil industry, and in subsequent decades other countries followed suit, weakening the grip of the seven great US and European-owned oil multinationals, known as the 'seven sisters'. Such was the importance of oil that governments were willing to incur US displeasure in the process, as when General Velasco's military government in Peru seized the installations of the International Petroleum Corporation in 1968.

In 1960 Venezuela joined Saudi Arabia and five smaller producers to found the Organisation of Petroleum Exporting Countries, OPEC, which became the king of commodity cartels. Mexico refused to join for fear of US trade sanctions, but both countries cashed in when OPEC shocked the industrialised world with large price rises in 1973/4 and 1978/9, taking oil from US$2.70 to US$40 a barrel. The oil producers paid the price for their defiance, as recession cut demand for oil and consumer countries responded to higher prices by investing in alternative sources of energy and energy conservation. In 1986 the ensuing price collapse took the price back down to US$10 a barrel.

State oil companies such as Petrobras in Brazil, Pemex in Mexico, and Venezuela's PDVSA became giants, wielding great economic power and channelling large amounts of cash back into exploration and development of new oil reserves, as well as funding the burgeoning public sector. Oil transformed Venezuela from a rural backwater to one of Latin America's wealthiest nations, although the poor did not always share in the bonanza. The price of success was pollution and debt, as Venezuela borrowed heavily

Oil exploration in the Amazon rainforest, in this case by Brazil's state oil company, Petrobras, has been blamed for deforestation and water pollution.

on the strength of its oil reserves. In Mexico, Pemex ran up a debt of US$15 billion by the early 1980s.

State companies ensured national control over a vital resource and were able to use profits to benefit their countries. By investing in exploration, they managed to quadruple Latin America's known reserves between 1974-88, as countries such as Colombia and Brazil became significant new oil producers. Yet they were also plagued by problems; a shortage of qualified managers was aggravated as governments made political appointments within the bureaucracy. Corruption and inefficiency reduced economic benefits, while nationalisation risked closing the door to the oil multinationals' modern technology.

Even in the late 1980s, as structural adjustment programmes obliged governments to privatise state assets, they were reluctant to sell off state oil companies. So far, only Argentina and Bolivia have gone for wholesale privatisation. Elsewhere, oil's enormous political significance has prompted huge domestic opposition to such a move, backed up by strikes by oil workers in countries such as Brazil, Peru and Bolivia. Yet governments badly need injections of foreign capital and technology in the oil and gas sector. As a result, they have opted instead for slowly opening up the oil sector by granting exploration and production licenses to multinational oil companies, and in some cases going into joint ventures with them.

Commodities and Development

Over the 500 years since the arrival of the Spanish, the commodity trade has exacted enormous social costs. In the mines the Spanish forced Indian labourers to work in inhuman conditions until hundreds of thousands died from the dust, poor food and disease. Today in Bolivia miners still die young, their lungs destroyed by dust and poisonous fumes which could have been removed by simple ventilation equipment.

In December 1922, Venezuela struck vast reserves of oil, changing the country's destiny overnight. Oil multinationals swiftly began operations, and by 1936, export earnings from oil were nine times those of coffee, Venezuela's other main commodity export. Yet oil wealth did not bring development. As dollars poured in, Venezuela's exchange rate became overvalued, destroying the competitivity of its other exports. Cheap imports undercut and wiped out domestic industry. Venezuela became an oil junkie, a consumer culture that produces nothing, its fortunes tied indissolubly to the international price of oil. When prices rocketed in the 1970s, government spending and corruption rose. When they fell back in the 1980s, Venezuela slumped into a debt crisis from which it is still to recover.

'Today, Caracas is a supersonic, deafening, air-conditioned nightmare, a centre of oil culture that might pass as the capital of Texas. Caracas chews gum and loves synthetic products and canned foods; it never walks, and poisons the clean air of the valley with the fumes of its motorisation; its fever to buy, consume, obtain, spend, use, get hold of everything leaves it no time to sleep. From the surrounding hillside hovels made of garbage, half a million forgotten people observe the sybaritic scene....

[Lake Maracaibo] is a forest of towers. Within these iron structures the endlessly bobbing pumps have for half a century pumped up all the opulence and all the poverty of Venezuela. Alongside, flames lick skyward, burning the natural gas in a carefree gift to the atmosphere. There are pumps even in houses and on street corners of towns that spouted up, like the oil, along the lakeside – towns where clothing, food and walls are stained black with oil, and where even whores are known by oil nicknames, such as "the Pipeline", "The Four Valves", "The Derrick", "The Hoist".'

Eduardo Galeano, *Open Veins of Latin America*, New York, 1973

In the countryside the introduction of each new export crop has led to more land coming under the control of big landowners and more peasants being expelled. The onward march of export agriculture has been largely responsible for the tidal waves of displaced peasants that broke over the continent's cities over the last fifty years, creating the sprawling shanty towns which surround the continent's small 'first world' city centres. By allowing peasant farmers, who generally grow food crops like maize and beans, to be driven out to make way for export crops, many countries have lost their self-sufficiency in food production – Mexico, where maize was first cultivated, now has to import it.

On a national level the commodity trade has proved an unreliable basis for Latin America's development. In the long term, commodities are liable to follow a boom-bust cycle, rather than steady growth, for a variety of reasons:

• Substitution: the discovery of a cheaper or better-quality substitute, as in the case of indigo in El Salvador.

TABLE 2: COMMODITY DEPENDENCE, figures for 1994

Country	Main commodity exports	% of total exports	All commodities as % of total exports
Argentina	oilseeds/oils	17.8	67.2
Belize	cane sugar	33.8	83
Bolivia	metals and metal ores	43.1	77.8
Brazil	iron ore	5.35	45.2
	coffee	5.1	
Chile	copper	33	83.6
Colombia	coffee	22.4	63.1
Costa Rica (a)	bananas	24.9	74.4
Ecuador	crude petroleum	31.2	92.6
	bananas	18.4	
El Salvador	coffee	32.5	55.3
Guatemala	coffee	21.2	68.7
Honduras	coffee	30.7	85
	bananas	18.2	
Mexico	crude petroleum	10.9	22.6 (b)
Nicaragua	coffee	21.7	86.9
	cattle	18	
Panama	bananas	38.3	82.3
Paraguay	soya	27.2	86.1
	cotton	18.5	
Peru	fish meal	16.9	86.1
	copper	16.6	
Uruguay	meat	10.7	57.1
Venezuela	crude petroleum and petroleum products	75.3	86.2

(a) 1992 figure   (b) includes maquiladora goods

Source: ECLAC Statistical Yearbook on Latin America and the Caribbean 1995

• Exhaustion: either the exhaustion of mineral deposits, as occurred with Bolivian silver, or impoverishment of the soil, as befell the sugar plantations of northeast Brazil.

• Development of cheaper production methods: the British smuggled out rubber seeds from Brazil and started a more cost-effective rubber industry in Malaysia; improved technology has allowed US tin can manufacturers to use less tin per can, thereby undermining demand for Bolivia's tin.

• Changes in patterns of demand: in recent years the taste for better coffee in Europe and the US has increased demand for high-quality beans from Central America and Colombia, and reduced demand for lower-quality Brazilian beans.

The price fluctuations common to commodities make planning extremely difficult and can lead to disaster. For example, in 1980, when sugar earned 17 cents a pound on the world market, the Nicaraguan government decided to build the Timal sugar mill, capable of producing sugar at 12 cents a pound. By the time the mill was ready in 1985, sugar's world price had dropped to 4 cents, invalidating the whole project. To make matters worse, countries are often extremely dependent on one or two commodities, exacerbating their vulnerability to any sudden fluctuations.

Even when prices rise, economies find difficulty coping with the windfall. Governments often spend the money on increasing public sector spending. Though in theory, this could lay the basis for future economic development through improving health and education, in practice, sudden and unplanned public sector growth has often encouraged corruption and inefficiency.

In 1996, when an analysis of 97 economies by two Harvard professors found hard statistical evidence that growth is higher among those economies with fewer natural resources, *The Economist* concluded, 'Next time you hear of a poor country that has suddenly struck oil or diamonds, do not sit back and give thanks that its future is assured. Tremble, rather, for its poor people – for they will be the last to benefit.'

In an attempt to avoid the problems of price fluctuations and trade wars between producer nations, many third world countries have joined forces in setting up price stabilisation agreements. But even when they have succeeded in guaranteeing more stable prices, these agreements have often merely encouraged producer nations to increase production, eventually leading to oversupply, a price war and the collapse of the agreement.

Many Latin American governments have recognised the pitfalls of commodity dependence and tried to avoid them. One obvious path was to develop local industry which would replace dependence on foreign imports. The rush for industry is discussed in chapter 5.

'Import substitution' has faced many problems. In order to protect fledgling local industries, governments had to prevent them being undercut by cheap foreign goods. This meant either an outright ban, or taxing imports to make them more expensive than locally-made products (tariff barriers). Any attempt to impose tariffs challenged the colonial, and later British or American, doctrine of 'free trade' and left the country open to all kinds of sanctions. As one Argentine minister explained in the early 19th century, 'We are not in a position to take measures against foreign trade, particularly British, because we are bound to that nation by large debts and would expose ourselves to a rupture that would cause much harm.' However, one nation in the Americas did successfully defy the British – the United States of America. In a prophetic speech the US President Ulysses S. Grant (1869-77) said:

> For centuries England has relied on protection, has carried it to extremes and has obtained satisfactory results from it. There is no doubt that it is to this system that it owes its present strength. After two centuries, England has found it convenient to adopt free trade because it thinks that protection can no longer offer it anything. Very well then, gentlemen, my knowledge of our country leads me to believe that within 200 years, when America has gotten out of protection all that it can offer, it too will adopt free trade.

President Grant apparently underestimated the speed of history – the US became the world's foremost economic power and its most determined advocate of free trade within seventy years of his death.

For fifty years, from the Great Depression of the 1930s to the debt crisis of the 1980s, Latin American governments turned to import substitution as their new development model, while still relying on commodities to bring in

Sean Sprague/Panos

The chewing of coca leaves, the raw material for cocaine, is traditional in the Andes. Coca is legal and sold in street markets, Bolivia.

most of their export earnings. Since 1982, the continent has returned to its historical reliance on commodities, as structural adjustment programmes across the region have put industrialisation into reverse and given new emphasis to 'export-led growth' based on commodities and cheap labour (see chapter 5). The emphasis has been on reviving traditional activities such as mining, and diversifying agriculture into new, luxury products such as fresh fruit and cut flowers. Although diversification reduces the extreme vulnerability produced by relying on a single product, it does not solve the more long-term problems of the commodity trade. The growth areas of the world economy are in high-tech industry and services, not commodities - successful economies produce computers, not kiwi fruit. Reliance on commodities risks confining Latin America for ever to the backwaters of the world economy, while the new products can have disastrous impacts on the environment (see chapter 3).

Cocaine - Just another Commodity?

'Were it not for the drug's effect abroad, coca would be lauded as an ideal export crop'
Financial Times, 15 February 1990

Over the last fifteen years, the surge in the production of coca, the raw material for cocaine, has provided Latin America's latest commodity boom. Although figures in this area are never more than informed guesswork, by 1990 the annual wholesale world cocaine trade was estimated at US$17 billion, making it the second most valuable commodity in the world after oil. Every gram was produced from coca leaves grown by Latin American peasants.

In the Andean countries of Peru, Bolivia and Colombia, thousands of small farmers depend on the scrubby coca bushes for their livelihoods. Many

18   *FACES OF LATIN AMERICA*

of them semi-process the leaves by treading them in pits filled with kerosene. The resulting coca paste is then smuggled to clandestine laboratories dotted about the inaccessible corners of the continent, where it is turned into refined cocaine powder before being shipped to the US, Europe and Japan. In 1992, the US government estimated there were 5.3 million consumers of cocaine in the US.

The cocaine boom began in the early 1980s, even though the drug had been known for over a hundred years and was used in various forms by such illustrious figures as Sigmund Freud and Queen Victoria. The trade differs from the normal pattern for commodities in that Latin American traffickers control the profitable stages of its journey to market and take the lion's share of the profits.

For the peasants, coca is a dream crop – its leaves can be harvested several times a year, and it needs minimal attention; buyers come to the peasants, solving the difficulties of getting the product to market which dog other crops in the remote areas where coca is grown. Moreover, its illegality ensures that big companies will not enter the market to compete and drive prices down.

However, coca's illegality has fuelled corruption and criminality, in many cases undermining Latin America's political stability. In Mexico, the brother of former president Carlos Salinas was arrested in 1995, suspected of amassing a drug-funded fortune during his brother's presidency; Colombia's President Samper spent his first two years in office fighting off allegations and investigations over the alleged financing of his 1994 election campaign by the Cali cartel; in Paraguay the general in charge of the country's anti-drug unit was gunned down while preparing to release evidence linking businessmen, military officers and the police to drugs. Drug gangs and drug use are both on the increase; in Rio, local drug lords effectively run many *favelas*.

Internationally, drugs remains one of the few Latin American stories which regularly makes headlines, chiefly because of its domestic importance within the US. Since 1989, successive US presidents have made the 'war on drugs' a national priority, spending US$80 billion on the effort by 1996, including arming and training Latin American governments and security forces to eradicate crops and intercept shipments, funding alternative crop programmes in producer areas, and running international interdiction efforts. Yet all the money and publicity have achieved remarkably little: cocaine use in the US has not fallen, the street price of cocaine has remained low and stable for much of the 1990s, while the trade has expanded into Europe and the former Soviet bloc.

Within Latin America the impact of the 'war on drugs' has been largely negative. Involving local armies in the drugs war has both boosted their influence and corrupted many officers at a time when Washington was attempting to consolidate human rights and democracy in the region. For all the high profile eradication efforts, the number of hectares planted with coca reached a record height in 1995.

Drug policy analysts compare the drug trade to a balloon: squeezing it in one area merely causes it to pop up in another. Crackdowns on producers in Peru and Bolivia have encouraged production in Venezuela, Panama and particularly Colombia, which now rivals Bolivia as the second largest producer after Peru.

A similar effect has been caused by the high-profile law enforcement effort in Colombia against the Cali and Medellín cartels, most of whose leaders were dead or in jail by 1997.

New drug mafias have sprung up in Mexico, Bolivia, Peru, Venezuela and Brazil. The most powerful newcomers are the Mexican cartels, which have forged direct links to Peruvian and Bolivian producers, cutting the Colombians out altogether, and taken maximum advantage from Mexico's 2,000-mile border with the US and the increased cross-border traffic resulting from the North American Free Trade Agreement (NAFTA). Money laundering operations and transhipment routes have also scattered to every corner of the continent, creating growing headaches for US drug control efforts. The drug trade's resilience has been extraordinary. The death of the infamous drug baron Pablo Escobar in a shoot-out in 1993 completed the dismantling of the Medellín cartel, which US officials in the 1980s had claimed was responsible for eighty per cent of the cocaine entering the US, yet Escobar's death had no discernible impact on the flow of cocaine.

Colombian or not, the drug cartels continue to thrive, developing, according to *The Economist*, 'all the acumen and professionalism of the big international tobacco companies.' In the 1980s, individual 'mules' were replaced by large-scale shipments by air and sea, but the cartels set their sights even higher: in 1997 a Miami businessman was caught trying to import a Piranha-class nuclear submarine from the Kronstadt naval base in St Petersburg, Russia, for use by Colombian cartels in shipments to California and elsewhere, according to officials of the US Drugs Enforcement Agency. The drug industry's growing complexity is also shown in its rapid move into heroin in Colombia and Mexico. Some drug experts believed that Colombia had outstripped Asian producers such as Burma and Thailand by 1996.

Although US drug policy has failed, few viable alternatives are on offer. Every so often, a courageous or foolhardy official suggests broadening the debate to include legalisation of some drugs, arguing that breaking the link with criminality would end much of the drug trade's most damaging impact on society. Parallels are often drawn with the end of prohibition in the US, which deprived gangsters like Al Capone of their control of the alcohol trade. Legalisation would also allow governments to tax drugs, a tantalising prospect for any administration trying to reduce its budget deficit. Given US domestic opinion, it is hard to see how legalisation could come about, but it is worth considering what effect it would have on the cocaine trade. Coca would become a normal commodity like tobacco; big farmers could move in and take over production from the peasant producers who currently grow the bushes, and the Colombian and Mexican cartels would suddenly be faced by a trade war with major multinational companies. Although it might bring an end to violence on the streets of the US, legalisation would not necessarily benefit ordinary Latin Americans.

The other option is for the US to recognise that as long as the demand persists, in the shape of millions of would-be cocaine users in the US, the supply will surely follow. That would involve a substantial shift from supply-side to demand-side policies, focusing on public education within the US, perhaps as part of a broader programme of inner-city regeneration aimed at breaking the cycle of poverty and exclusion which creates new generations of drug users. Yet such a strategy would require significant public spending at a time when Washington is hard pressed to cut its budget deficit, an unlikely eventuality given the current state of US politics.

Shanty town resident shows the remains of squatters' shacks after they were burned down by police in an eviction, Cali, Colombia.

Chronology

1519-35	Spanish conquest: colonisers introduce new animals and crops and take back to Europe novelties such as tomatoes, maize, tobacco and potatoes; Spanish hand out land and forced labour to their officers through the *encomienda* system
1538	First slaves brought from Africa to work Latin America's sugar plantations
1881	Communal land-ownership by Indian peasants banned in El Salvador, enabling coffee plantations to expand onto Indian lands
1899	United Fruit establishes a monopoly over Central American banana production
1917	Beginning of Mexican land reform – the greatest in Latin American history
1950s on	Expansion of commercial agriculture throughout Latin America
1952	Bolivian revolution redistributes land and ends the near-feudal status of Indian 'serfs'
1959	Cuban revolution: state farms take over sugar production
1961	Washington launches Alliance for Progress, which supports land reform programmes throughout Latin America
1964	Military coup in Brazil: new government promotes agro-exports and the colonisation of the Amazon basin
1979	Nicaraguan revolution: half of the country's farming land is included in a land reform
1982 on	Under pressure from debt crisis, governments try to increase agro-exports, in many cases by giving more power to large landowners
1990	FSLN loses elections, new government starts to reverse agrarian reform
1994	Zapatista uprising in Chiapas, Mexico, prompted by government's attempts to privatise communal land-holdings
1996	Proportion of Latin Americans living in the countryside falls to a quarter

Promised Land 2

Land Ownership, Power and Conflict

The priest is holding an open-air mass for the Indian coffee pickers. Women in their bright traditional costumes listen on rough benches under the hot sun, the men sit on the ground, hats in hands. Round about are their tents, made of transparent plastic sheets stretched over sticks. Maize grinders, essential for the staple food, *tortillas*, are mounted on branches stuck into the earth. A few possessions are hung from other branches, clear of the pigs.

In Guatemala such scenes are re-enacted every December, as the coffee harvest starts and Indians are trucked down from their tiny plots of land in the highlands of Chimaltenango to live rough and pick coffee for several months. The wages are US$3 to US$4 a day, the food is worm-ridden and insufficient, but they come every year because they have no choice. Their land does not grow enough food to keep them going all year round, so they must pick coffee.

As the priest says mass, the owner of the coffee plantation, Loren, opens a beer on the verandah of his estate house. He has driven out in his jeep from his town house in Guatemala City to visit his farm, a crumbling but still beautiful building with whitewashed walls, palm trees and a stagnant swimming pool full of tadpoles. Green fields of coffee bushes cloak the hillsides.

Loren is white, owns a great deal of land, speaks French, English and Spanish, and is very rich. Back in Guatemala City, he plays the international coffee market by computer. 'His' Indians inhabit a different world; they own minute plots of land, are mostly illiterate, speak Kekchi and broken Spanish, and will probably never see either a computer or Guatemala City. Loren makes his excuses: 'I can't give them meat and vegetables on top of everything else or I'd go bankrupt. Anyway, those people are not used to it – they don't want it.' Outside, the priest exhorts the coffee pickers to 'work hard and be humble.'

Guatemala is an extreme example of the abyss that separates peasant from large landowner in most of rural Latin America. In this essentially apartheid system, the struggle for land and the other farming essentials such as water, credit and roads, has been a source of political conflict and instability throughout the 20th century, producing revolutions, massacres and innumerable simmering disputes. The recent wave of market reforms in the region has further exacerbated such tensions.

In 1993, 26 per cent of Latin Americans lived in the countryside. Of these 122 million people, around half lived below the poverty line. The continent has vast underused areas of cultivable land, climates and soils to suit every crop, and good water resources, yet at least six million children are malnourished, a million of them severely so. The roots of this hunger amid plenty lie in the patterns of unequal land ownership established from the first days of the Spanish conquest.

Before the conquistadores came, most land was communally owned and largely used for arable crops. The most advanced civilisation, the Incas in Peru, had large scale irrigation systems, crop terracing whose remnants can still be seen today, and a sophisticated storage and distribution system.

The Spanish and Portuguese introduced cows, sheep, horses, wheat and sugar-cane and raised them alongside traditional crops like maize, beans, tobacco and potatoes. Both Spanish and Portuguese Crowns rewarded their troops and settlers with grants of land and Indian slaves. Under the *encomienda* system in the Andes, conquistadores had the right to exact forced labour from specified Indian communities. In return they had to send a percentage of the proceeds to Madrid and, in theory, convert the Indians to Catholicism.

From these massive land grants, three main forms of land ownership became established during the colonial period:

Plantations: these were large farms geared to exports, often using foreign capital and slave labour (the first slaves were brought from Africa to Brazil in 1538). They were mainly in areas where the indigenous population was less advanced and soon wiped out by the European conquerors. The first great plantation crop was sugar in northeast Brazil, coastal Peru, parts of Colombia, and the Caribbean. On the plantations African slaves worked in gangs, often in the harshest of conditions, watched over by armed guards. Plantation owners were businessmen, motivated by profit, and their farms were usually both efficient and brutal.

Haciendas: these produced for the domestic market, rather than export. They grew food crops for pack animals and raised cattle to feed the Spanish armies and mine workers. The haciendas were mainly in regions with advanced

On the haciendas of Bolivia, prior to the revolution of 1952, *pongos* were peasant farmers who did three or four days of unpaid work a month for the owner in exchange for the right to farm a small piece of often substandard land.

'The pongo must bring his own food, even though he has a right to the leftovers from the master's table. So when he goes to fulfil his obligation, he takes with him an earthenware or copper cooking pot, quite covered in soot, a faggot of kindling wood and a sack of llama turds for fuel, and some supplies of food.

The pongo is given a spot in the great house for his quarters, some alleyway near the mangers and pigsties, and here he builds a fire to prepare his soup, boil up his corn-grits or toast his corn. But like a watch-dog he must sleep in the lobby ready to open the door for the master's children and for the master himself if he is a night-bird and likes to spend his time at the club or in a tavern.

His work occupies him from dawn until far into the night, amongst his labours are the following: to help in the kitchen, to look after the harness and mind the poultry. He must sweep out the rooms, the courtyards, clean the stables and pigsties and do the garden. The traditional colonial estate house is a little world, a kind of Noah's ark with every kind of animal in it. The pongo is builder, messenger, nanny and brewer of *chicha* (corn beer). He fills in the gaps in the phalanx of servants during the day. And at night he has other tasks to complete the dark rosary of his obligations: spinning, weaving, husking corn, *mukeo* (chewing corn for chicha, fermented with saliva) and of course, minding the doorway.'

Rafael Reyéros, *El Pongueaje*, La Paz, 1949

Indian civilisations at the time of the conquest, such as Peru, Ecuador and Mexico. Rather than profits, hacienda owners valued the power and status conferred by land ownership; they more closely resembled aristocrats than businessmen and their farms were frequently underused and inefficient. The workers on the hacienda had a feudal relationship with the landlord, renting land in return either for a share of their crop (sharecropping), or for cash, or more often paying by working on the landowners' estate for a certain number of days a year. Hacienda owners controlled every aspect of their lives – some even ran their own local police and jails. The hacienda was a closed world where the owner was the main channel for contact with the outside.

Smallholder Communities: residual Indian communities in inaccessible areas tried to carry on as before, despite the heavy tribute and labour payments exacted by the colonial authorities. The Indian farmers retained many pre-Columbian practices, such as communal ownership of land, a strong spiritual bond with the soil, and the use of simple technology such as hoes and digging sticks. As time went by, their numbers were swelled by poor *mestizo* (mixed blood) farmers, many of whom spoke Spanish.

A typical peasant family today still lives in a one or two room shack made of wood or adobe. They own a few animals and handtools, and plough by

Sean Sprague/Panos

Small-scale farming, peasant farmers harvesting potatoes, a staple food crop, Bolivia.

hand or oxen rented from a better-off local family. Families are large, sons helping from an early age in the fields, while daughters work both in the home and on the land. They usually grow traditional food crops such as beans, maize, or potatoes.

Unbridgeable Gulf

The legacy of the colonial system has been an extreme and growing concentration of land, wealth and power in the hands of a tiny minority of big landowners, while the vast majority of rural people have insufficient or no land, are poor, hungry and excluded from the political system. In Mexico at the turn of the century one per cent of farmers owned an extraordinary 97 per cent of the land, while as recently as 1962 one per cent of Peruvian farmers owned eighty per cent of the land. These dry statistics hardly convey the almost unbridgeable cultural and economic gulf which still divides the rich elites from peasant farmers.

After independence, and especially in the second half of the 19th century, Latin America became increasingly bound in to the world economy. Foreign investment from the new industrial powers such as Britain and the US started to arrive, turning the old plantations into modern capitalist farms. Waged labour replaced slavery, which was abolished everywhere in Latin America by the end of the 19th century, and farmers began to invest more capital in machinery and fertilisers. This model proved extremely profitable, and grew at the expense of the traditional, but inefficient hacienda system. As each new crop was introduced, the plantation system and the power of the plantation owners grew.

At the end of the 19th century, US companies started to buy up land themselves, rather than work through local farmers. The pioneers were the multinational banana companies, like United Fruit, which set up banana enclaves in Central America and the Caribbean. On these enclaves workers lived in barracks, permanently in debt to the company store, while the multinational built its own railways to take the bananas to ports and its waiting ships. The system brought scant benefit to the host country, which usually received very little tax income from the banana trade.

The concentration of land in very few hands, which grew as capitalist agriculture expanded, made Latin America the most unequal continent in the world. Big farmers, whether local or foreign, became rich and used their influence to ensure government policies favoured their own interests. Governments duly encouraged exports, kept taxes low on the luxury imports the elites desired, and made sure that the big farmers received the lion's share of state spending through bank loans, investment in roads and railways, and training and technical advice for their administrators. As they grew richer, the big farmers bought more land, whereas the peasant farmers were deprived of state help, credit and social services like health care and education. The gap between rich and poor grew ever wider. In her autobiography *I, Rigoberta Menchú*, the Guatemalan Indian leader and Nobel Peace Prize winner Rigoberta Menchú recalls how her parents lost their land to incoming *ladinos* (Spanish-speaking Guatemalans of mixed race)

They weren't exactly evicted but the ladinos just gradually took over. My parents spent everything they earned and they incurred so many debts with these people that they had to leave the house to pay them. The rich are always like that. When people owe them some money they take a bit of land or some of their belongings and slowly end up with everything.

As the rural population grew, families had to subdivide their land between their children. Broken up, their small plots proved unable to sustain a family and both adults and children were forced to seek work on the plantations at harvest time. Millions more abandoned the countryside for the shanty towns that were springing up around the major cities. The combination of peasant farming and seasonal labour, known as semi-proletarianisation, has become the norm in much of the countryside. In Central America, seventy per cent of the rural population are seasonal migrants, joining the coffee pickers of Guatemala in their annual trek to the plantations. For the plantation owners, this system provides a cheap labour force at harvest time, with no need to pay year-round wages to regular employees.

Factory Farms

After the Second World War many politicians and economists saw further modernisation as the solution to Latin America's inadequate agricultural system. This meant increasing productivity and making Latin America's farms more like the capital-intensive farms of the United States and Canada. Since the 1960s, a new wave of state and foreign investment has transformed Latin American agriculture. In Colombia, state spending on agriculture increased fifty-fold between 1950 and 1972. Most of the money went on grandiose schemes favouring large-scale export agriculture; for example, the Mexican government irrigated the arid Northwest of the country which subsequently became a major producer of fruit and vegetables for the US market.

Driving through the rich Cauca valley of Colombia, one passes through mile after mile of lush new sugar and sorghum fields, punctuated by billboards advertising the latest in tractors and pesticides. In Mexico's Northwest, the fast-growing fruit and vegetable industry has transformed the fertile river valleys into a vast patchwork of irrigated fields and packing sheds resembling those of California's Imperial Valley. In southern Brazil, more than a dozen multi-million dollar soybean processing plants owned by US multinationals are scattered through the region, surrounded by large-scale mechanised soybean farms, none of which existed two decades ago. While a few countries such as Brazil, Colombia, Mexico and Argentina,

Sean Sprague/Panos

are clearly in the forefront of the agricultural revolution, no part of the countryside has been left untouched by capitalist development.
Roger Burbach and Patricia Flynn, *Agribusiness in the Americas*, New York, 1980

Migrant coffee pickers move into their dormitory on a cotton estate, Bolivia.

Following the military coup of 1964, Brazil provided the most dramatic example of government involvement in boosting agro-exports. Through lending, tax concessions, state investment and a guaranteed minimum price for farmers growing export crops like soybeans, southern Brazil has been transformed into one of the most modern agricultural regions in the hemisphere. Although a few Brazilian families have grown very rich in the process, they remain heavily dependent on foreign banks and multinationals to finance and buy their crops. For the mass of the population, the new crops have meant yet another round of land concentration, increasing inequality of wealth, and growing malnutrition as food crops are once again squeezed out by commodity exports. Rather than abolishing hunger in the countryside, modernisation has often made it worse.

In some cases foreign investors have bought and farmed land, but in recent years multinational companies have largely drawn back from the direct control which made them so unpopular in the past, leading to extensive nationalisation of their operations in the 1960s and 1970s. Instead, they prefer to sign contracts with local farmers, under which the companies provide credit and agricultural inputs such as fertilisers and equipment in return for buying the farmer's crops at a guaranteed price. This leaves the multinational in control of the profitable processing and marketing of a product, while the local farmers must deal with the local labour force and run the risk of a failed harvest. The multinationals lose little through this arrangement: one study

When Del Monte first sent its technicians to look at the Bajio [valley in Mexico] in 1959, they found a region ill-suited to the needs of the world's largest canner of fruits and vegetables. Grain production predominated, with corn and beans serving as the mainstays of the local diet. In Del Monte's own words, 'vegetable production was small and limited to a few crops grown exclusively for the local fresh market.'

The Bajio's land tenure system was also incompatible with Del Monte's needs. Due to the valley's population density, and the break-up of the large landed estates under Mexico's agrarian reform laws, the average land holding was small, ranging from 10 to 20 acres. Some of the land was held in *ejidos*, large state-owned farms that are subdivided into many small plots and worked by peasants. Mexican law prohibited the sale of these lands, and it also placed restrictions on land ownership by foreign corporations. For a company used to owning plantations and working with US growers who own hundreds or even thousands of acres, the conditions in the Bajio did not appear auspicious.

But Del Monte found the perfect tool for changing the valley's agriculture - contract farming. Under the contract system, the farmer or grower agrees to plant a set number of acres of a particular crop, and the company in return provides financial assistance which usually includes seeds and special machinery, as well as cash outlays for purchasing fertilisers and hiring farm labour. All these costs are discounted from the farmer's income when the crop is delivered to the cannery.

In a country like Mexico, where agricultural credit is limited or non-existent, contract farming is a powerful instrument. Del Monte revealed just how influential its crop financing was when it noted that 'in the early 1960s Productos Del Monte was practically the only source that many of its growers could turn to for short term crop loans.' By skilfully using its financial leverage, Del Monte affected the valley in several ways: it introduced crops that had never been grown there, favoured the development of the larger growers at the expense of the smaller more marginal producers, and gained operating control over large tracts of land.

'Canned Imperialism', *Report on the Americas*, New York, September 1976

in the early 1970s showed that of each US$1 earned by bananas in the marketplace, only US$0.11 finds its way back to the producer country.

In today's Latin America, high-tech farms resemble islands of modern capitalism in a sea of traditional peasant agriculture. The two worlds are intimately connected – peasant farms provide seasonal labour and often sell their produce to local agribusinesses. But power lies firmly in the hands of the big farms, with their near-monopoly on capital, credit, state support and access to world markets.

Fighting For Land

The three forms of land ownership – haciendas, plantations and peasant farms – have competed for land, and the expansion of one at the expense of the others has generated conflict, land seizures, political unrest and even war.

As commercial agriculture has spread onto lands traditionally farmed by peasant families, the big landowners have forced them out through a combination of money, legal trickery (for example, over the deeds to the land) and brute force. In the Brazilian Amazon, landowners commonly hire gunmen to expel peasant farmers from land they want to turn over to cattle. Peasants have responded by seizing land left idle by the landowners and organising political movements to demand agrarian reform and access to social services.

On the plantations disputes have been over wages and conditions, rather than demands for land and credit. Since plantation owners are determined to keep wages as low as possible, these disputes have frequently been bloody, often involving the army and police on the side of the owners. One of the worst-hit areas has been Colombia's banana-growing Urabá region.

A typical incident was the arrest by members of the [local army] battalion of 19 banana plantation workers in the municipality of Apartadó in March 1989. They were taken to the battalion headquarters in Carepa and twelve were later released. Four others were released after several days during

which they were tortured, and three needed hospital treatment for their
injuries. The bodies, or rather the remains, of two other workers were
found on 4 April. They had been killed by having charges of dynamite
attached to their bodies and exploded.
Jenny Pearce, *Colombia: Inside the Labyrinth*, London, 1990

In many cases when local disputes were met with repression, they escalated
into national political protest movements. In El Salvador in the 1970s frustrated
peasant activists decided they could not improve conditions in the
countryside without a radical change of government. As a result, many
joined new guerrilla movements, fighting in a bloody civil war in which over
70,000 people died, mostly at the hands of the army and their associated
death squads.

Over the last fifty years governments have tried to alleviate pressure on
the land through colonisation programmes. These have consisted largely of
irrigation projects which have reclaimed arid land in countries such as Mexico
and Peru, and the deforestation and occupation of the Amazon basin in
Brazil and the neighbouring Andean nations of Bolivia, Peru, Ecuador and
Colombia. Governments have often seen these programmes as an alternative
to agrarian reform, since they can ease pressure on the land by sending
landless peasants off to colonise new areas. Unfortunately, the lands being
colonised in the rainforest have often proved unsuitable for sustained
agriculture, and have been in remote areas, making it expensive or impossible
for small farmers to get their produce to market. Colonisation programmes
have often been chaotic and violent, as in Brazil where large landowners
have moved in to throw peasants off the land, once they have cleared it for
farming. In her autobiography, *Mi Despertar*, (My Awakening), Ana María
Condori, a Bolivian Indian woman describes the colonisation programme of
the 1950s:

My father went there because our farm at home was all divided up and
wasn't producing enough for all the children. Going on the colonisation
seemed like a solution to him, because the government at that time promised

people heaven and earth. They gave out publicity at the fairs in the Altiplano [high plateau region of the Andes where most Bolivians live] trying to get people to sign up – leaflets, posters, adverts on the radio offering ready-made houses, a hectare of land already cleared, schools, hospitals, paved roads, technical assistance and credit for the farm. But once people got to the colonisation zone, they found nothing of all that; the government handed out food to make sure people didn't actually starve to death, but apart from that they were left to their fate.

The conflicts generated by growing inequality in the countryside have made agrarian reform one of the hottest issues in Latin American politics. For both rich and poor, land is literally a matter of life and death.

The first, and greatest Latin American agrarian reform followed the Mexican revolution of 1910-17. Over the ensuing decades, especially during the radical presidency of Lázaro Cárdenas (1934-40), Mexico's vast haciendas were broken up and given out to 1.5 million families in the form of *ejidos* - communally-owned land administered by Indian communities along traditional lines. The reform consolidated the ruling party's grip on the countryside, laying the foundations for fifty years of one party rule.

The Mexican government gave out land, but failed to back up the programme with a reform of credit and investment to benefit the peasants. Credit is the essential oxygen supply for all farmers because of the cyclical nature of agriculture. Every year a farmer has to borrow cash to buy seeds and fertiliser, pay employees, and hire or buy equipment before the harvest brings in a lump sum which must pay off debts and maintain the farmer's family until the next harvest. Even after the agrarian reform in Mexico, big farmers have continued to receive most of the credit, and government spending on roads and irrigation has benefited their farms most. Agrarian reform has provided the security that goes with owning a piece of land, but has done little to improve the living standards of Mexico's peasantry.

In 1991 even such limited gains were endangered when Mexico's President, Carlos Salinas, announced a constitutional reform to allow the piecemeal privatisation of ejido lands. Henceforward, *ejidatarios* would be allowed to sell their land or go into joint ventures with private companies. The reform, coupled with the impact of the North American Free Trade Agreement (NAFTA), is expected to drive millions of peasant families off the land over the coming 15 years. Its explosive impact was seen in the uprising in the southern state of Chiapas in early 1994, when the Zapatista rebels named the reversal of the land reform as one of the principle reasons for their decision to take up arms.

The Bolivian revolution of 1952 led to a radical reform of its almost feudal rural society, directly benefiting three quarters of the country's peasantry. Large estates were divided up among the sharecroppers who had previously been forced to give the landowner a large proportion of their crop in exchange for farming the land. Titles were established for Indian communities and the worst forms of labour exploitation were made illegal. In Guatemala a similarly radical land reform after 1952 came to an abrupt end when the Arbenz government was overthrown by a US-backed military coup.

Agrarian reform on a continental level took off in the 1960s. Following the Cuban revolution in 1959, the US government decided it had to end social unrest in the countryside of Latin America if it was to pre-empt further

'Now we too have land!'
Peruvian peasant
farmers celebrate after
receiving land titles
through the agrarian
reform.

revolutions. In 1961 President Kennedy launched the Alliance for Progress, a joint Latin American – US initiative under which the US gave money and advice for agrarian reform programmes in countries such as Chile, Colombia and Venezuela.

However, agrarian reform as understood by Washington had two often incompatible aims: it sought to increase productivity by modernising agriculture along capitalist lines, and at the same time to redistribute land and wealth to the rural poor. In practice, modernisation came first, often causing further land expulsions and impoverishment for the peasantry. Landlords successfully resisted US pressure to reduce their influence, and instead benefited from the drive for modernisation. Landlord opposition and government incompetence meant that even when apparently progressive reform laws were passed, they were seldom implemented. Such laws have become a focus of discontent as peasants in countries such as Honduras and Brazil occupy idle lands and try and force the government to enact their own laws, expropriating the farms and distributing them among landless peasants.

The Brazilian government seems to specialise in making extravagant promises of agrarian reform which it never keeps. Most recently, President Cardoso has promised to settle 280,000 families by the end of his first term in 1999. The Landless Peasant Movement (MST), which organises protests and land occupations across the country, argues that even this is insufficient, claiming that there are 15 million desperate Brazilian peasant farmers currently without any land. Land conflicts continue to exact a deadly toll in Brazil - in April 1996, nine peasants and two policemen died in a clash when squatters moved in to occupy a ranch in the remote Amazon state of Rondônia.

In the 1980s two land reform programmes in Central America exemplified the gap between rhetoric and reality. The Sandinista government in Nicaragua and the Christian Democrat government in El Salvador both instituted agrarian reform programmes at about the same time, but with very different results. The Salvadorean reform fizzled out in the face of opposition from the coffee-growing elite and lack of credit and training, while the Nicaraguan reform succeeded in radically redistributing land and wealth in the countryside, breaking up much of the old landowning system and affecting about half of the country's farming land. After an initial emphasis on state farms proved unpopular, the Sandinistas rewrote the reform first to benefit peasants grouped into co-operatives, and then to hand out land to individual families. Although the Sandinistas' ideological conversion from state farms to individualism took only five years, thousands of Nicaragua's more conservative peasants had already been outraged by the government's initial opposition to the peasants' age-old hunger for their own piece of land. Many ended up supporting or joining the US-backed Contra rebels who fought to overthrow the Sandinista government. Since the Sandinistas' electoral defeat in 1990, the return of expropriated land to former landowners has become one of the most conflictive political issues, while subsequent governments' espousal of market forces and the cuts in bank credit to small farmers, have led to land once again accumulating in the hands of the few.

Where agrarian reforms have worked to the advantage of the rural poor, they have generally been associated either with revolution (Mexico, Bolivia 1952, Cuba 1959, Nicaragua 1979) or with the election of left-wing government (Chile 1970-73, Guatemala 1950-54). In both Chile and Guatemala, the governments were overthrown by military coups, in part because of the hostility of the landed elite to their agrarian reforms. In Peru one of Latin America's few radical military governments, the regime of General Velasco (1968-75) also transformed the country's semi-feudal land system with a radical reform.

In the 1990s, the wave of structural adjustment programmes which have tried to open up the Latin American economy to market forces has had a significant impact on agriculture. As part of the drive to encourage private investment in agriculture, especially in non-traditional agro-export crops, governments in countries such as Peru, Mexico, Ecuador and Nicaragua have put past reform processes into reverse in a new wave of 'modernisation' which has had serious implications for the peasants. As credits have been cut back, and land opened up to private buyers, peasant unrest has broken out in many countries, the most notable examples being the 'First National Indigenous Uprising' in Ecuador in 1990, and the Zapatista rebellion in 1994.

Although the growing urbanisation of the continent has reduced the relevance of rural questions to many Latin Americans, over a quarter of the region's people still live in the countryside, where they suffer the consequences of unequal land distribution and a system which invariably favours the rich farmers over the peasants. The modernisation of agriculture seems only to exacerbate the situation, while half-hearted colonisation programmes and agrarian reforms have done little to change the system, and in some cases, may have made matters worse. Experience shows that government initiatives like agrarian reform can only work when they are carried out democratically, in consultation with their supposed beneficiaries, and are willing to challenge the power of the big landowners. Only if such reforms take place, is there hope that a more just society can grow in rural Latin America, one which does not perpetuate poverty, hunger, sickness and an endless flight to the cities.

Unregulated industry in Latin America pollutes air, land and waterways. Chemical works, Colombia.

Chronology

1930s   Industrialisation leads to explosion of shanty towns and environmental deterioration in cities

1966   Brazil's new military government unveils 'Operation Amazonia' to colonise and industrially develop the rainforest

1980   Brazilian government decrees tax incentives for enterprises taking part in the Grande Carajás development programme

1984   Opening of giant Itaipú dam between Brazil, Argentina and Paraguay

1985   US Congress forces World Bank temporarily to suspend road-building loans due to their environmental impact and include environmental criteria in its project assessments

1988   Chico Mendes, leader of Amazon rubber-tappers, assassinated by landowners

1980s   500,000 gold prospectors pour into the Amazon, bringing disease and destruction to the Yanomami Indians

1990   Chilean government declares first ever 'environmental state of emergency' in Santiago

1992   World Summit on the Environment and Development held in Rio de Janeiro

1992-94   15,000 square kilometres of rainforest burned every year in Brazilian Amazon

1995   Disaster at the Omai gold mine, Guyana, spills cyanide-laced toxic waste into the Essequibo river

A Land in Flames   3

The Environment

The burning season starts in June in the Brazilian Amazon. The sky turns a dirty ochre, as a pall of smoke closes local airports and cuts off whole towns from the outside world. Each year the flames engulf a vast and irreplaceable area of virgin rainforest – in the mid-1990s, the forest was disappearing at the rate of three hectares a minute and the burn rates were rising.

Although many people in the industrialised nations see environmental questions in Latin America as synonymous with the Amazon rainforest, the damage stretches to every corner of the continent, blighting cities and countryside alike.

• Indian groups from the Ecuadorean Amazon stunned the mighty Texaco oil company in 1993 by filing a US$1.5 billion lawsuit against it for damage caused during twenty years of drilling which had poured toxic waste into the waterways, destroying fish stocks on which the Indian communities depend.

• On the Pacific Coast of Central America, fishermen must watch as their catch is poisoned twice a year: when the rains start in May they wash accumulated pesticides from the cotton fields into the sea, killing marine life for miles around. When the rains end, and crop-spraying begins, a new dose of chemicals flows into bays and estuaries.

• In Mexico, acid rain from oil refineries is threatening to obliterate the region's history: it is eating away the stone inscriptions at the Mayan temple of Palenque, while at the great ruined city of Chichén-Itzá walls have been covered in a black soot left by the polluted rains.

The Conquest of Nature

The conquest of the Americas lessened one kind of environmental pressure, but introduced many new ones. Recent archaeological evidence suggests that indigenous agriculture in Mexico and the Andes was in a state of crisis when the Spaniards arrived, as population pressure and soil erosion combined to produce a food crisis which may have been an important factor in enabling the Spaniards to win against the odds. After the conquest, the collapse of the Indian population, through disease and forced labour, did much to ease the immediate pressure on the ecosystem. The population of Latin America did not return to its pre-conquest levels until the 19th century.

The subsistence economies of the great Indian civilisations were replaced by a colonial gold-rush mentality which aimed to plunder Latin America's resources, whether mineral or agricultural, as quickly as possible and send them abroad. When one resource was exhausted, another was found, with no attempt to build long-term sustainability. The philosophy was even applied to people: when Indian labourers began to die out on Brazil's sugar plantations, the plantation owners chose to ship in Africans to do the job, rather than try and reduce the death rate among the indigenous population. As the centuries have passed, Latin America has become ever more bound in to the world economy, raiding its natural resources to pay for imports of manufactured goods.

In this century, an urban environmental crisis has taken off following the aggressive industrialisation programmes introduced in the 1930s and 1940s. Cities have sprung up, sucking the rural poor into shanty towns with few facilities. Unregulated industry has poured effluents into the air and the water and millions of dilapidated cars have choked the cities with carbon monoxide.

Big is Beautiful

Since the Second World War, governments and international lenders have added to the damage done to Latin America's environment through their predilection for 'pharaonic' projects. Especially attractive to military governments, giant dams, huge road building programmes, nuclear power, and vast mining complexes have wrought enormous human and environmental damage to the continent.

Roads are the kiss of death for the rainforest. Seen from the air, Amazonian roads are bordered by a corridor of deforested land, spanning roughly a day's walk either side for the peasant farmers who move in as soon as a road is built and start hacking back the forest.

Dams were originally hailed as a clean and renewable energy source – every environmentalist's dream. Small-scale dam projects, such as those of Costa Rica, which relies on hydro-schemes for 99 per cent of its energy, are indeed environment-friendly. They affect a small area, and do not create the social, economic or environmental disruption caused by the great dams. Elsewhere, notably in Brazil and Argentina, governments have built gigantic constructions, flooding vast areas of the countryside, displacing indigenous peoples and local farmers, and causing unpredictable climatic change.

On the border between Brazil and Paraguay, the Itaipú dam has been described as 'a monument built of raw superlatives'. For five years Brazilian construction companies poured enough concrete every day to build a 350-storey building. The construction contract alone weighed 220lb. The dam began operation in 1984, straddling the giant Paraná river which flows out to the sea as the River Plate between Argentina and Uruguay. It produces as much electricity as ten average nuclear power stations.

Dams on this scale carry costs not associated with smaller projects. The initial investment adds enormously to the country's debt burden – Itaipú cost Brazil US$20 billion, roughly twenty per cent of its entire foreign debt at that time. Dams are usually accompanied by other developments, such as industries using cheap energy. Since they are often built in relatively untouched parts of the country, this can cause great environmental damage. A prime example is the Grande Carajás project (see below), for which Brazil built the Tucurui dam, fifty per cent bigger than Itaipú. Furthermore, flooding leads to a massive loss of forest, and kills wildlife. The Tucurui dam flooded 216,000 hectares in 1984, killing 2.8 million trees which were first sprayed with chemical defoliants. In populated areas the valleys flooded by dam

projects are often the most fertile farm land. In some regions, the sudden increase in standing water has led to epidemics of parasitic diseases such as malaria, and can even substantially alter the local climate. Finally, deforestation upstream can increase siltation rates, shortening the dam's lifespan and turning it into a huge loss-maker, even before environmental costs are included in the balance sheet.

Megaprojects; megadestruction. The Grande Carajás iron ore mine, Brazil.

The generals' fascination for giant projects has been shared by many western governments and multilateral lenders like the World Bank. In 1981 the World Bank signed a US$330 million agreement with Brazil to fund a highway and feeder roads linking the industrialised south with the forested areas of Rondônia and Mato Grosso. At the time, David Price, a consultant anthropologist to the Bank, warned in a report:

> If [the project] is carried out, land values will rise vertiginously, there will be an influx of settlers, and the pressures on the native population will be redoubled. More than 8,000 Indians in Mato Grosso and Rondônia will be affected. To entrust their welfare to [the government Indian agency] as it is now constituted would be criminal.

According to Price, officials prevented the report from being distributed within the Bank. Other World Bank staff pointed out that the road could provoke uncontrollable colonisation and that the soils which would be deforested would be unsuitable for agriculture. Despite these warnings the project went ahead and the road was inaugurated in 1984. Six days after the road's inauguration, the US Congress began hearings on the environmental devastation caused by the project, leading it in 1985 to pressure the World Bank into temporarily suspending payments on the loan. It was too late for Rondônia. By the following year the state's governor was lamenting, 'Rondônia is being trampled down by a migration of 180,000 people a year.'

Pressure from environmental groups has forced organisations like the World Bank to reassess the impact of their lending on the environment. US Congressional legislation in 1985/6 obliged the Bank's officials to include environmental criteria in their project assessments. However, western governments have done little to ease the pressure exerted by the debt crisis and structural adjustment policies (see chapter 5). The debt burden has forced governments to give top priority to exports, in order to earn the hard currency needed to pay the interest on their debts. Environmental concerns have therefore taken second place to the need for quick returns. Not only did much of the initial lending go to environmentally damaging projects, such as dams, but now further damage must be done to pay the debt back!

Extractive Industries

In August 1995 disaster struck at the Omai gold mine in Guyana, jointly owned by two Canadian multinational mining companies. A huge pit, into which were piped waste products from the gold extraction process, ruptured and over the next three days spewed three million cubic metres of cyanide-laced toxic waste into the Essequibo, Guyana's largest river. Guyana's president, who only years before had sung the praises of the mine, was forced to declare the area an 'environmental disaster zone'. Indians, traders and miners living along the river bank reported dead fish and wild hogs floating belly up, and for two months suffered skin rashes and blistering after using river water.

The Omai disaster was just the latest proof of the environmental damage caused by Latin America's pursuit of 'extractive industries' such as mining and oil drilling. Damage is not confined to unexpected accidents, but in many cases is an integral and unavoidable part of the industries. In 1967, oil was discovered by the Texaco oil multinational in the Ecuadorean Amazon, leading to an oil boom which had a devastating impact on the Amazonian ecosystem. The company built access roads, paving the way for deforestation by incoming landless peasants and ranchers; hundreds of wells now generate millions of gallons of toxic waste every day which leaks into the waterways, destroying the fish stocks on which local Indian communities depend. In 1993 lawyers representing local Indians filed a US$1.5 billion lawsuit against Texaco in a federal court in New York, yet the Ecuadorean government opposed it, fearful that the action would scare off other foreign investors.

The most spectacular mining complex is Brazil's Grande Carajás project, the largest in the world, costing an estimated US$62 billion, and occupying an area the size of Britain and France put together. The EU has contributed US$600 million to the project, while the World Bank is also a major funder. Its centrepiece is the giant Serra dos Carajás open-cast iron ore mine, which lies at the heart of a string of open-cast mines producing manganese, bauxite (for aluminium), copper, chrome, nickel, tungsten, cassiterite and gold. Carajás alone could provide ten per cent of the world's iron ore.

Clustered round the mines are processing plants, steel and aluminium mills, hydro-electric dams and railways. The environmental impact of the project became obvious soon after its inception in the 1980s. 1.6 million acres of timber were cut annually to make charcoal for the pig iron smelters, dwarfing the project's attempts at reforestation. The smelters and foundries have no pollution controls, and emphysema, bronchitis and other respiratory diseases are on the increase. The men working in the furnaces have already

started coughing up black phlegm, as have nine-year-old children who toil in the charcoal ovens at the edges of the receding forest, inhaling smoke and dust for twelve hours a day. 'People have just charcoal in their chests,' one charcoal burner told an Anti-Slavery International researcher. As in Potosí four centuries ago, the poor are losing their lungs to enrich others.

Massive projects are not the only environmental villains. Following a steep rise in the price of gold in 1979, 500,000 impoverished gold prospectors (*garimpeiros*) poured into the Amazon, invading lands occupied by the Yanomami Indians on Brazil's northern border. The Yanomami were previously

A poor gold prospector toils in the mud, pursuing a dream of sudden riches. Mercury used by the prospectors is poisoning Amazonia's waterways.

one of the largest and most isolated of Brazil's indigenous groups. The
miners brought guns, diseases such as malaria and TB, and mercury, which
they used in a crude process to separate gold dust from mud. According to
Survival International, 1,500 of the 9,000 Yanomami died over a two year
period, while in settlements near the mining camps there were almost no
children under the age of two.

Fight for the Forest

Deforestation has galvanised the green movement outside Latin America.
Public opinion has been horrified at the spectacle of vast tracts of rainforest
falling under the chainsaw, and the possible (though often exaggerated)
implications for the global climate. Latin America contains 62 per cent of the
world's remaining tropical rainforest, chiefly in the Amazon Basin countries
of Brazil, Bolivia, Ecuador, Peru, Colombia, Venezuela and the Guyanas. There
are also smaller areas in Mexico and Central America, where the process of
deforestation is both more rapid and much more advanced.

Accurate figures are hard to come by, but about 12 per cent of the Amazon
rainforest had been destroyed by the mid-1990s, some 50 million hectares.
Following a decline at the start of the decade, the burn rate was once again
picking up, approaching the peak year of 1988-89, when 19,000 square
kilometres of forest were destroyed.

In the Amazon, forests are burned in order to turn the land over to pasture
for cattle. The huge, inefficient cattle ranches have been encouraged by the
Brazilian government with a variety of tax concessions and other incentives
as part of its scheme for colonising the Amazon. One study in the 1970s
showed that each ton of beef received US$4,000 in subsidies, yet earned
only US$1,000 on the international market. Although the farms made little
commercial sense, they were seen as an inflation-proof investment by
companies or individuals living in the industrialised south.

The forest is also hacked down by poor peasant colonisers using 'slash and burn' methods. The precise division of blame between peasants and cattle barons is controversial. Up until 1980, cattle ranching accounted for 72 per cent of the deforestation. Since then, however, hundreds of thousands of peasants have marched in along the new roads like an army of leaf-cutter ants, while some of the tax incentives for cattle ranching have been removed in response to international pressure. Many of the peasant colonisers are themselves environmental refugees from soil erosion elsewhere or have lost their land to the onward march of soybean and other agribusiness in the south. Frequently they migrate following government advice to seek their fortunes as pioneers in the Amazon. What the government fails to tell them is that rainforest soil is unsuitable for sustained agriculture. Stripped of its trees, the fragile ecosystem rapidly collapses, nutrients are washed out of the soil, and within two or three years, declining fertility forces the peasant farmer to move on and cut down more forest.

Devouring the forest. Twenty-four hour burning, wood-fired gasifiers for lime-kilns, São Paulo state, Brazil.

In Central America, the hamburger, epitome of US consumerism, is the driving force behind the breakneck pace of deforestation. Unlike their Brazilian counterparts, whose meat is destined largely for domestic consumption, cattle ranches in countries like Costa Rica are commercial ventures aimed at the US fast food market. As in the Amazon, peasant farmers enter the forests and do the work of clearing the land for agriculture, but are soon squeezed out by declining fertility and pressure from cattle ranchers coming in behind them. Under cattle, the soil deteriorates further over 7-10 years, leaving an increasingly barren scrubland supporting fewer and fewer animals per hectare. By one calculation, Costa Rica loses 2.5 tonnes of topsoil for every kilogram of beef exported. Even though beef production has boomed, squeezing out other food crops like beans and maize, domestic meat consumption has actually fallen as more and more of Central America's beef heads north. The average US housecat now eats more beef than a typical Central American.

FIGHT FOR THE FOREST

The fight by local people to defend the Amazon gained world-wide attention when Chico Mendes, the leader of the Brazilian rubber tappers, was assassinated by a landowner in 1988. Mendes pioneered the idea of 'extractive reserves', using the forest sustainably to produce fruit, rubber and nuts.

'We realised that in order to guarantee the future of the Amazon we had to find a way to preserve the forest while at the same time developing the region's economy.

So what were our thoughts originally? We accepted that the Amazon could not be turned into some kind of sanctuary that nobody could touch. On the other hand, we knew it was important to stop the deforestation that is threatening the Amazon and all human life on the planet. We felt our alternative should involve preserving the forest, but it should also include a plan to develop the economy. So we came up with the idea of extractive reserves.

What do we mean by an extractive reserve? We mean the land is under public ownership but the rubber tappers and other workers that live on that land should have the right to live and work there. I say 'other workers' because there are not only rubber tappers in the forest. In our area, rubber tappers also harvest brazil nuts, but in other parts of the Amazon there are people who earn a living solely from harvesting nuts, while there are others who harvest babaçu and jute.'

Cachoeira ('rapids') was the name of the rubber estate in the forest outside Xapuri where Chico Mendes was brought up and started life as a rubber tapper. He worked on the Cachoeira estate from the age of ten until his early thirties, when he began devoting most of his time to the rural workers' union.

In 1987 Cachoeira was bought by Darli Alves da Silva. Using a mixture of inducements and threats, he tried to drive out the sixty families of rubber tappers who had lived and worked on the estate for generations. Chico Mendes invested a great deal of effort and all his powers of persuasion and leadership to convince the rubber tappers of Cachoeira to stay where they were, and Darli issued death threats against him. In the second half of 1988, following the shooting of two youths during the *empate* [confrontation] at the Ecuador rubber estate in May and the assassination of Ivair Higino in June, the federal government sought to defuse the situation by signing expropriation orders for three extractive reserves. One of these was Cachoeira, where 15,000 acres were allocated to the rubber tappers.

This victory for the rubber tappers was also the death sentence for Chico, as the family of Darli Alves sought to avenge their defeat. The attempts on his life became systematic and on 22 December 1988 he was murdered.

Chico Mendes, *Fight for the Forest*, London, 1989

The costs of deforestation are enormous:
• Deforested land is quickly eroded, and tons of topsoil are washed into the watercourses, silting up streams and rivers, clogging hydroelectric installations and disrupting marine ecosystems along the coast. In Panama,

deforestation has increased soil erosion, threatening to silt up the Panama Canal just as it is handed back to Panama by the US in the year 2000.

Soil erosion turns rich farmlands into barren wastes, Oaxaca, Mexico.

• Deforestation disrupts the local climate, since the trees regulate the storage and release of rain water. By returning water vapour to the atmosphere, trees also encourage further rainfall. The loss of forests therefore makes both drought and flooding as well as mudslides more likely.

• Many of Latin America's poor rely on firewood for fuel. As the forests become depleted, they must travel farther afield to scavenge for supplies, and in the towns the price rises to reflect wood's increasing scarcity.

• Indigenous peoples who live in harmony with the forest have little hope of surviving sustained contact with incoming settlers, although some Indian groups are now fighting to survive and even benefit from the environmental onslaught (see chapter 11).

• The rainforest is a repository of plant and animal species which, besides their intrinsic value, are a vital source of new genetic material – a quarter of all pharmaceutical products are derived from rainforest products, even though only one per cent of all Amazon plants have been intensively investigated for their medicinal properties. Tropical forest plants have provided treatments for leukaemia, Hodgkin's disease, breast, cervical and testicular cancer and are currently being used in AIDS research.

• A number of investigations show that the commercial potential of the forest is far greater than that of the pasture which replaces it. In addition the forest can be farmed in a sustainable way, yielding rubber, brazil nuts and many kinds of fruit.

• Most western attention has centred on the issue of global warming. The burning itself releases greenhouse gases (especially carbon dioxide which accounts for half the global warming effect) into the atmosphere, and the forests are no longer there to convert carbon dioxide to oxygen through photosynthesis. However, developing countries point out that 75 per cent of the world's carbon dioxide emissions come from the factories and cars of the industrialised nations, who long ago destroyed their own forest environments. They say the North has not yet put its own house in order, and therefore has little moral authority to tell Latin America what to do with its rainforests.

Soil erosion

Over-intensive agriculture can produce just as much soil erosion as deforestation. In Central America forty per cent of all lands suffer a degree of erosion which undermines their productivity. The worst case is El Salvador, where an estimated 77 per cent of arable land is eroded. Ravaged by years of civil war, this tiny country is the most densely populated in Latin America and has an extremely unequal system of land distribution. In the Salvadorean countryside peasant farmers hand-tend tiny plots of maize and beans on steep hillsides, while down below on the fertile valley floor the rich landowners' tractors prepare the land for cotton or sugar. When the rains come, they wash the soil off the hillsides by the ton, yields decrease and the poor peasant becomes even poorer.

Downstream the silt, often laden with pesticides, devastates the marine environment. Siltation, pollution and wood-cutting have reduced El Salvador's 300,000 acres of mangrove estuary to a pitiful 6,800 acres. The loss is also an economic one: mangroves provide a rich breeding ground for marine life, and one square kilometre of mangrove estuary is worth US$100,000 a year in fish and shellfish. Siltation has also greatly reduced the lifespan of a number of hydroelectric dams in the region, (themselves often damaging to the environment) by clogging up the lakes which feed the generators.

Despite efforts to show poor farmers the virtues of terracing, crop rotation and tree-planting, hard-pressed families are likely to continue to plough up hillsides or cut down trees unless a serious land reform gives them better lands elsewhere. In Nicaragua, one of the Sandinista government's main contributions to the environment was their land reform programme, which eased pressure on the country's remaining tropical forests by giving peasants land.

Pesticide Poisons

An early morning bus ride through the cotton-growing area of Central America provides a stinging glimpse of everyday reality. As the bus passes plantations, its windows film over. Most of the passengers, knowing what to expect, close their eyes, slow their breathing, and cover their nose and mouth with a scarf. Those riders caught unaware feel their eyes begin to smart, their lungs involuntarily contract, and a bitter chemical smell starts to clog their noses.

Visitors to the area will likely rush off the bus to change clothes and to wash their stinging skin with soap and water. The local population is not so fortunate; their exposure to agricultural chemicals for the day has only begun. They will toil long hours in the fields, drenched with chemicals that crop dusters sprayed earlier that morning. Three out of four farm workers have no running water in their homes to wash off the day's accumulation of pesticides. Many bathe in irrigation canals or streams contaminated with still more agro-chemicals, or try to wash off with water stored in a discarded pesticide drum.

Tom Barry, *Roots of Rebellion*, Boston, 1987

Crop-spraying on the outskirts of Lima, Peru.

All over rural Latin America glossy roadside billboards peddle the wares of the big agro-chemical multinationals. Names like Bayer, Ceiba-Geigy, Shell, Monsanto and Du Pont adorn adverts promising farmers prosperity if they administer just one more dose of chemicals to their crops. In jeeps and village bars, the plantation owners sport brand names such as Tordon or Gramoxone on their T-shirts and baseball caps. The pesticide companies claim to sell their wares in philanthropic pursuit of an end to world hunger, and that, in the words of one Bayer annual report, 'emotional attacks against conscientious agro-chemicals research are attacks against humanity.'

In fact, nearly all pesticides are used on export crops, not food for local people, and the cotton and banana plantations of Central America provide some of the worst examples of pesticide abuse in the world. In the 1970s Central America consumed forty per cent of all US pesticide exports. Chemicals like DDT which were illegal in the US were routinely exported and sold in the region, where about 75 per cent of the pesticides used were either banned, restricted or unregistered in the US. In 1990 the US Congress finally took action and passed laws preventing the 'dumping' of banned pesticides on third world markets.

Several thousand people are poisoned every year. In 1987, in just one children's hospital in El Salvador, more than fifty children died from pesticide poisoning. A number of factors exacerbate the damage:

• Cotton spraying is mainly done by light aircraft. Over half the sprayed chemicals miss the cotton fields altogether, drifting over neighbouring villages, streams and crops. Most workers on cotton farms live near the fields, and therefore suffer almost constant exposure to toxic chemicals during the spraying season.

• Chemicals for hand-spraying frequently carry instructions in English, but even those in Spanish mean nothing to illiterate farmworkers. Governments and companies typically provide no education for plantation workers on the risks of pesticide poisoning and how to avoid them.

• Safety gear such as masks and gloves is either not provided, or is designed for temperate climates and is unbearable in the sun-baked fields of Central America.

• Farm managements are often extremely irresponsible towards their workforce. In the words of one United Brands foreman in Panama, quoted in *Roots of Rebellion*, 'If you get careless and forget to rotate [the workers], the next thing you know the damn Indian's bleeding at the nose all the time and you gotta pay for his sick care for the next couple of weeks.'

• Saturation spraying leads to the so-called 'pesticide treadmill', whereby pests increase their resistance, requiring more spraying and a greater range of chemicals. Between the mid-1950s and the late 1960s, cotton growers moved from spraying five chemicals five to ten times a year, to using a cocktail of 70 chemicals 28 to 35 times a year. Across Central America, growers in the mid-1970s applied over four pounds of pesticides for every man, woman and child in the region.

• Any protective legislation is almost entirely ignored and rarely enforced.

From the plantations, the pesticides enter the food chains of animals and humans alike. Milk in some Guatemalan cotton regions has registered ninety times the highest level of DDT permitted in the US, while Central American beef exports are increasingly refused entry to the US market because of pesticide contamination. They are sent home to be eaten by Central Americans, who have the world's highest levels of DDT in their body fat. No one knows how many will die from the carcinogenic organochlorines literally imbibed at their mothers' breast – women in the cotton regions have been found to have as much as 185 times more DDT in their breast milk than is considered safe by the World Health Organisation.

In the early 1980s, the Sandinista government in Nicaragua won praise from environmentalists for challenging the multinationals and big agribusiness interests. It prohibited pesticides that were banned in their country of origin, began an education campaign among rural workers on the dangers of pesticides, and insisted that all instructions be in Spanish and colour-coded for the illiterate. It also revived a previous pilot programme of integrated pest management (IPM). IPM involves finding alternatives to chemical overdoses as a means of controlling pests. The programme used natural predators, particularly viruses and bacteria, to prey on the pests, with the advantage that once the predators have eaten all the pests, they themselves then die out. Another technique is that of 'trap rows' – planting a strip of the crop earlier than the rest, which then attracts all the local pests. An application of pesticide to that smaller area can then greatly reduce the total number of pests.

Lost Volcanoes

The cities of Latin America are losing their volcanoes. In Santiago, Chile, people recall the days when the snow-capped Andes loomed over the city. Now they rarely break through a dense blanket of smog. The Chilean government even proposed blasting a hole through the mountain chain to

CURITIBA: UTOPIA BY BUS

The city of Curitiba in southern Brazil has attracted international attention and praise for its innovative and successful approach to urban planning. Despite being one of the fastest-growing cities in Brazil, it has achieved substantial improvements in the quality of life, introducing an innovative public transport system, preserving the city's cultural heritage, expanding the numbers of parks, carrying out environmental education and pioneering new ways of recycling waste.

The keys to Curitiba's success have been planning and public transport. In the 1960s, city planners decided to avoid large-scale, expensive transport systems such as a metro. Instead, they built five main 'trinary' roads with two exclusive bus lanes in the centre for express buses. Passengers switch from the express buses to slower local buses to reach their final destination. The city authorities then used planning permission to encourage high density housing programmes along the five main bus routes, matching people and public transport and taking pressure of the city centre, which was then turned over to pedestrians. The results have been spectacular: over a quarter of the population switched from using cars to the public transport system, saving money, fuel and air pollution.

Other successful programmes include a recycling scheme in which over seventy per cent of the population separates out organic and inorganic garbage for weekly collection. In the remaining *favelas* (slums), home to about ten per cent of the city's population, poor families can exchange bags of garbage for bus tickets and food. The cost to the city authorities is roughly the same as paying a private company to collect the garbage. Thanks to the scheme, dumping in rivers and waste ground has fallen and infant mortality rates are down substantially in the poor areas. The authorities have planted 1.5 million trees in the last twenty years, and the ratio of open space per inhabitant has increased from 0.5 square metres to 52 square metres, one of the highest averages in the world.

Jonas Rabinovitch, 'Curitiba: towards sustainable urban development', in *Green Guerrillas*, London, 1996

allow the wind through to clear away the murk. 'They think it's easier to move mountains than to control the bus drivers,' explained a resident.

In Mexico, the two great volcanoes of the Aztecs, Popocatepetl and Ixtaccihuatl have similarly been lost to sight. Average visibility has dropped from twelve kilometres to just three in the last forty years. Air pollution exceeds internationally acceptable levels in São Paulo, Buenos Aires, Santiago, Caracas and Mexico City. Mexico is probably the worst, as any visitor will agree who has had the misfortune to be there on one of the 225 days a year when a thermal inversion prevents the city's filth from escaping. Pedestrians weep as they walk through the streets in air that does as much damage as smoking forty cigarettes a day. Mexico is uniquely damned by geography – it lies in a natural bowl where pollution collects, and at its high altitude of 7,400 feet car engines produce twice their sea-level amount of carbon monoxide. For the inhabitants of such cities, air pollution is far more than an irritant. Seventy per cent of all babies are born with unacceptable levels of lead in their bloodstreams.

Following the Great Depression, all of the larger Latin American nations embarked on a programme of industrialisation aimed at reducing their dependence on commodity exports and manufactured imports (see chapter 5). The consequence was a sudden surge in unchecked industrial growth and a chaotic exodus of impoverished farmers from the countryside to the cities. Latin America's cities rapidly became some of the biggest in the world – Mexico City and São Paulo both had about 15 million inhabitants by 1995. A thousand migrants currently flood into Mexico City every day.

Three-quarters of Mexico City's pollution comes from its 2.5 million cars and its huge and filthy industrial complex. 'If the [US] Environmental Protection Agency standards were applied to this country,' comments one US embassy official, 'Mexico would surpass the highest tolerable levels for sulphur dioxide, cadmium, lead, zinc, copper and particulate matter.' What he omits to mention is that many US and other multinational companies have been quick to relocate some of their dirtiest factories to Latin American countries precisely to avoid those EPA standards, and the increased costs they imply.

The growth of the cities seems inexorable, but could be slowed if governments undertook serious agrarian reform in the countryside and used regional planning to decentralise the economy. In the towns, the environmental damage could be reduced if factories and vehicles were regulated, and there have been some encouraging signs in recent years, with the Brazilian city of Curitiba offering some impressive lessons to city planners around the world (see box). City schemes to encourage lead-free petrol and make people leave their cars at home for one working day a week have helped cut air pollution in Santiago, Mexico City and São Paulo.

Structural Adjustment

Since 1982, pressure on Latin America's environment has been stepped up by structural adjustment programmes and a regional push for growth based on exporting ever-greater quantities of raw materials.

The squeeze on the environment started with the debt crisis, (see chapter 5) as governments stepped up exports to meet escalating repayments to the western banks. As time went on, the broader processes of 'structural adjustment', which pursued an 'export-or-die' approach to development, have further increased pressure on the ecosystem.

Governments desperate to find new sources of hard currency have shown little interest in longer-term issues such as environmental protection. In Guyana, largely untouched forests have come under the hammer as part of an adjustment programme agreed with the International Monetary Fund (IMF) in the late 1980s. Guyana has duly parcelled out its forests and rivers to an unholy alliance of Canadian, Brazilian and Asian mining and logging companies. In return for a fifty-year licence on a 4.13 million acre concession, the notorious Sarawak-based logger, Samling Timbers, promised to export 1.2 million cubic feet of Guyanese timber a year (compared to national exports of just 94,000 cubic feet in 1989).

One of the growth areas has been so-called 'non-traditional exports' of higher value agricultural products such as cut flowers of fresh fruit. These require enormous doses of pesticides and fungicides in order to reach supermarkets in the North in pristine condition. In a 1990 survey of Costa Rican farmers growing melons (one of its most successful non-traditional exports), seventy per cent of the farmers using such agro-chemicals as Tamaron, Paraquat and Lannate (metomil) reported seeing animals die after spraying and 58 per cent of them knew of water supplies poisoned by the sprays. In Jacona, Mexico, farmworkers pay a high price for getting 4.5 million kilograms of strawberries a year to US tables in the middle of winter. According to his death certificate, Blas López Vásquez, 36, died in December 1992 from a 'respiratory insufficiency' caused by 'intoxication from organophosphates' after backpack-spraying a strawberry field. Three other workers died that year in Jacona, and 14 more were hospitalised.

Green Guerrillas

In recent years, the environmental movement has taken off in Latin America and has already achieved some notable successes. Environmental groups were initially largely urban and middle-class, taking their cue from the burgeoning green movement in Europe and North America. They were also boosted by the 1992 UN 'Earth Summit', held in Rio de Janeiro, which by explicitly linking the two concepts of environment and development, gained general acceptance of the importance of 'sustainable development'.

The work of the middle-class environmentalists and the international green lobby can clearly be seen in the increased media coverage for green issues within the region and the 'greening' of political debate. Even ranchers and loggers now feel obliged to dress up their language in green rhetoric. Pressure from the urban environmental movement has also been instrumental in forcing the region's cities to begin to try and control air pollution. In some cases,

DIRTY INDUSTRY

Apart from raw materials, the other growth area in Latin American exports are the *maquiladoras*. These are assembly plants run by multinational companies in Mexico, Central America and the Caribbean which take advantage of low wages and lax environmental laws to produce goods for re-export to the US market:

'"Twelve years ago we came to live here," says Maurilio Sánchez Pachuca, the stout president of the local residents' committee in a dingy *colonia* just outside Tijuana, Mexico. "We thought we'd be in glory because it was an ecological reserve – lots of vegetation, animals, birds. Two years later the maquiladoras started to arrive up there." A fat thumb gestures up at the plateau overlooking the colonia, with its clean blue and white maquiladora assembly plants. "Now many of us have skin problems – rashes, hair falling out, we get eye pains, fevers. My kids' legs are really bad – all the kids have nervous problems and on the way to school the dust and streams are all polluted. We've tried to stop them playing in the streams, but kids are kids." He flicks despairingly through a treasured folder full of blurred photocopies of the hand-typed letters he has written to the authorities and their replies, a nine-year Kafkaesque exercise in futility. "The first thing [the maquiladoras] do is buy the local officials. There are too many vested interests – dark interests, dollars. I have so many lovely letters from the government – but they aren't real."

Up on the plateau, huge container trucks are at the loading bays, gorging themselves on the products of the 189 factories – Maxell cassettes, a crisp new Sanyo plant, Tabuchi Electric de México. A security guard ushers unwelcome visitors from the site. A black and pink slag-heap of battery casings is piled up by the fence surrounding the factories, where truckloads of old batteries from the US are broken up to recycle the lead and acid. By law, the remnants should be returned to the US, but they are just dumped here on the edge of the plateau.'

Duncan Green, *Silent Revolution: The Rise of Market Economics in Latin America*, London, 1995

governments and the private sector found that environmentalism could also be good for business. One of the most successful green industries is ecotourism, which in Costa Rica brought in US$500 million in 1993, as northern holidaymakers were lured in by a combination of beaches and spectacular national parks.

Another wing of Latin American environmental activism comes from the grassroots, involving those directly affected, usually poor communities such as those championed by Chico Mendes. Often led by the region's burgeoning Indian revival (see chapter 11), these groups have led campaigns against polluting oil industries in Mexico and Ecuador and have taken up numerous other causes.

Such developments offer hope for the future, but there are also ample grounds for gloom. The greed and short-sightedness of both local and foreign interests have changed little since the conquest – they still mistakenly treat

Harriet Logan

the New World and its people as an inexhaustible and indestructible source of riches. Since the 1980s, the region's uncritical adoption of a development model based on the unregulated market and ever-more rapacious exploitation of its ecosystem has worked against attempts to improve the environment, forcing campaigners to swim against the prevailing economic tide. When, as part of its commitment to opening up the economy, the Brazilian government removed the tariffs which had protected domestic rubber producers, cheap Malaysian rubber flooded in. The price of latex in Brazil fell from US$1.80 per kilogram in 1980 to under 40 cents in 1992, and Amazon-grown rubber saw its market share slide from 85 per cent to just 28 per cent. The first to suffer were the rubber tappers, who in the wake of Chico Mendes' murder had pressured the government into establishing extractive zones covering millions of hectares. Their joy turned sour as they watched prices slump. Thousands of families have been forced to leave the new reserves in search of a living wage in the cities, or join the ranks of the *garimpeiros* in the ecologically disastrous gold rush. The blind forces of economics have turned them from defenders of the environment into its destroyers.

Protesters supporting Kayapó Indians in a campaign against the great hydro-electric project at Altamira, Brazil.

City of contrasts. Rich city centre and poor shanty towns, La Paz, Bolivia.

Julio Etchart

Chronology

1920	First shanty towns recorded in Rio de Janeiro
1930s	Start of industrialisation leads to mass migration to the cities
1950	41.2% of Latin Americans live in towns
1960	500 people invade land in Lima to found the Cuevas settlement
1970	Population of Cuevas settlement reaches 12,000
1978	Argentine military government bulldozes shanty towns in clean up campaign before World Cup
1979	Informal sector now accounts for over half Colombia's jobs
1980	64.7% of Latin Americans live in towns
1982 on	Debt crisis and ensuing structural adjustment programmes lead to massive rise in informal sector
1985	Mexico City earthquake, thousands made homeless
1990	23 million Hispanics now constitute 10% of the US population
1994	74% of Latin Americans live in towns

Mean Streets 4

Migration and Life in the City

The tourist hotels along Ipanema beach in Rio de Janeiro are some of the most expensive real estate in the world. Luxury tower blocks, their balconies bursting with foliage, overlook beaches strewn with perfect brown bodies sporting skimpy swimsuits known locally as 'dental floss'. Far above the beach, dozens of hang-gliders circle lazily down from one of Rio's extraordinary bare-rock mountains, to which clings the Rocinha *favela*, a shanty town which is home to 350,000 of Rio's poor. Shimmering in the heat haze, Rocinha looks down on the beaches like a bad conscience.

Shanty towns surround most Latin American cities, bulging with migrants from the countryside or the city's youth, fleeing the overcrowded tenements of the inner city in search of a house of their own. In Peru the poor have built their settlements on the barren desert around Lima. In Ecuador, sixty per cent of Guayaquil's population have built shacks over the muddy and polluted water of the swamps, their houses suspended on stilts. Some homes are a forty minute walk along rickety boardwalks to dry land.

The growth of the cities has been astounding. In 1930, Latin America's total urban population was 20 million, out of a total population of around 100 million. Now 350 million Latin Americans live in cities, out of a total of some 470 million. Since the 1930s, millions of peasant families have left their farms and villages and joined the great trek to the cities. The driving forces behind this great human tide include war, famine, the shortage of land and the often illusory glitter of the city, with its promise of jobs, education and excitement. If present trends continue, Latin America will be more urbanised than Europe or the US by the early 21st century. Already the majority of people live in towns and cities in all but five Latin American nations – Haiti, Honduras, El Salvador, Guatemala, and Costa Rica.

Contrary to the common image of poor, desperate peasants trailing into the cities, most migrants are literate young adults, frustrated with the lack of opportunity in the countryside. In Latin America, unlike Asia and Africa, women migrants outnumber men, reflecting women's lesser role in agriculture compared to the other continents. However, catastrophes like war and famine change the pattern, as people of all ages and educational backgrounds flee to the cities *en masse*.

The way people migrate has been determined by the changes in public transport. As roads and bus and truck services have improved, migration has become a less daunting prospect. Not only has it made it easier for people to move to big cities from once-remote rural villages, but better transport now means that the move need no longer be a definitive break with the past. Increasing numbers of poor Latin Americans now divide their time

TABLE 3: PERCENTAGE OF POPULATION LIVING IN URBAN
AREAS, 1960-93

Country	Urban population as % of total population	
Most developed	1960	1993
Argentina	74	88
Costa Rica	37	49
Uruguay	80	90
Chile	68	84
Intermediate		
Colombia	48	72
Brazil	45	77
Ecuador	34	57
Paraguay	36	51
Least developed		
Honduras	23	43
El Salvador	38	45
Nicaragua	40	62

• Most developed, intermediate and least developed categories based
on Human Development Index ranking, see table, page xi
Source: World Development Report, 1996

between town and country, visiting the family farm at weekends. The distinctions between urban and rural lifestyles are becoming blurred.

The increased contact between town and village has in turn stimulated further migration, as one Aymara Indian woman in Bolivia recalls:

At that time I was nine years old, and was already seeing the older girls coming back from working as servants saying: 'I'm happy in the city. Life is great there.' To me they seemed physically happier; they talked beautifully, they had lovely clothes with embroidered shawls, with luxurious skirts. Pretty Indian girls, they looked. So I said 'Ah! I'm going too.'
Ana María Condori, *Mi Despertar*, La Paz, 1988 (author's translation)

Unless driven by war or natural disaster, migration is usually a carefully planned operation; for example, a family will send an eldest daughter on ahead to find work and establish a base before other family members follow. Since they are mainly young people, migrants then have their children in the city, further boosting urban population growth. For those that stay behind, money sent by relatives in the city, or increasingly from abroad, has become vital to the survival of many rural communities. One study of Mixteca Indians in Mexico showed that remittances from family members working in New York now pay for everything from a new drinking water system to the religious festivals which bind the villages together.

The growth of the cities is a consequence of Latin America's drive for industrialisation (see chapter 5). As industry grew from the 1930s onwards,

the prospect of jobs pulled in the rural population. In addition, as commercial agriculture spread further into the countryside, peasants were forced off the land and left with the choice of seasonal labour on the plantations or moving to the city in search of a better life. Although many migrants never found regular employment, they still lived better in urban squalor than in rural poverty. Their children were more likely to get some schooling, and there was more chance of winning eventual access to basic services like water and electricity. At a national level, wealth in Latin American countries is disproportionately concentrated in the urban areas, especially the capital. This enduring inequality is the driving force behind the continued drift to the cities. One of the consequences of the debt crisis and recent structural adjustment programmes has been a sharp rise in urban poverty, which has tarnished the glitter of the cities and reduced migratory pressures in many countries.

Indian woman selling chewing gum at the traffic lights, Mexico City.

The lopsided division of wealth between urban and rural areas also occurs between countries. Table 1 shows that those countries which remain predominantly rural, such as Bolivia and Paraguay, are among the poorest in the continent, while the more urbanised countries are among the best off.

Urbanisation is a serious headache for Latin America's planners, swamping existing services, and stretching such resources as water and food dangerously thin. In recent years pollution and congestion have added to their problems. Governments' attempts to check urban growth have had little impact, however, since they have failed to question the logic of the development model which was fuelling migration. The only exception has been Cuba, where the Castro government used its central planning of jobs, housing and food-distribution to dissuade would-be migrants to Havana, while investing in other, smaller cities and rural improvements. As a result, it managed to reverse Havana's growing share of the population. In some of

City	Population (thousands)	Year
Mexico City, Mexico	15,047	1990
Buenos Aires, Argentina	11,382	1990
São Paulo, Brazil	11,128	1990
Lima-Callao, Peru	6,414	1990
Rio de Janeiro, Brazil	6,042	1990
Bogotá, Colombia	4,177	1985
Santiago, Chile	4,099	1990
Caracas, Venezuela	2,784	1990
Belo Horizonte, Brazil	2,415	1990
Havana, Cuba	2,096	1988
Salvador, Brazil	2,050	1990

TABLE 4: POPULATION OF LATIN AMERICA'S LARGEST CITIES

Source: J Wilkie et al, *Statistical Abstract for Latin America*, 1996

the giant cities like Buenos Aires, congestion and pollution have started to make life so difficult that some companies are relocating to nearby cities.

Crossing the Border

Many migrants, especially those from Mexico, Central America, the Caribbean and Colombia, decide to leave their country altogether. Their usual destination is *El Norte*, the promised land of the US, where they work illegally in factories, on farms, or in restaurants in the hope of one day acquiring the coveted green card, or work permit. The route to the US is uncertain and dangerous, and involves running the gauntlet of unscrupulous *coyotes* or guides, as well as US Immigration Service patrols. Migrants caught at the border are swiftly returned to their home country, often to begin another attempt to head north and find safety in the anonymity of the Hispanic quarters of major US cities.

The exodus has changed US society. By 1990 an estimated nine per cent of the US population, some 23 million people, were 'Hispanics', over half of them hailing originally from Mexico. Hispanics are concentrated in a few states, notably California, where by 1991 they made up over a quarter of the population. Successive immigration amnesties have swelled the number who hold green cards to prove legal citizenship and the right to vote, although so far Hispanics have made little impact on national politics. Although Cuban émigrés dominate political life in Florida, the Hispanic community has not found national leaders to play Jesse Jackson's role in galvanising black voters; there are as yet no Hispanic senators, and only a handful of Hispanics in the House of Representatives. Part of the reason is that the Hispanic community is fragmented – Puerto Ricans and Dominicans dominate in New York, whereas Mexicans and Central Americans are the main groups in Los Angeles.

Within the US, attitudes to Hispanic immigrants have depended on the state of the economy. After the Second World War, when US agriculture was suffering a labour shortage, Mexicans were encouraged to migrate on the *bracero* farm-worker programme. In recent years, however, a rising tide of anti-immigrant feeling has prompted discrimination and attacks against Hispanics. In California, 59 per cent of the electorate voted in 1994 for Proposition 187, depriving undocumented immigrants of the right to medical care and education and obliging teachers, nurses and others to inform on suspected illegal immigrants. Politicians have been swift to capitalise on the issue, with Newt Gingrich, the Republican Speaker of the House of Representatives, predicting 'the decay of the core parts of our civilisation' as he urged Congress in 1996 to pass a law declaring English the official US language.

Not all migrants head for the US; inequalities of wealth and opportunity between neighbouring countries often force Latin America's migrants over the nearest border. In Buenos Aires the people of Ciudad Oculta (Hidden City) are shorter and darker than the rich white inhabitants of the city centre. Indian features denote the thousands of Bolivians and Paraguayans who have come to Argentina in search of a decent living. City centre stores are full of the latest labour-saving gadgets, yet the women of Ciudad Oculta cook in mud ovens, and watch over scruffy, barefoot children. Infant mortality is four times higher than the national average – one child in ten never reaches its first birthday.

Builders and Squatters

Recently-arrived migrants in Latin America's cities frequently stay with friends and relatives until they get used to their new surroundings, and find some way of earning a living. With space at a premium, however, they soon come

Helping yourselves.
Tapping into the
electricity supply,
Mexico City.

under pressure to find a place of their own. Choices are limited. They can rent a tiny room in an overcrowded inner city tenement, but the development of bus and other mass urban transport networks in the last fifty years has given them another option – joining the increasing number of squatters in the shanty towns on the outskirts of the cities.

Shanty towns have transformed Latin America's urban landscape. In Rio de Janeiro the first were recorded in 1920. Today they house over a third of the city's inhabitants. In Caracas that figure is nearer two-thirds. Each country has a different word for them – in Brazil they are *favelas*, in Argentina the evocative term is *villas miserias* (towns of poverty), in Peru the progressive military regime which came to power in 1968 insisted on the more dignified *pueblos jovenes*, (young towns). In Chile they are simply *callampas*, (mushrooms), springing up overnight on the outskirts of Santiago.

Shanty town homes are built by their residents and are nearly always illegal, either because the squatters do not own the land, or because they have no planning permission to build. Many squatter settlements begin with a 'land invasion'; a group of the urban poor, often including recent migrants, invades a piece of ground at night and hastily raises temporary shacks. If they succeed in fending off initial attempts by the authorities or the landlord to evict them, the temporary homes stand a chance of becoming permanent.

As time goes by and the settlement's prospects improve, residents start the long process of improving their homes. The improvements take up much of their spare time and money. The first cardboard and plastic shacks are replaced by planks or corrugated iron. Over the years brick houses start to appear, some even acquiring a second storey. Eventually they come to resemble other parts of the city, and become absorbed into the city's economy as increasing numbers of the houses are sold or rented out by their original inhabitants.

THE INVASION OF LA VICTORIA, SANTIAGO, CHILE

At last the great and historic moment arrived in which we had to risk everything. On the 29th, a trail of gunpowder reached our door bringing the news: the *toma* [invasion] is on. That night the final orders were given in all the committees. Essential qualifications: being poor, having kids, three poles and a flag. The hour of decision had arrived for each of us.

There were women who went without their husband's agreement, risking a good hiding if things went badly. But when you have suffered the lack of a roof, when your babies have died and no one listens to you, you have to use other methods. You heard people saying:

'Listen, kids, your dad doesn't want us to go to the toma, but I'm going anyway; I'll take the youngest kids with me. You wait for your papa, give him his dinner, and tell him I went to the toma.'

The orders, the taking down of the shacks, getting the dog and the mother-in-law onto the carts; all this began from early in the morning. At last, everything was sorted out.

At 8pm the most militant started to gather at the site. The three poles and the flag, some household goods and blankets, started to form a caravan. We started to look like the tribe of Israel in search of the promised land. Many Christians who were with us that night said the hand of God was with us.

Silently we crept towards our goal, coming from different directions we arrived at the four sides of the La Feria farm. We could see the lights of the Los Cerillos airport. In the darkness we moved forward, with frequent bumps. As dawn broke, each person began to clear a piece of scrubland, to put up their hut, and to raise the flag.

Constructores de Ciudad, Santiago, 1989, author's translation

Squatter settlements face enormous initial problems. Often the land they have occupied was empty precisely because it was unsuitable for building. In Rio the poor cling to sheer hillsides, risking landslides every time it rains. In El Salvador's capital, San Salvador, shanty towns are strung terrifyingly close to railway lines or huddled into ravines, often side by side with the local rubbish tip. In Lima the pueblos jovenes are built into the desert, leaving the new arrivals at the mercy of private water suppliers. Typically, the most urgent problems are water and sanitation. In São Paulo, over a third of the city's houses, mainly in the peripheral shanty towns, have no sewer connections or cesspools. People use open holes or dry latrines, which often contaminate the shallow wells that provide their only water supply.

The key to improving living standards is organisation, and squatter settlements have produced some of Latin America's best-organised and most vocal neighbourhood organisations. The list of demands is dispiritingly long: roads, drinking water, sewers, electricity, schools, rubbish collection, health clinics and bus routes. Another major battlefield concerns their illegality, since without proper legal title to the land, the inhabitants will never be secure in their homes. Once a settlement is established it can grow rapidly. In Lima 500 people organised a land invasion in 1960 and founded the Cuevas settlement. By 1970, 12,000 people lived there.

BUILDING A SELF-HELP HOME

Alfonso and Isabel Rodríguez live with their three children in a low-income settlement in the south of Valencia, a Venezuelan city with around 800,000 inhabitants. The population has grown rapidly as manufacturing plants have moved to the city in preference to the crowded conditions found in Caracas. Alfonso works in the Ford plant. He was born in the mountain state of Mérida and arrived in Valencia in 1975 after an uncle told him that work was available. He stayed with his uncle for a while in a consolidated self-help house in the south of the city and then moved into rental accommodation nearer the centre. He met Isabel, who had been born in Valencia, six months later. They rented a new home together and stayed there for 18 months. Two years later, he managed to obtain a plot of land through an invasion. The invasion was organised by an employee of the local authority who was trying to win support for a councillor who was hoping to be re-elected that year. One hundred and twenty families established rudimentary shacks early one Sunday morning. Because of the protection given by the councillor there was little trouble with the police and the settlers soon began to improve their accommodation. Since Alfonso had a reasonably well-paid job, he could afford to buy cement and bricks with which to improve the house. In addition, he sold half of the 20 by 35 metre plot he had obtained to two other families; this was sufficient to buy the rest of the materials he needed. He could also employ, on an occasional basis, a friend who worked in the construction industry. Progress on the house was slow but steady. Since he had to work at his paid job during the week, he could do little except at weekends. Even then there were interruptions, family visits, the occasional fiesta, demands by the children to go out. Isabel helped with some of the lighter jobs when she could, but three rapid pregnancies and a miscarriage limited her participation in the actual building.

By 1985, five years later, the house had three rooms. It was not pretty to look at but it was solidly built and the roof kept out the rain. It had electricity, stolen from the mains by a neighbour who worked for the electricity board. Water had been provided by the government during the last election campaign, but sewerage was still lacking. There was a school in the next settlement, and the eldest child would start to attend it in a couple of years' time.

Alan Gilbert, *Latin America*, London, 1990

The authorities may respond to land invasions with violent attempts at eviction, but in the long term many recognise that illegal settlement and self-build housing are the only solution to the shortage of accommodation. In cities like Lima and Mexico, local politicians support squatters in exchange for votes, while political parties frequently try to co-opt the neighbourhood organisations' leaders. In Argentina, on the other hand, the military government bulldozed the 'villas miserias' while cleaning up the city for the World Cup in 1978. Bolivian and Paraguayan migrants were beaten up, then herded onto trains and trucks for deportation. Often, however, the

At the settlement Márquez del Callao, hundreds of children line up in front of the dining hall. They begin two hours before noon, every day, plate and spoon in hand. They beg and shout in hopes of getting a free portion from the mothers who organised this communal kitchen. Forty mothers cook 400 portions a day, half for member families and half for the hungry children.

These organisations depend on donations of oil, oatmeal and flour, and on their own purchases. In their search for better prices, the women will frequently contact the producers directly. This form of organising has proven so successful that, by 1986, 800 *comedores* (communal canteens) were represented by a National Commission of Comedores. Some are independent while others may be funded by the Church, the state, political parties or development agencies.

Rosario de Meléndez, recently laid off from a stocking factory, is a new member of the Glass of Milk committee of the neighbourhood of El Carcamo. When it is her turn, she gets up at five in the morning, turns on the stove and begins to heat a huge pot of milk, oatmeal, some sugar, cloves and cinnamon. She knows that at seven the children will begin lining up at the door of her house waiting for the hot milk. Each member of her committee contributes less than ten cents a week for the purchase of kerosene, cocoa and cloves.

By working together, these women come to see their oppression as a social ill and open up new horizons for themselves. The voice of the women, before silent, is making itself heard. Formerly taboo subjects are now discussed. The mere fact that they are no longer shut up in their houses cooking for their husbands transforms relationships within the home. The women like to talk about the time one leader arrived at a meeting barefoot because her husband had hidden her shoes to keep her from going.

Carolina Carlessi, 'The Reconquest', *Report on the Americas*, New York, November 1989

settlements' successes produce a spirit of optimism and self-confidence which is lacking in the gloomy tenements of the city centre.

The only alternative to the current uneasy coexistence between authorities and squatters is a serious urban land reform. There are many parallels between the rural land crisis and that in the cities. Like agrarian reform, an urban land reform requires far more than mere distribution of land if it is to succeed. Settlers also need access to credit to enable them to buy building materials, physical infrastructure such as roads and electricity, and technical advice on building. Just as in the countryside, the big urban landowners resist any attempt to challenge their control, and are usually successful in their efforts.

Visitors to Latin America may see little of life in the shanty towns and tenements, since tourists' hotels and friends or contacts are usually in the wealthier areas, either pleasant suburbs or modern city centres. In the middle-class areas, families lead a relatively comfortable existence, aided by servants and access to household appliances. As a proportion of the total population the middle class in Latin America is far smaller than in Europe or the US, and a vast gulf separates it from the poor masses of the slums. The middle-class

A community comes together to build its own street, Cusco, Peru.

enclaves are often little more than islands of 'modernity' in vast surrounding expanses of poverty. Along the main road north out of Recife, in Brazil, sensitive car drivers are even spared the sight of the long lines of cardboard and wooden shacks. A municipal billboard hundreds of yards long apologises for the 'inconvenience caused by temporary housing'. The billboard can hide the houses from view, but not the hot stench of the canal passing through the encampment. Scrawny children swim in the polluted waters. In places the canal banks are made up entirely of rubbish.

Scraping a Living

New Year's Eve on the road to Mexico City's airport. When the cars pull up at the traffic lights, a firebreather steps out in front of the queue. A jet of flame lances across the night, lighting up a shiny face, glazed eyes and a hand clutching a bottle of petrol. After the show, the ragged performer goes up the line of car windows, hand outstretched. On New Year's Eve the drivers are in a good mood and he does well.

Although many migrants come to the city looking for regular paid jobs in industry, few find them. Despite Latin America's attempts at industrialisation, most of the investment has been in capital-intensive industry where machines do the work instead of people. Consequently, manufacturing employment has failed to keep up with the demand for jobs. In most Latin American nations, social security provisions only apply to those in regular employment for the state or big companies – unemployment and maternity benefits or pensions are not available to the majority. Without the safety net of a welfare state, migrants unable to find a way of earning an income face starvation, and most of the inhabitants of the shanty towns are forced to find work in what has become known as the 'informal sector' of the economy.

The informal sector is the umbrella term for a mass of different tasks including street selling, domestic service, odd-jobs, casual building labour, small-scale industry recycling tyres into sandals, picking through garbage for tin cans and paper, or even firebreathing at traffic lights.

Such work is in stark contrast to the formal sector of waged jobs more familiar to those in the industrialised nations. Formal-sector jobs are provided by large private and state-owned businesses, subsidiaries of multinational companies, and the public sector. Often such jobs take place in the westernised centres of the cities, with their office blocks, government departments and shops, while economic life in the poor fringes of the city operates through the networks of the informal sector. Perhaps the clearest distinction between the two is over the level of protection: if someone in the informal sector is injured or sacked, they are on their own. Increasingly, the deregulation of workplaces and spread of activities such as subcontracting to sweatshops by textile companies, means that the informal sector is encroaching on what were once formal-sector occupations.

To the visitor, the street traders are the most striking members of the informal economy. In La Paz, the Avenida Buenos Aires and adjoining streets are the site of the capital's biggest street market. Young men dressed in denims sell the latest line in microwaves or stereos, smuggled in from Brazil, while one street along, Indian women sit patiently in their bowler hats and ponchos, selling dried llama foetuses which are buried under the foundations of new houses to bring good luck. Herbal remedies, BMX bicycles, imported disposable nappies, toiletries and pots and pans – the list of available goods is endless.

As the numbers of the urban poor have grown, so has the informal sector. In Colombia it rose from employing 30 per cent of the economically active population in 1960 to 52 per cent in 1979. During the recession of the 1980s and the structural adjustments of the 1990s, the informal sector has acted as a gigantic sponge, soaking up those who have been sacked, or who are entering the work force for the first time. As Latin America's streets have become clogged with vendors desperately seeking customers, incomes have fallen. In La Paz, where sixty per cent of the workforce is now in the informal sector, there is one street trader for every three families – there are just not enough buyers to go round.

The comparison between formal and informal sectors has led some economists to talk of two parallel circuits existing within the urban economy. The first circuit is a formal, western-style world of banks, factories and supermarkets, existing alongside a second circuit of street traders, money lenders and casual labourers. The two worlds are linked, however, since the informal sector provides low-cost services which often benefit the formal economy. The system resembles agriculture, where modern capital-intensive commercial agriculture exists alongside traditional labour-intensive peasant farming, which supplies it with cheap labour at harvest time.

Future Cities

Latin America is now an urban continent, and will remain so. In many ways, its cities have been remarkably successful, absorbing nearly 300 million new inhabitants over a sixty year period. The fact that more keep arriving is proof that, whatever the difficulties of city life, for many it is still preferable to the struggle for existence in the countryside.

Yet if a better future for the region is to be forged in the cities, much has to change. The energy and dynamism of the self-help housing movement must be channelled into community development; governments must help, rather than hinder the process, by passing urban land reform laws, providing support for the informal sector and ensuring that the next generation gets adequate education and health care. The ability of city authorities and national governments to provide such a future for their citizens is largely determined by the performance of the economy and the role of the state. It is to these subjects that we now turn.

The great divide. Cleaning car screens, Lima, Peru.

Chronology

1929	Wall Street Crash and ensuing depression in the US and Europe pushes Latin America into industrialisation
1958	Brazil becomes Latin America's leading industrial power
1973/4	First oil price rise leads to wave of loans to Latin America. Foreign debt soars.
1982	Mexico defaults on interest payments on its foreign debt, swiftly followed by most other Latin American governments
1982-91	Latin America pays a net US$219 billion in debt repayments to the North – US$500 for every Latin American.
late 1980s	Structural adjustment gathers pace throughout Latin America
1989	Announcement of austerity package in Venezuela provokes riots in which at least 276 people die
1994	Start of the North American Free Trade Agreement (NAFTA), between Mexico, the US and Canada
1994	Mexican currency crisis and subsequent economic recession raises fresh doubts over neoliberal model
1995	Start of Mercosur, or Southern Cone Common Market, comprising Argentina, Brazil, Uruguay and Paraguay
1997	One million people, mostly women, employed in cheap-labour assembly plants in Mexico, Central America and Caribbean

Growing Pains

5

Industrialisation, the Debt Crisis and Neoliberalism

São Paulo is made of cheap concrete. Millions of tons, poured in a hurry, spewed forth to make houses, tower blocks, factories and flyovers. Within a few years rain and sun leave it stained and crumbling, but quantity matters more than quality, for dilapidated buildings can always be replaced by bigger and newer constructions, using yet more concrete. The flood of concrete that created the great megalopolis of São Paulo is part of Brazil's rush for industrialisation, a titanic effort which has turned a relatively primitive coffee-exporter into a great industrial power, the tenth largest economy in the world. However, like the concrete, Brazil's industrial development is flawed and vulnerable. To pay for it, the national economy ran up huge debts in the 1970s, driving the country to the verge of bankruptcy during the debt crisis of the 1980s. State-led industrialisation has also failed the Brazilian people. In the main thoroughfares of São Paulo, the rush-hour is a stampede of the well-heeled, the manicured and beautiful beneficiaries of Brazil's growth. On the street corners the losers, the old and unemployed, earn a pittance working as human billboards. Standing in bored clumps all day, they wear T-shirts saying 'I buy gold', with a phone number.

For a half century after the Great Depression of the 1930s, Latin Americans saw industrialisation as the path to development. The satanic mills whose fumes now choke Caracas or Mexico City may seem unlikely saviours, but the region's planners pointed to the experience of the rich countries, like the UK, US or Japan, where the growth of industry had led to a rise both in political power and the standard of living. Industrialisation, they argued, offered Latin America a way out of its crippling dependence on commodity exports, and its humiliating reliance on foreign governments and multinational companies for aid and manufactured goods. In recent years, the failings of Latin America's industrialisation efforts have forced a rethink, and industrialisation in many cases has gone into reverse as governments have abandoned local industries to sink or swim in the global economy, in many cases reverting to commodity exports as the path to economic growth.

Latin America's industrial quest started late. During the colonial period, the Spanish and Portuguese governments did everything they could to prevent the growth of domestic industry, which they feared would disrupt the continent's dependence on commodity exports which provided a lucrative trade for the colonial powers. In 1785 a royal decree from the Portuguese crown banned all industry in its Brazilian colony, ordering all textile looms to be burnt. When independence arrived in the early 19th century, Britain's cheap manufactures soon undercut what little local industry had arisen as the colonial ties had weakened. Nevertheless, most countries managed to achieve a first stage of industrialisation; they semi-processed agricultural crops and minerals for export, and local industries produced simple goods like soap, clothing and bottled drinks. European immigrants set up many of the first local industries – in Argentina and Uruguay, British immigrants built slaughter-houses, freezer plants and tanneries to serve the beef export industry, while Germans set up Peru's beer industry and controlled ninety per cent of Brazil's textile production by 1916.

Despite these primitive local industries, Latin America remained a commodity exporter, dependent on manufactured imports, until the late 1920s. By then, the cattle and grain trade had made Argentina the fifth richest country in the world, and coffee had established São Paulo as Brazil's economic powerhouse. In 1929 the Wall Street Crash and the ensuing depression in the industrialised world rudely awoke Latin American governments to the perils of commodity dependence. Brazil's exports fell by sixty per cent between 1929-32, and the country suddenly had no hard currency with which to import manufactured goods.

Latin America learned its lesson. Just like the US government under Roosevelt's 'New Deal', or the followers of John Maynard Keynes in the UK, they concluded that the state had to play a much greater role in running the economy if future crashes were to be avoided. In Latin America, as local entrepreneurs moved in to start producing simple manufactured goods to plug the gap left by the import collapse, several governments began looking at ways to encourage 'import substitution'. By the late 1930s they were taking the first steps to improve transport, electricity and water supplies for local factories. When the Second World War came, the dilemma of the Great Depression was reversed; the industrialised nations were now desperate for Latin America's exports, but had fewer manufactures to spare as factories were converted to war production. The largest Latin American economies accumulated great wealth during the war, and afterwards used it to begin import substitution in earnest.

Besides improving national infrastructure, countries such as Argentina, Brazil and Mexico set up state-owned companies in strategic industries such as iron and steel and raised taxes on imported manufactured goods. These tariff barriers were essential to protect fledgling local industries from being undercut by cheap imports. At the same time, governments encouraged multinational companies to set up factories on Latin American soil, arguing that this would create jobs, while providing the technology and capital that the region lacked. Volkswagen built its first factory in Brazil in 1949, with other car producers from the US, Germany and Japan hot on its heels. By 1970, eighty per cent of the country's cars were assembled in Brazil itself.

The initial results of import substitution were impressive. From 1950-70 Latin America's Gross Domestic Product (GDP, a measure of all the goods and services produced by a country) tripled, and even in per capita terms it rose by two-thirds. In the mid-1950s, Latin America's economies were growing faster than those of the industrialised West. By the early 1960s, domestic industry supplied 95 per cent of Mexico's and 98 per cent of Brazil's consumer goods. By this time, however, there were already clear signs that the model was approaching exhaustion, as state-led development in Latin America began to suffer much the same fate as the state-run economies in Eastern Europe. Protected industries had no need to invest or innovate, and fell behind the rest of the world in technology and productivity; political interference encouraged corruption and incompetence, as people were

Liba Taylor/PANOS

appointed to run state companies on the basis of political favouritism rather than merit. The ever-growing state sector began to outspend meagre revenues (rich Latin Americans have always been adept at avoiding taxes), generating growing inflation.

In social terms, import substitution also failed. Latin America and the Caribbean have always had hugely unequal societies and import substitution further aggravated the situation. In order to keep wage costs down in industry, governments held down food prices, penalising the peasant farmers who grew the food and creating growing poverty in the countryside. Millions of peasants gave up hope of earning a living from the land and drifted to the cities, where they joined the armies of hopeful job-seekers in the shanty towns that sprang up on the edges of the continent's cities. Some achieved their ambition of a steady, waged job, but most ended up as street sellers, domestic servants or doing odd jobs.

The local market for manufactured goods was limited because most people in Latin America were too poor to buy more than the most basic necessities. This prevented industry from growing and reducing costs through mass production. Even Brazil, the most populous country in the region, faced this problem, although among its 140 million people, there was at least a significant middle class to buy locally-produced goods, enabling Brazilian industry to outperform its Spanish American counterparts. The problem of a small domestic market could have been solved if wealth were redistributed to allow more people to buy goods, an option ruled out by the wealthy elite.

Initially, governments responded to the lack of an internal market by establishing a variety of free trade agreements with other Latin American nations. Organisations like the Latin American Free Trade Association and the Central American Common Market, both established in 1960, soon foundered, however, because the smaller countries opened their markets to the more industrialised nations in the agreement, but received little in return.

Much of Latin America's industry has been dominated by multinational companies. Volkswagen plant, Puebla, Mexico.

The Dance of the Millions

Many Latin American governments were forced to adopt austerity programmes to cope with the slowdown in growth. In Brazil and Argentina, military governments seized power in order to implement such unpopular policies. They used both the law and brute force to suppress trade unions and lower the living standards of the poor majority. The major economies then set off in pursuit of the elusive third stage of industrialisation, the move from import substitution to becoming an exporter of manufactured goods. This meant large-scale investments, which had to be funded by foreign capital. Latin America turned to the international loan sharks. The initial results were astonishing. In just thirteen years, from 1967 to 1980, Latin America's manufactured exports increased in value forty-fold, from US$1 billion a year to US$40 billion.

Brazil led the field in both industrialisation and the race for foreign loans. In 1958, it overtook Argentina as the region's leading industrial power. By 1961 it was self-sufficient in electric stoves, refrigerators and television sets. Vehicle production boomed from 31,000 in 1957 to 514,000 in 1971. In 1968 Brazilian industry finally outstripped agriculture as the major wealth producer

---

TABLE 5: INDUSTRIALISATION IN LATIN AMERICA

Country	A	B	C
Brazil	555	39	23
Mexico	377	28	24
Argentina	282	30	32
Colombia	67	32	23
Venezuela	58	42	27
Chile	52	-	25
Peru	50	37	18
Ecuador	17	38	19
Uruguay	16	23	27
Guatemala	13	19	17
Dominican Republic	10	22	29
Paraguay	8	22	22
Costa Rica	8	24	27
El Salvador	8	24	21
Panama	7	16	16
Bolivia	6	-	18
Honduras	3	32	20
Nicaragua	2	20	26
Haiti	2	12	9

A: Gross Domestic Product (US$billion), 1994
B: Industrial output as % of GDP, 1994
C: Percentage of the workforce employed in industry, 1990
Sources: UNDP *Human Development Report 1996*, World Bank *World Development Report,* 1996

---

in the country. By 1994 Brazil's industrial output was over twice that of Mexico, and nearly three times greater than Argentina's, and by 1996 four out of Latin America's top five companies were Brazilian. The one-time coffee producer has become the region's superpower.

As the factories multiplied, so did the foreign debt. The big borrowers were the state corporations which dominated the politically vital areas of steel, petroleum and electricity production. By the early 1980s, Mexico's petroleum corporation, Pemex, had run up a debt of US$15 billion. State and private banks also borrowed heavily abroad, in order to re-lend to local businesses.

The 'dance of the millions', as the round of frenzied foreign borrowing became known, took off after the oil price rise decreed dby the Organisation of Petroleum Exporting Countries (OPEC) in 1973-74. OPEC oil producers recycled their new wealth to western banks, who in turn were anxious to find outlets for their 'petrodollars'. Latin America seemed the ideal borrower; it had decades of steady growth and industrialisation already behind it, and countries such as Mexico and Venezuela were sitting on huge oil reserves. Foreign bankers fell over themselves to lend as much as possible, as fast as possible. Since they assumed that governments could not go bankrupt, they paid little attention to where the money was actually going. In practice, it went into a number of unproductive areas, such as capital flight, where government officials and business leaders siphoned billions of dollars back out of the country into US bank accounts; on prestige 'megaprojects' such as hydroelectric dams and roads, and on arms, as military governments splashed out on the latest hardware for their troops.

In all, US$60 billion in foreign loans entered Latin America between 1975 and 1982. Sixty per cent of the money went to Brazil and Mexico, as they and Argentina became the Third World's top three debtors. In Mexico, the rain of dollars funded exploration and development of the oil industry; in Brazil it fuelled the country's further rise as an industrial power. Brazil was the only country successfully to make the leap to the third stage of industrialisation as an exporter of manufactured goods. From 1970-78 it doubled its proportion of the region's exports, becoming a producer of everything from computers to aircraft.

The dance of the millions ended abruptly in August 1982, when the Mexican government announced it could no longer pay the interest due on its foreign debt. Many US and other banks suddenly realised that what had seemed a safe and lucrative loans business in Latin America could drive them into bankruptcy, if other countries followed Mexico's lead. The announcement sent a shudder through the international banking community, raising fears of a run on the banks and a possible collapse of the world financial system. The following weeks established the pattern for years to come. The banks and creditor governments worked together to find a solution – not to the problem of Mexico's excessive debt repayments, but to remove the threat to the global banking system. The initial remedy was a band-aid affair whereby the banks rescheduled debt repayments and lent Mexico new money, purely so that it could give it straight back as interest payments. This avoided the banks having to write off Mexico's loans as bad debts, which would have damaged their profits and sent their shares plunging on the stock market.

By early 1984, every Latin American nation except Venezuela, Colombia and Paraguay had been forced into similar rescheduling deals. Cuba and Nicaragua also avoided such agreements, since Washington was imposing an effective financial boycott on both left-leaning governments. In every case the creditors stuck together, but insisted on negotiating with each debtor nation separately. Rescheduling was good business for the banks, since they could exact particularly high interest rates in exchange for deferring repayments. In return for rescheduling US$49.5 billion in loans, the banks earned an extra US$1.7 billion. At the same time, they ended virtually all new lending to Latin American nations, other than that needed to enable them to keep up with interest payments on the original loans.

The immediate cause of the debt crisis was the sudden rise in US interest rates announced by newly-elected President Reagan in 1981. Since Latin America's debts had been largely contracted at floating interest rates, this meant a massive increase in its interest payments. Each time the international interest rate rose by one per cent, it added nearly US$2 billion a year to the developing countries' bills. At the same time the austerity policies of 'Reaganomics' and the second OPEC price rise of 1979 produced a sharp recession in the industrialised nations which cut demand for Latin America's manufactured exports and sent commodity prices tumbling. Latin America earned less hard currency for its exports, just as it needed to pay more interest on its debt.

For Sir William Ryrie, a top World Bank official, the debt crisis was 'a blessing in disguise'. It forced Latin America into a constant round of debt negotiations, providing the Reagan government, along with the International Monetary Fund (IMF) and the other international financial institutions controlled by the wealthy industrialised countries, with all the leverage they needed to overhaul the region's economy, in alliance with northern commercial creditor banks and the region's home-grown free-marketeers. The state-led model was discredited, monetarism was in the ascendant with champions in the White House and 10 Downing Street – Latin America was ripe for a free market revolution.

Since then, almost all of Latin America and the Caribbean has followed a similar path. In the initial stage of reform, known as 'stabilisation', the IMF and banks pressured governments both to crack down on inflation by cutting spending, and to keep up their debt repayments by cutting their imports and generating a trade surplus. At the same time, commercial banks decided Latin America had become a bad risk, and stopped lending. Throughout the 1980s, capital flowed out of Latin America, destined for the rich countries of the north. This perverse flow of wealth from the poor to the wealthy squeezed out US$218.6 billion, over US$500 for every man, woman and child in the region.

With time, reforms have moved on to a broader process known as 'structural adjustment', involving a relentless assault on the state's role in the economy, including cuts in social spending, privatisation, and deregulation of everything from trade to banking to employers' abilities to hire and fire at will. The aim of such measures is to move Latin America and the Caribbean rapidly to a dynamic market-based economy, but up to now, the panorama has largely been one of recession and austerity.

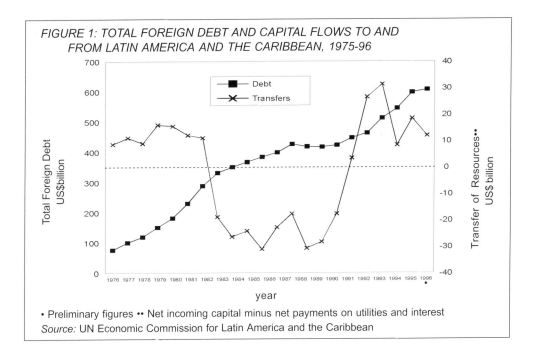

FIGURE 1: TOTAL FOREIGN DEBT AND CAPITAL FLOWS TO AND FROM LATIN AMERICA AND THE CARIBBEAN, 1975-96

• Preliminary figures •• Net incoming capital minus net payments on utilities and interest
Source: UN Economic Commission for Latin America and the Caribbean

Silent Revolution

The slump in Latin America's economy which followed the Mexican collapse contributed to one war and several bloody 'IMF riots'. Argentina's military leaders invaded the Falklands/Malvinas islands to divert attention from a collapsing economy, while riots, protests and looting afflicted cities across the continent. Prior to the 1980s, Latin Americans were accustomed to a growing economy. In every year between 1964 and 1980, the regional economy grew by more than four per cent, making the recession that hit in 1982 all the more painful. In 1982 Latin America's economy shrank in real terms for the first time since the Second World War. Chile was the worst hit, with per capita GDP falling by 14.5 per cent in a single year. The despair of Chile's unemployed workforce was captured in the lyrics of one of its top rock bands in the late 1980s, *Los Prisioneros*

> They're idle, waiting for the hands
> that decide to make them run again
> The mist surrounds and rusts them ....
> I drag myself along the damp cement,
> remembering a thousand laments.
> Of when the misery came, when they said
> don't come back, don't come back, don't come back
> The factories, all the factories have gone.

The cause of the collapse was the austerity programmes implemented under IMF pressure to keep debt repayments flowing. The extraction of wealth from the region left a large hole in the economy, in the form of an investment collapse. Governments forced to adopt IMF austerity measures found it less politically costly to cut public investment than to sack employees in the middle of a recession, (although many did that as well), while the

Julio Etchart

Workers scramble to finish a turbine of the giant Itaipú dam and hydro-electric complex, Brazil/Paraguay.

private sector was deterred from investing both by the impossibility of borrowing abroad and the recession and high interest rates at home, as governments lifted interest rates to fight inflation. Foreign investors also took fright. Across the region, gross domestic investment (which includes both local and foreign investment) collapsed from US$213 billion in 1980 to just US$136 billion in 1983. The level of investment is crucial to any economy's prospects; Latin America was mortgaging its people's future to pay its debts.

Falling investment and the domestic recession brought about by austerity programmes provoked an industrial collapse. By 1983, the degree of industrial development in Latin America had regressed to the levels of 1966. In Argentina and Peru it was back to 1960 levels, while in Chile and Uruguay it was more like 1950.

The 1980s was a period of recession and false starts, as governments desperately sought a way out of the debt crisis and continued to send billions of dollars to overseas creditors. By 1991, the capital tide had turned. Although debt repayments continued, foreign investors rediscovered the region, and started pouring money in again. Partly, they did so because pickings were thin elsewhere, partly they were lured in by the latest component of Latin America's structural adjustment programme: from the late 1980s, governments have been privatising the state assets built up over fifty years of import substitution.

The pressures on governments to privatise seem irresistible. The growing fiscal crisis of the state sector, provoked by both foreign and domestic debt payments, has forced governments to increase revenue or cut expenditure; privatisation achieves both, shedding loss-making companies while raising substantial amounts of cash. In Argentina, President Carlos Menem's selling spree raised US$9.8 billion in cash, and enabled the government to lop a further US$15.6 billion off its foreign debt between 1989 and 1993 as multinational corporations bought up debt paper and swapped it for a stake in the newly privatised companies (a process known as 'debt for equity swaps'). In Mexico, the family silver raised a total of US$13.7 billion in 1990-91, during which time privatisation receipts provided just under a tenth of government revenues.

Privatisation is also part of a broader ideological shift, since neoliberals believe in cutting back the state and passing ever-larger chunks of the economy over to the private sector. Once privatised, they argue, management will be able to take decisions based on economic efficiency rather than politics and a company's performance is bound to improve. The rhetoric employed is the same as in Mrs Thatcher's Britain, the only country to surpass the large Latin American economies in its privatising zeal. In Latin America, privatisation provides a juicy carrot with which to attract foreign investment back into the region after the capital famine of the debt crisis. Multinational corporations are expected to introduce capital and new technology into a region starved of both.

State airlines and telecommunications companies have gone on the block throughout the region, but so far only Argentina and Bolivia have allowed the rush to market to sweep away their state oil companies. Elsewhere, governments have been reluctant to hand over such strategic or highly profitable companies, preferring instead to encourage joint ventures with multinational corporations to attract technology and investment while retaining some degree of overall control. The track record of privatisations has varied enormously. Areas which urgently required injections of capital and cutting-edge technology, such as telecommunications, have clearly benefited, but critics of the privatisation process argue that governments have missed the chance to divide up giant companies and introduce competition, and have been lax in regulating the newly-privatised companies. Privatisation programmes are, however, extremely good news for the local business class with the capital (often through joint ventures with foreign companies) to snap up the bargains. Mexico's stock of billionaires rose from 2 to 24 during the privatising presidency of Carlos Salinas de Gortari (1988-94), all of them with close ties to the ruling Institutional Revolutionary Party (PRI). In another echo of the British experience, Chile's pioneering privatisers in the 1970s operated a highly questionable revolving door system, moving from government posts in which they oversaw the privatisations to top jobs in the big conglomerates who cashed in on the sell-offs.

In Mexico and Argentina, the sudden inflows of dollars produced a short-lived rerun of the 'dance of the millions', as governments abandoned austerity in favour of reducing inflation by using the exchange rate. Overvalued currencies made imports artificially cheap, keeping prices down at home. Not surprisingly, imports boomed, but governments were able to use the incoming capital, as long as it lasted, to cover the resulting trade gap. It lasted until 1994, when a series of political crises, including the Zapatista uprising in Chiapas and the assassination of the PRI's anointed successor to Carlos Salinas, made foreign investors reassess Mexican risk. Capital flows to Mexico fell away, producing a run on the peso, a devaluation, and a devastating recession, costing two million jobs over the course of 1995. In the so-called 'tequila effect', foreign investors also pulled out of Argentina which was pursuing a similar policy to that of Mexico, provoking massive recession and unemployment there during 1995. By 1997, capital inflows had still not recovered their pre-tequila levels, and for the time being, governments had little option but to return to the 1980s-style, more painful form of adjustment.

By disposing of loss-making companies and pulling in one-off windfalls, the privatisation bonanza has played a crucial part in curbing governments' spending deficits and getting inflation down in many Latin American countries in the early 1990s. Inflation in the region as a whole peaked at around 1,200 per cent in 1989 and 1990. Since then, privatisations, further government cut-backs in spending and investment and improved tax collection have all helped to get fiscal deficits down, reducing inflation to a regional average of 19 per cent in 1996.

Trade

Under the new neoliberal regime, countries are encouraged to trade on the basis of their 'comparative advantage' – economic jargon for sticking to what you are good at. In the case of Latin America, this means raw materials and cheap labour. In a return to the course of development followed since the conquest (see chapter 1), Latin America has gone back to exporting commodities, both traditional products such a minerals and oil, and a whole range of new, non-traditional exports, covering everything from cut flowers to fresh salmon. The other side of the export drive is an attempt to increase the exports of manufactured goods, usually low-tech products such as shoes or textiles, or the output of assembly plants, such as the *maquiladoras* strung along the US-Mexican border, where imported components are assembled by cheap Latin American labour. By 1997, these were employing close to a million people in Mexico, and many more factories were dotted around Central America and the Caribbean.

Although exports have boomed in the 1990s, Latin America's attempt to get in on the ground floor of the global economy as a purveyor of raw materials risks confining it to one of the most sluggish areas of world trade, continuing its traditional reliance on the fickle prices of the commodity markets. The recovery in its exports has been matched by a flood of imports, following blanket trade liberalisation, bankrupting potentially competitive local producers and raising fears that the 'opening' has undermined the region's industrial future. Furthermore, the boom in non-traditional exports has been achieved at a high social cost, exacerbating inequality and undermining the region's food security, while both assembly plants and pesticide-intensive agriculture have damaged the environment (see chapter 3).

Regional Integration

The region's shift away from import substitution towards the merits of 'export-led growth' has also seen a renewed interest in free trade agreements. Within Latin America dozens of bilateral and multilateral agreements have been signed since the late 1980s, the largest being the Southern Cone Common Market (Mercosur). Mercosur, which came into operation in 1995, brings together Argentina, Brazil, Uruguay and Paraguay.

The best-known free trade agreement in the region is the North American Free Trade Agreement, NAFTA, between Mexico, the US and Canada, which came into force in 1994. Over a period of 15 years, NAFTA will phase out all trade tariffs and restrictions on foreign investment between the three countries. Its many critics argue that it is little more than a 'charter of corporate rights', working to the benefit of large corporations, at the expense of the poor. Big companies in the US can relocate to Mexico in order to cut wages, thereby

SOFT FRUIT, HARD LABOUR

Orchards fill the Aconcagua valley north-east of Santiago de Chile. Parallel rows of peach trees stretch off to infinity, playing tricks with the eye. The monotony is punctuated by the occasional fat-trunked palm tree or weeping willow, shining with new leaf on a cold and dusty spring day.

Carlos Vidal is a union leader, president of the local *temporeros*, the temporary farm labourers who plant, pick and pack the peaches, kiwi fruit and grapes for the tables of Europe, Asia and North America. A shock of black curls streaked with grey fringe his round, gap-toothed face. A freezing wind off the nearby Andes blows across the vineyards as Carlos tells his story.

'On this land there were 48 families who got land under [former President] Allende. We grew vegetables, maize and beans together, as an *asentamiento* [farming co-operative]. There were a few fruit farms then, but we planned them. After the coup the land was divided up between 38 families – the others had to leave. Then it started to get difficult, we got the land but nothing else – the military auctioned off the machinery.

Then the *empresarios* started to arrive, especially an Argentine guy called Melitón Moreno. The bank started taking people's land – foreclosing on loans – and Moreno bought it up. Three *compañeros* committed suicide here because they lost their farms. Melitón got bank loans and bought yet more land and machinery. He planted nothing but fruit – grapes at first, then others.

My father was a leader of the asentamiento. The first year after the coup we were hungry, lunch was a sad time. We began to sell everything in the house, then we looked for a *patrón* to sell us seeds and plough our land for us, and we paid him with part of the harvest. Next year we got a bank loan and managed to pay it off, but the following year they sold us bad seed. We lost all the maize and the whole thing collapsed. We had to sell the land and Melitón Moreno bought it.

Of the 38 families, most are now temporeros. We all sold our land but kept our houses and a small garden to grow food. Trouble is, even the gardens are no good, the water's full of pesticides from the fruit. This area used to be famous for water melons and now they don't grow properly any more. They chuck fertiliser and pesticide everywhere, it doesn't matter that the earth is dead because the fruit trees live artificially. No one grows potatoes or maize any more – it's cheaper to buy the imported ones from Argentina.'

Duncan Green, *Silent Revolution: The Rise of Market Economics in Latin America*, London 1995

increasing unemployment in the US; although some Mexicans will find jobs in the new factories, far more will suffer the impact of ending tariffs on imported maize, which is produced on commercial US farms at a fraction of the cost of Mexican-grown maize. By the Mexican government's own admission, over a million Mexican farmers and their families will be put out of business by the flood of cheap imports.

Those hoping to extend NAFTA to the rest of the region received a boost in December 1994, when President Clinton went to Miami to host the 'Summit of the Americas' with every Latin American head of state bar Fidel Castro.

The summit agreed to establish a 'Free Trade Area of the Americas' by the year 2006. However, two years later, domestic opposition to further free trade agreements within the US has effectively stalled progress. Into the vacuum has stepped Brazil, which is keen to expand Mercosur into a Latin American counterweight to US economic might in the hemisphere. Mercosur has already added Chile to its ranks (after Chile was rebuffed by NAFTA) and is currently negotiating free trade agreements with Bolivia and Venezuela.

The Lost Decade

The Third World War has already started – a silent war, not for that reason any the less sinister. This war is tearing down Brazil, Latin America and practically all the Third World. Instead of soldiers dying there are children, instead of millions of wounded there are millions of unemployed; instead of destruction of bridges there is the tearing down of factories, schools, hospitals, and entire economies.
Luís Inácio da Silva (Lula), Brazilian labour leader, 1985

Such a profound economic transformation has only been achieved at enormous social cost. Throughout the region, after decades in which the percentage of Latin Americans living in poverty had been falling (though not their actual number), poverty is once again on the rise. By the end of the 1980s, sixty million new names had joined the grim rollcall of the poor, leaving 46 per cent of the population, nearly 200 million people, living in poverty. Almost half of them were indigent, barely existing on an income of less than a dollar a day. As the poor got poorer, the rich got richer, especially the very rich: according to *Forbes* magazine, the number of Latin American billionaires rose from six in 1987 to 42 in 1994.

The problem of rising poverty in Latin America is one of political will, not resources – there *is* enough money to go round. Latin American inequality is on such a scale that a comparatively minor move towards a fairer distribution of income could eradicate poverty overnight, According to the World Bank's 1990 *World Development Report*, 'Raising all the poor in the continent to just above the poverty line would cost only 0.7 per cent of regional GDP – the approximate equivalent of a 2 per cent income tax on the wealthiest fifth of the population.'

Structural adjustment programmes have exacerbated poverty and inequality in numerous ways. According to the UN, the main cause of increasing poverty and inequality has been the 'massive decline in real wages,... the rise in unemployment and... the number of people employed in very low-productivity jobs.' State cutbacks, recession and unemployment have all combined to suppress wages, as have adjustment policies to 'flexibilise' the labour market. In practice, this has meant cracking down on trade unions and making it easier for managers to hire and fire employees, shift to part-time work and to cut costs by sub-contracting work to smaller companies, often little more than sweatshops. By the early 1990s, 23 per cent of wage-earners in the manufacturing sector were living below the poverty line, whereas before the debt crisis a job in a factory virtually guaranteed a pay packet big enough to keep a family out of poverty.

Although curbing inflation has undoubtedly improved the quality of life of the poor, adjustment policies have also exacerbated poverty by removing food subsidies and other price controls. The combined impact of changes to

prices and the labour market under adjustment has shifted poverty away from the rural to urban areas. From 1980 to 1990 the number of poor Latin Americans in rural areas increased from 73 million to 80 million, but was overtaken for the first time by the battalions of the urban poor, which jumped from 63 million people to 116 million.

Cheap labour. Making shorts for Levi's to reexport to the US, Honduran Free Trade Zone.

Women have borne the brunt of adjustment. Many of the new, low-waged or part-time jobs generated by adjustment go to women, while many men have lost their role as family breadwinner as full-time waged jobs disappear, or wages fall so far that a single income becomes insufficient to feed a family. On top of this 'double day' of work and running the home, the deterioration of social services, especially in urban areas, has forced women into a third role, taking responsibility for running their communities, fighting or substituting for inadequate state services in schools, health, drainage, water supply, or roads.

Adjustment has made all these tasks more vital to the family's survival and more exhausting: 'flexibilisation' often means lower wages, longer hours and greater insecurity, just as cuts in state subsidies have brought steep price rises in basics like food and public transport. One study of women in a shanty town in Guayaquil, Ecuador gives a graphic picture of the impact of adjustment on women. The research found that the women were affected differently by adjustment. About thirty per cent of the women were coping, juggling the competing demands of their three roles in the workplace, home and community. They were more likely to be in stable relationships with partners who had steady jobs. Another group, about 15 per cent of the women, were simply 'burnt out', no longer able to be superwomen 24 hours a day. They were most likely to be single mothers or the main breadwinners and were often older women, physically and mentally exhausted after the effort of bringing up a family against such heavy odds. They tried to hand over all household responsibilities to their oldest daughter, while their younger children frequently dropped out of school and roamed the streets. The remaining 55 per cent were described as simply 'hanging on', sacrificing their families by sending sons out to work or keeping daughters home from school to help with the housework. If nothing is done to change the impact of adjustment policies, many of these women will also 'burn out', swelling the number of families broken by the impact of Latin America's silent revolution.

Latin America is still searching for a development model which benefits all its people. Import substitution failed because it produced uncompetitive industries and an ineffectual and corrupt state bureaucracy while aggravating social inequality. Now Latin America's renewed infatuation with the market is needlessly destroying local industry and ratcheting up inequality still further, although admittedly it has got inflation under control, and produced a return to fitful growth. Across the region, the search is on for a new, more genuinely Latin American economic model of development which can combine the elusive goals of growth and economic equity. But the search is taking place under heavy constraints, not least because the flawed neoliberal model has such powerful allies – the United States, the IMF, the World Bank and the World Trade Organisation, in alliance with foreign investors and the global money markets will all resist any move away from neoliberal orthodoxy. For the foreseeable future, Latin America seems destined to sink or swim in a Darwinian free-market world order.

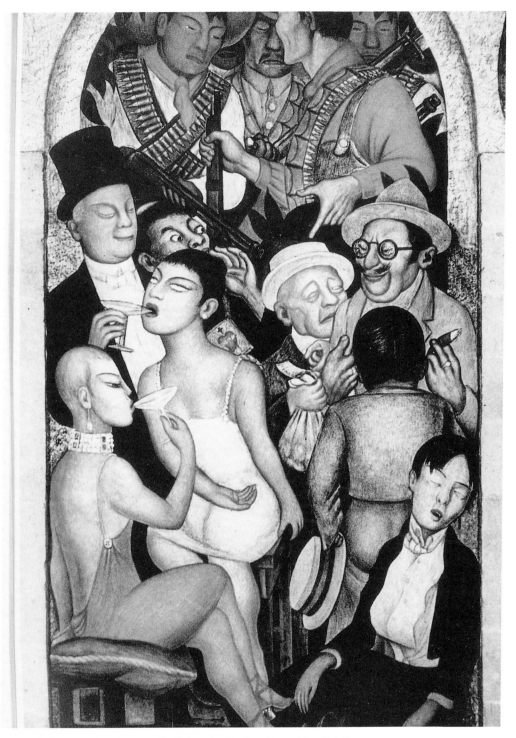

Unacceptable faces. Diego Rivera's portrait of the Mexican elite at the time of the revolution, 1910-17.

Chronology

1896	First moving picture shown in Buenos Aires
1910-17	Mexican revolution begins attempt to construct a new mestizo consciousness, especially through the work of muralists such as Diego Rivera
1923	Brazilian government sets up country's first radio station which soon bows to popular demand for broadcasts of samba music
1959	Cuban revolution promotes attempt to build a radical and distinctive Latin American cultural movement
mid 1960s	First telenovelas broadcast in Brazil and Mexico
1967	Gabriel García Márquez publishes *One Hundred Years of Solitude* which sells more than twenty million copies world-wide
1971	Cuban government arrests the dissident poet, Heberto Padilla
1973	Singer Víctor Jara killed by the army following military coup in Chile
1982	García Márquez wins Nobel Prize for literature
1990	Peruvian novelist Mario Vargas Llosa loses presidential elections to Alberto Fujimori
1992	Columbus quincentenary prompts continent-wide soul searching. Televisa's soap 'The Rich Also Weep' takes Russia by storm
1994	Zapatista rebels in Chiapas use the Internet to bypass government censorship
1996	Ninety per cent of Latin Americans have access to a TV set

Writing on the Wall

6

Culture, Identity and Politics

Every evening the suburbs and shanty towns of Latin America grind to a halt as anyone with a television settles down in front of the latest *telenovela*, or soap opera. TV-less neighbours drop by for the show and an animated discussion about the latest twist in an often bewildering plot. In Mexico in the late 1980s forty million people – half the country's population, regularly tuned in for *Cradle of Wolves*, a lurid account of a ruthless heroine with an eye-patch who committed a series of gruesome murders. When the last episode was shown, Mexico's underground drivers refused to go to work and the public transport system closed down.

In Europe and North America, Latin America is better known for its literature and music than for its soaps. *Salsa* and *merengue* are favourites on European dance floors, like the *tango* and *bossanova* before them. Latin American literature has become so popular that, in the words of critic and translator Nick Caistor, it 'has become the equivalent of the Amazon rainforest, providing oxygen for the stale literary lungs of the developed world.' Yet although Latin America's novelists have become international celebrities, at home the audience for one of the top Mexican or Brazilian soaps exceeds the entire continent's readership for writers such as Mexico's Carlos Fuentes, Peru's Mario Vargas Llosa, or Gabriel García Márquez, Colombia's Nobel Prize-winning author of classics such as *One Hundred Years of Solitude*, which has sold twenty million copies world-wide and is considered by Fuentes to be the greatest novel in Spanish since *Don Quixote*.

In his work, García Márquez draws heavily on the traditional 'popular culture' of his native Colombia, filling his books with the tales of travelling singers and story-tellers, remembered from his childhood. He has turned his hand to other genres, from journalism to film to writing soaps, and challenges those intellectuals and critics who have in the past derided telenovelas as cheap, tacky melodrama churned out by Latin America's media giants. Such critics frequently hark back to a 'pure' popular culture in the countryside, free of the taint of capitalism and technology, yet such views risk reducing the idea of 'popular culture' to a quaint, but increasingly irrelevant folklore destined for the museum. Popular culture would paradoxically cease to be the culture of the people, with its constantly evolving mix of traditional and modern styles.

Ever since the conquest, Latin America's dispossessed peoples: the Indians, descendants of African slaves, and poor *mestizos*, have developed varied and unique cultural forms by constantly absorbing new influences into a bedrock of tradition. The Indians of the Andes and Central America kept alive pre-conquest textiles and pottery, while adopting Spanish stringed instruments and combining them with their own panoply of flutes and drums.

Day of the Dead, Peru.
Miners go to the
cemetery to be with
and remember dead
relatives.

Traumatic events such as the conquest and murder of the Inca emperors are today recalled through the cultural memory of street theatre and dance, yet traditional styles are still evolving. In Guatemala, widows of men killed or 'disappeared' by the military during their counter-insurgency campaigns in the early 1980s now include stylised images of helicopters in their traditional weaving patterns, where they join images of Spaniards on horseback from the time of the conquest. In Brazil the Kayapó Indians expertly wield imported video cameras to record their traditional dances and rituals for future generations. The Kayapó explain that they find their own ceremonies more interesting than Brazilian national TV. The cameras also come out at meetings with the Brazilian authorities, to be played back to the bureaucrats should they try to go back on a promise.

The survival of ancient cultural traditions was frequently achieved in defiance of the colonial authorities' attempts to impose European ways. The greatest battleground for the defence of tradition was religion. Traditional Indian religion and culture are inseparable; music, costumes and dance are part of an annual round of rituals and feast-days linked to the seasons and the agricultural cycles of sowing and harvest. To the Catholic Church, charged with a mission to convert the heathen, the pantheon of Indian deities had to be crushed, the temples overthrown and practices such as ancestor worship stamped out. In order to appease the authorities, Indian communities adopted Catholic forms, but subverted their content. The Christian saints took on the characters and powers of the different Indian gods and All Souls Day, known in Spanish as the 'day of the dead', became an opportunity for ancestor worship. Every year on 2 November, Mexican families still go to the cemeteries to picnic with their dead. Throughout the continent the cycle of fiestas, carnivals and saints' days plays a central role in community life:

In all of these ceremonies the Mexican opens out. They all give him a chance to reveal himself and to converse with God, country, friends or relations. During these days the silent Mexican whistles, shouts, sings, shoots off fireworks, discharges his pistol into the air. He discharges his soul. This is the night when friends who have not exchanged more than the prescribed courtesies for months get drunk together, trade confidences, weep over the same troubles, discover that they are brothers, and sometimes, to prove it, kill each other.
Octavio Paz, *The Labyrinth of Solitude*, London, 1950

In Mexico, visions of the Virgin Mary began to occur soon after the conquest, the most famous being the Virgin of Guadalupe, who appeared to an Indian at Tepeyac, north of Mexico City, the site of a traditional Indian shrine to Tonantzin, the Aztec earth goddess. A flow of miracles forced the disapproving Church authorities to recognise the event and the Virgin of Guadalupe's shrine became the most important holy place in the Americas. She also became a symbol of emergent Mexican identity, representing both earth goddess and dark-skinned Virgin Mary, who had chosen to appear to an Indian rather than to a member of the white elite. In Bolivia, paintings by mestizo artists of the colonial period transformed the Virgin into Pachamama, the Andean earth goddess. Sometimes the subversion of Catholicism was even more deliberate. The Mexican muralists of the 1920s were particularly influenced by contemporary accounts of a religious dance around the statue of the Virgin in a Puebla village, during which the statue toppled over to reveal a small stone carving depicting the goddess of water, hidden beneath the Virgin's skirts for centuries, and worshipped throughout that time.

In the Bolivian mines, Catholic and pre-Columbian beliefs are fused in the figure of the *tío*. The *tío* (uncle) is the god of the underworld whose domain includes the tin mines where many of Bolivia's Indians toil in unhealthy and dangerous conditions. Since the Christian God resides in heaven, the *tío* has become equated with the Christian devil, but without the qualities of evil normally ascribed to him. In the mines, the *tío* must be placated and asked for help to avert the all-too-frequent rockfalls and explosions. His statue glares out from niches cut into the walls of the mines, but the miners seem on affectionate terms with him, handing him cigarettes or coca to chew. At carnival time they offer him the blood and heart of a llama. As they prepare to cut the llama's throat, the miners, their cheeks bulging with coca, cry out 'for the health and prosperity of our section,' 'may there be no more accidents.' Blood collected in a chipped china plate is then smeared on the walls of the mine to bring good luck for another year.

Above ground, the carnival brass bands and 'devil dance' of young men dressed in the elaborate, horned and multicoloured masks of the *tío* have moved down from the pitheads to the town centre and become a tourist attraction. These days it is the shopkeepers and middle classes who dance in the masks, which have become too elaborate and expensive for a miner to buy. In the dance the Archangel Gabriel, a pink-skinned, blue-eyed European representation of good, fights the devils in ritual combat. The god of the mines, like the miners he protects, comes off worst in this clash of cultures.

In traditional Indian beliefs, sacred properties belonged not just to a God, but filled everyday objects, which could themselves be worshipped or asked to bring good luck. Everything from a hill, to a tree or a carving could be seen

BLESSING CARS IN BOLIVIA

'Bless this vehicle. May the driver drive in a Christian way. May the motor not use too much petrol.' So goes the much-repeated blessing by the old Irish priest as he totters along a queue of new cars, jeeps and trucks decked out in garlands of yellow and red flowers.

Copacabana, on the shores of Bolivia's Lake Titicaca, the highest lake in the world. The cars have come from all over the country to be blessed at the shrine of the country's favourite Virgin.

The priest sprinkles holy water on the driver, the upholstery and the engine and moves on. After the blessing the owners shower petals over their new (and now sanctified) cars. Next comes the beer, shaken vigorously then squirted over wheels, upholstery and down expectant throats. Off go the firecrackers, as the smells of gunpowder and beer blend in the clear Andean air.

On the outskirts of the town another ceremony is taking place half-way up a small, rocky outcrop topped by another shrine to the Virgin. Here, overlooking the silver-blue expanse of the lake, Bolivia's Indian traditions take over from Catholicism.

A family arrives with a toy pick-up swathed in bright paper streamers. An elderly Indian priest blesses them and their cherished vehicle, mumbling in a mixture of the Spanish Mass and the native Aymara language.

Little bells ring. The fizz and splat as he sprays beer to the four points of the compass. A palpable sense of calm and spirituality. If the blessing wins divine approval, the family will get their dream car and bring it to the church below to be blessed. The services mix prayers to Pachamama, the Indian earth mother, with invocations to God and the Virgin Mary. Pachamama and God; petrol consumption and incense. In Bolivia there is no dividing line between 'traditional' and 'modern'.

as holy. To the Catholic Church, these practices were idolatrous, and public worship of objects (other than saints) was stamped out, but many of the beliefs were passed down through the family, principally from mother to daughter.

Along the way, they were fragmented and transformed into what became known as 'folk magic', involving faith healing and other 'magical' practices. Today, throughout Latin America, such beliefs as *mal de ojo* (evil eye) and the sale of love potions are commonplace amongst Indians and mestizos alike. Even such eminently rationalist, western figures as 'the liberator', Simón Bolívar, have been turned into quasi-religious icons. Stores throughout Venezuela sell 'Liberator' aphrodisiacs and his name is invoked in faith-healing.

This interweaving of the sacred with everyday life is one reason why writers such as García Márquez insist that their style, often labelled 'magical realism', is merely an accurate portrayal of the life and stories of their native world. In Latin America everyday 'magic' and 'reality' are so interwoven as to be inseparable. Márquez has particular trouble separating life from art: in 1996, hours after he had sent off the final proofs of his latest book, *News of a Kidnapping,* real-life kidnappers abducted the brother of ex-president César

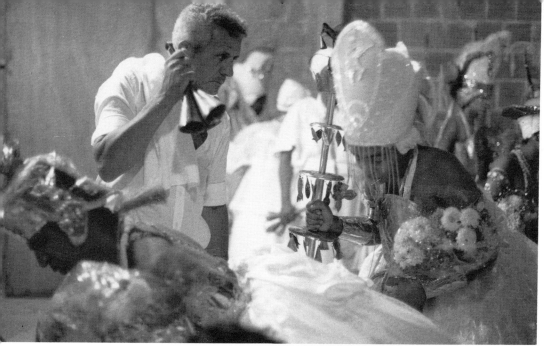

Gaviria. Their main demand? That García Márquez take over as president to 'save the fatherland'.

African-based religions such as Candomblé have flourished alongside Christianity in Brazil. Candomblé ceremony.

In Brazil, the African slaves on the sugar plantations of the Northeast managed to retain their cultural identity through music and dance. Plantation owners even encouraged erotic dances to keep up morale amongst their slaves. Today on Rio's beaches young black men can still be seen performing *capoeira*, a traditional slave dance combining both dance and ritualised martial arts. As increasing numbers of blacks left the sugar plantations and moved to the shanty towns and tenements of the cities, African religions resurfaced in the shape of Candomblé. Candomblé is based on the personal relationship between an individual and a pantheon of African deities, each with a different personality and tastes. As in the Andean religions, music, dance and worship are inseparable. The gods appear through the possession of chosen 'sons and daughters' and receive ritual offerings, songs and dance.

African and Portuguese cultures combined to produce samba and carnival, a joyous three day euphoria of dance, music, sex and beer which has become synonymous with Brazil:

In the official parade grounds – the Sambadrome – I thought the silence eerie until I realised it was in fact a solid wall of sound, a percussive din that did not sound like music and advanced gradually towards the spectators on an elaborate loudspeaker system set up on either side of the central 'avenue', or parade space. At the head of the noise was a gigantic waggling lion's head that floated down the avenue and overtook us, giving way to dazzling hordes in red and gold. A marmalade-thick river of people swept past; outlandish dancers in feathers and capes, ball gowns and G-strings, hundreds of drummers, thousands of leaping princes singing at the top of their lungs. Drowning in red and gold, I struggled to

focus. In the ocean of feathers and banners faces emerged: brown, white, pink, tan, olive. Young men bopping in sweat-drenched suits; old women in cascades of flounces whirling ecstatically; middle-aged men and women with paunches and eyeglasses bouncing happily in their head-dresses and bikinis.
Alma Guillermoprieto, *Samba*, London, 1990

Carnival's origins lay in festivals brought from Portugal, messy affairs in which the populace pelted each other with flour and water and indulged in gargantuan feats of eating and drinking. Over the years dance and music acquired increasing importance and local carnival associations grew up to organise floats for processions through the streets of Rio. The centre of carnival culture moved from the rich European suburbs to the poor black *favelas*, provoking one well-to-do reader of the *Jornal de noticias* in Bahia to write in 1901:

'the authorities should prohibit those [African drum] sessions and candomblés that in such quantity are overflowing on our streets these days, producing such great cacophonous noise, as well as those masquerades dressed in [typical black costumes] singing their traditional samba, because all of that is incompatible with our current civilised state.'

The associations metamorphosed into the samba schools, enormous permanent organisations based in Rio's favelas which each year take on the task of building the increasingly monumental floats, and organising thousands of drummers and costumed dancers into their various 'wings'. The vast expense of carnival and the elaborate costumes have so far not forced the samba schools out of the favelas, but there has been a slow erosion of the poor communities' involvement in carnival as a whole. Outside designers and artists are now hired to create the floats, costumes are farmed out rather than made by the women of the favela, and each school's procession is now fronted by TV stars, usually white.

Two Cultures Clash

In Latin America culture and politics have been inextricably linked since Pizarro's conquistadores ransacked the temples of Cusco and melted down the Inca empire's finest wrought gold and silver into ingots to be sent home to Spain. After the conquest the Spanish authorities initially banned fiction, fearing it would excite the minds of the Indians and fan subversion. During the colonial period the social and economic divide between the white ruling elite and the dark-skinned masses was mirrored in the gulf between their two cultures. In their art academies and concert halls Latin America's elites pursued a purely European aesthetic and made regular visits to its cultural capitals of Paris or Rome. Werner Herzog's film, *Fitzcarraldo*, recounts one particularly bizarre example of the forced implantation of European culture – a rubber baron's folly in the shape of a 2,000 seat opera house in Manaus, in the heart of the Amazon jungle. After it opened in 1897, companies from Milan, Paris and Madrid sailed up the Amazon to sing at the theatre, which boasted curtains from Alsace, stone from Portugal, Venetian crystal and English wrought ironwork. When the rubber boom came to an end, the theatre closed down, until its restoration in 1990, when Plácido Domingo came to sing *Carmen* to a full house. Meanwhile, away from the paved streets of the city centres, a rich and separate popular culture was actively combining ingredients of Indian, African and European culture into a uniquely Latin American cocktail.

Many 19th-century writers, notably Argentina's essayist and president Domingo Faustino Sarmiento, portrayed popular culture as a form of barbarism which must be fought through the introduction of civilised (i.e. European) values, described by one author as 'the civil war between the swallow-tailed coat and the poncho.' Yet popular culture also offered middle-class writers and artists an apparent solution to a conundrum that has dogged the continent's intelligentsia since the conquest, the riddle of Latin America's

LATIN AMERICA'S MELTING POT

Little Tamales from Cambray
To make 4,200,000 small tamales
by Claribel Alegría

Two pounds of mestizo cornmeal
a half-pound loin of Spanish immigrant
all finely chopped and cooked
with a packet of ready-blessed raisins
two tablespoons of Malinche's milk
one cup of troubled water
then fry the conquistadors' helmets
with three Jesuit onions
one small sack of multinational gold
two dragon's teeth
add one presidential carrot
two tablespoons of pimps
the fat from Panchimalco Indians
two Ministry tomatoes
half a cup of televised sugar
two drops of volcanic lava
seven pito leaves
(don't get me wrong, it's a soporific)
set it all to boil
over a slow fire
for five hundred years
and you'll discover its unique aroma.

Lovers and Comrades: Women's Resistance Poetry from Central America,
Amanda Hopkinson (ed), London, 1989

Note: 4,200,000 is the population of El Salvador, of which tamales are the
national dish. Malinche was the name of the Indian mistress of Cortés, who
betrayed the Aztec emperor Cuauhtémoc to the Spaniards.

identity. As the 'liberator', Simón Bolívar lamented, 'We are not Europeans, we are not Indians, but a hybrid species between the aborigines and the Spaniards.' After independence, and particularly as modern nation states began to form towards the end of the 19th century, the search for a national and continental identity played an essential role in the formation of a common sense of nationhood. The influence of European romanticism made writers and artists look for such an identity in Latin America's own version of the 'noble savage', an authentic innocent untainted by tawdry modernity. In Argentina the romantic figure of the *gaucho*, the self-reliant cowboy of the pampas, spawned a series of novels and poems in the dying years of the century, glorifying rural life at a time of massive migration to the cities. Although a caricature, *gauchismo* offered a sense of belonging to a distinctive culture, playing much the same role as the glorification of the cowboy and the 'winning of the west' in the US.

The search for a Latin American identity and debate over politics and art took on greater urgency in the political and cultural ferment that followed the Mexican revolution of 1910-17. The revolutionary Mexican government set about forging a new national consciousness. Under the patronage of a dynamic education minister, José Vasconcelos, a group of Mexican artists began to cover the walls and ceilings of public buildings with murals depicting scenes from Mexican history and allegorical portraits of the revolution. In preferring walls to canvas, the muralists sought to make art the property of the people, not a commodity for sale to the highest bidder. The movement came to be dominated by the 'big three', Diego Rivera, José Clemente Orozco and David Alfaro Siqueiros. Between them, they developed what has been called the greatest public revolutionary art of the century, a maelstrom of unforgettable images of Indians, conquistadores, farmers and bloated capitalists. Rivera, in particular, drew heavily on pre-Columbian designs and the popular artists of his time, notably the skull images of José Guadalupe Posada, who had earned fame for his satirical cartoons prior to the revolution.

Although perhaps unintended by the artists, the murals helped the state establish enduring myths of a new Mexico which had thrown out the rich, white capitalists and now belonged to the poor mestizos and Indians. The muralists' combination of revolutionary zeal with an unquestioning faith in technological progress both excited and enraged the US art establishment. In California in 1933, Rivera's patron, John D. Rockefeller, ordered his 'Man at the Crossroads' destroyed because Rivera refused to remove the figure of Lenin from an allegory of progress in the modern age.

The work of the Mexican muralists has inspired political street art throughout Latin America ever since. In Nicaragua following the Sandinista revolution of 1979, the walls of the cities became littered with revolutionary iconography. Figures like Che Guevara, Sandino, Allende and Zapata joined Bolívar and others on the roll call of Latin America's secular saints. When the Sandinistas fell from power in 1990, one of their opponents' first actions was to whitewash the walls of Managua.

The Mexican experience was the first example of a phenomenon repeated throughout the continent in the coming years. Populist governments took power, combining limited social reform with a drive to turn the major nations such as Mexico, Brazil and Argentina into industrial powers. By promoting a sense of patriotic identity with its own myths and symbols, populist leaders such as Brazil's Getúlio Vargas and Argentina's Juan Domingo Perón could build the national unity needed to implement their model of development and ensure the legitimacy of the state. In Brazil, Vargas seized on samba, carnival and football and used state money to turn them into national icons. Vargas built the Maracanã stadium, the biggest football ground in the world, and transformed carnival into a major international event. Both samba and football were ideal for the purpose, being poor people's pastimes which the state could use to weld people together at both local and national level.

Football also acquired an important political role under the military dictatorships in Brazil and Argentina. The 1964 coup came when Brazilian football was at its height, the national team having won two successive world cups and turned their stars into national heroes, many of them black. Unfortunately the generals could not resist the temptation to meddle, appointing a military official as head of the Brazilian Confederation of Sports who sought to impose greater discipline and teamwork on the individualist genius of Brazilian football. The national team promptly went into decline. The 1978 world cup took place in Argentina, two years after a military coup and amidst a wave of army human rights violations and disappearances. The junta used the national team's victory to seek both national and international legitimacy. Two years later, the goals from the cup final were still being shown every lunchtime on the main shopping precincts of Buenos Aires, a source of enduring national pride in a country with a conspicuously fragile sense of identity.

The political importance of literature and art also showed in the great political weight acquired by the intellectual, a figure of far greater status in Latin America than in Britain or the US. In the 19th century, poet José Martí fought for Cuban independence, while Sarmiento played a key role as president in forging modern Argentina. Rómulo Gallegos, author of Venezuela's classic novel, *Doña Barbara*, was also that country's president. In this century, two accomplished historians, Joaquín Balaguer and Juan Bosch, spent several decades vying for the presidency of the Dominican Republic, while writers and poets such as Chile's Pablo Neruda, Mexico's Carlos Fuentes and Octavio Paz and Guatemala's Miguel Angel Asturias have served their countries as ambassadors. In 1987 Peru's Mario Vargas Llosa decided to abandon the pen for the campaign trail and run for president. His political career came to an abrupt end following his defeat by Alberto Fujimori in the general election of 1990. Even musicians got in on the act when top salsa singer Ruben Blades unsuccessfully ran for Panamanian president in 1994.

Mexican political scientist Jorge Castañeda believes that intellectuals fill serious gaps in Latin American political life, acting as a conduit for ideas from abroad, and speaking on behalf of groups in society: 'Intellectuals are nearly always substituting for someone or something... They fight for labour rights in lieu of unions and denounce human rights abuses in the place of judges or the courts. They decry injustice, oppression and electoral fraud on behalf of weak or nonexistent political parties, and write pamphlets revealing and condemning corruption, substituting for a fettered, often marginal press.'

Electronic Ambassadors

The rapid pace of urbanisation since the turn of the century has had a seismic impact on popular culture. Towns and cities act as the entry point for foreign influences, while the most remote rural areas remain repositories of traditional culture. As the rural poor flocked to the shanty towns around the major cities, they brought with them traditional customs, which blended with the new influences. In Peru this melting pot has produced what is known as *chicha* culture, named after a potent local brew. Chicha music has combined the traditional wailing lament of the Andean *huaynu* with tropical music and electric guitars to become the sound of Lima's shanty towns.

Salsa, probably Latin America's most successful musical export in recent years, is itself a mongrel mixture of Cuban dance styles such as *son, rumba* and *chachacha*. In the late 1960s, Fania Records, a Latin record label in New York, had the inspired idea of repackaging this baffling range of musical styles as 'salsa', and the music took off, becoming a central part of the Latino identity movement in the ghettos of New York during the 1970s.

The introduction of new electronic media has transformed popular culture in the present century. Film, radio and TV have become the main channels of

Julio Etchart

Football crowds celebrate at the Brazilian cup final, Maracanã stadium, Rio, Brazil.

public communication in society, thereby acquiring a central role in creating and passing on cultural values. The mass media has also become a battle ground in the struggle to define Latin America's identity. Increased dependence on Western technology has given huge influence to films and TV programmes, with the film industry in particular dominated by Hollywood. Other media, such as radio and TV, have shown greater success in becoming largely Latin American in character, playing an important role in forging national identities.

It is difficult to overestimate the importance of the US as a purveyor of mass culture. The record shops of Latin American cities blare out Michael Jackson and Madonna (reborn in 1996 as Eva Perón in the musical *Evita*). Middle-class youth covet the latest Levis or Nike trainers just as much as their North American or European counterparts. Dubbed or subtitled US films of the *Rambo* and *Rocky* school form the staple diet of scruffy cinemas throughout the continent. Especially since the Cuban revolution of 1959, many artists and writers have come to see North American influence in the media as another facet of US political and economic domination of the continent. They argue that its domination allows the US to instil its values into Latin Americans, acting as a subliminal ambassador which can reach into the poorest home with a dazzling image of the giant to the north. Latin America's intellectuals have stressed the political importance of creating and sustaining a separate Latin American culture in the mass media, as part of the search for a political alternative to US domination.

The high cost and advanced technology required in film-making has meant that Latin America's cinema has lived in the shadow of films from the US and other industrialised nations, but at different moments it has managed to produce high quality films which have challenged the Hollywood monopoly. Until the 1960s most Latin American cinema consisted of low budget musicals, comedies and melodramas whose characters and themes were summed up by the critic John King as 'good women who bear the stigma of fate, weak men caught in the trap of a man-eater, rooms and brothels reeking with smoke and moral turpitude, eyes bloodshot with alcohol and grief, innocence, violent death.'

Yet Latin American cinema has also been intimately involved in politics since the days when the Mexican revolutionary, Pancho Villa, signed an exclusive contract with the US Mutual Film Corporation, granting it exclusive rights to film his battles. For $25,000 he agreed to fight in daylight whenever possible, to rerun scenes of battle if the cameras had missed the real thing, and to reschedule firing squad executions from 4am until after dawn.

The Cuban revolution marked a watershed for the continent's film-makers, as Havana quickly became the centre of a politically committed 'New Cinema', dedicated to portraying Latin America's conflicts, especially with the US, through a brand of social-realist cinema and documentary. The 1960s and early 1970s saw young radical film-makers using a low budget, hand-held camera style to film life, warts and all, in favelas and villages across the region, producing classics such as *Blood of the Condor* (Jorge Sanjinés, Bolivia) and *Battle for Chile* (Patricio Guzmán, Chile). Havana became the host of an annual Latin American Film Festival and invited film-makers from every corner of the Third World to come and study at its international film school.

The New Cinema dominated the 1960s, but soon afterwards the optimism began to wear thin as military dictatorships in the Southern Cone drove film directors into exile and the Cuban government started to show growing intolerance towards dissident writers and directors. Cuba illustrates a problem which has beset the Latin American cinema since its inception. In the absence of private capital, it has frequently had to rely on state support, leaving it open to manipulation and censorship, or simply asphyxiation by a state bureaucracy which cares little for artistic innovation.

In the 1980s and 1990s, government austerity programmes cut state funding and led to a slump in film production in many countries. Recently, however, there have been renewed signs of life. In Argentina, a percentage of box office and video sales is recycled as credits to film-makers. In Brazil, Embrafilme, the state industry, was shut down in 1992, and film production fell to one or two a year, before bouncing back to forty or so, when laws were passed granting tax breaks to film investors. In Mexico some joint ventures of private and public capital have scored successes with films such as *Danzón* and *Like Water for Chocolate*, directed by Alfonso Arau, which became the biggest foreign language success in the history of US cinema. Cuba, on the other hand, is cash-strapped in the 1990s and now produces few films – one recent success being *Strawberry and Chocolate*, a mild critique of gay issues directed by Tomás Gutiérrez.

Latin America's film audiences are dwarfed by its TV networks, which are relatively recent creations – Brazil's system did not become consolidated until the 1960s. Heavily patronised by the state, which recognised its political potential, Latin American TV has grown rapidly. There are now ninety million TV sets in the region, reaching ninety per cent of the population, and their favourite viewing is the telenovelas which dominate prime time. From the mid-1960s, when the first national telenovela was filmed, Latin America's soaps have built on the melodramatic tradition in popular theatre and film, developing rapidly into a major cultural commodity dominated by Brazil and

Mexico and their giant media conglomerates, TV Globo and Televisa, which rank fourth and fifth in the world league table of media giants.

Brazil and Mexico have even become TV exporters, breaking into the US market to build a large following for their soaps among the growing Hispanic population. Harder to understand is Russia's fascination with Latin soaps. In 1992 Televisa's *Los Ricos Tambien Lloran* (The Rich also Weep) broke all viewing records, while Boris Yeltsin's successful bid for reelection in 1996 was partly put down to his brainwave in engineering a special scheduling of TV Globo's *Tropicaliente* to dissuade Russians from leaving town on polling day. *The Strange Return of Diana Salazar*, shown by Televisa in 1988, described the reincarnation in today's Mexico of a 17th-century aristocratic woman who had been burned as a witch by the Inquisition. The plot illustrated several key themes in the soap genre. It contained a struggle between good and evil, in which one was often mistaken for the other; it included the obligatory love story, complete with a baroque plot which only addicts could disentangle, and it emphasised individual emotion and melodrama, rather than wider social or political themes. In addition, the soap added a new ingredient to the successful recipe – Diana Salazar could exert special powers over computers, another sign of the assimilation of new influences into existing forms.

An analysis of telenovela plots in Brazil showed that the affair usually takes place between lovers from different classes. In a country as profoundly unequal as Brazil, where social mobility is minimal, the soaps raise important issues, but unlike real life, they provide a happy ending as love triumphs over class barriers. In recent years, telenovelas have taken on a number of political issues such as landlessness and the environment in *O Rei do Gado*, in Brazil, or the highly topical question of government corruption in Mexico's *Nada Personal* or Venezuela's *Por Estas Calles*. Unfortunately, the ratings

Chicha culture achieves a unique and dynamic blend of traditional Indian and modern imported styles and fashions, Peru.

for such programmes have not always lived up to expectations, as script writers have struggled to reconcile the conflicting demands for escapism and social comment.

The 1990s has brought the digital revolution to Latin America. The big conglomerates are currently preparing to slug it out over control of the lucrative cable and satellite TV markets (one in ten of the region's homes already pays for cable TV). The battle shows both the risks and potential benefits of the new electronic age. While the big players may dominate the main stations, the proliferation and fragmentation of communications channels create spaces for other voices which in the past had no way of making themselves heard. Until the *New York Times* published Herbert Mathews' Sierra Maestra interview with Fidel Castro in 1957, the revolutionary movement in Cuba was virtually unknown to the rest of the world. In 1994, the Zapatistas' charismatic Subcomandante Marcos was issuing lyrical communiqués on the internet within hours of their uprising. Anyone with a laptop and a modem could follow the struggle unfolding in the depths of the Lacandón jungle, and there was nothing the Mexican government could do about it.

The Impact of Cuba

The cultural impact of the Cuban revolution spread far beyond the cinema. In a continent preoccupied with its identity, Cuba became a symbol of resistance to US domination and the search for a new Latin America, where culture was at the service of the people. In the early years of the revolution, the Cuban National Ballet performed classical and folk dance in factories during the lunch breaks, mobile cinema vans took film to isolated villages for the first time, and Havana became an international centre for writers, poets, film-makers and musicians. According to García Márquez, 'the definition of a Latin American "intellectual of the left" became the unconditional defence of Cuba.'

In the 1960s everything was new; 'New Song' in Chile blended traditional Andean music with folk ballads and revolutionary lyrics, 'New Cinema' recorded real life rather than cinematic fantasies, and the 'New Novel' established a worldwide readership for writers like Márquez, Mexico's Carlos Fuentes, Cuba's Alejo Carpentier and the Argentine Julio Cortázar. While the 1960s phenomenon in Europe peaked in 1968, Latin America's cultural boom reached its zenith a year earlier. In 1967 the Guatemalan author Miguel Angel Asturias became the first Latin American novelist to receive the Nobel prize, Gabriel García Márquez published *One Hundred Years of Solitude*, and Che Guevara was killed in Bolivia. With Che died the optimism of a generation who had grown to believe in imminent revolution. In Cuba the beginning of the 1970s saw the government curtailing cultural freedom and arresting the dissident poet Heberto Padilla, leading many leading figures such as Mario Vargas Llosa to part company with the revolution, after fiercely criticising Fidel Castro.

Since the Cuban revolution, students, radicals and social movements throughout Latin America have tried to create more democratic alternatives to the mass media dominated by big business. This conscious attempt to build a counter-culture to national and international TV, film and music involves myriad grassroots initiatives, using audio cassettes, community radio, theatre, the internet, film and video.

Borje Tobriasson/Panos

In a dusty square in one of Recife's poorer neighbourhoods, 'TV Viva' is showing community videos on a six-feet-square screen atop a VW van. Their team of radical journalists makes a monthly fifty-minute programme which combines cartoons, community news and radical politics, a typical example of the slick, high-tech Brazilian left. Barefoot children run in and out of the crowd as their parents guffaw at street interviews on the theme of 'when did you last have sex'. Another piece shows how property speculators have been moving in on community football pitches – serious politics in Brazil. When a more traditionally 'political' piece on death squad assassinations comes on, two-thirds of the audience drift away – raising awareness is not always easy.

Sex and violence fail to interest bored film-goers, Mexico

In developing their community video, TV Viva have learned that broadcasting left-wing diatribes is useless; they must adapt their message to the forms of popular culture if they hope to win an audience. In Lima, a community radio broadcast in a market square to a largely female audience only took off when the women were asked to make their own programmes about their home regions' traditions. Out of this experiment grew a radio soap about a woman migrating to the city, full of political content, but based in the lived experience of the audience.

The 1970s saw gloom settle over much of Latin America. Coups in Chile and Uruguay (1973), and Argentina (1976), coupled with the growing intolerance in Havana, led to repression and exile for many intellectuals, and a climate of hostility, fear and censorship for those that remained. The clampdown's best-known victim was Víctor Jara, Chile's top exponent of 'New Song'. Jara was murdered, along with thousands of others, in Santiago's infamous football stadium shortly after the coup. In an act of extraordinary malice, the soldiers crushed the guitarist's fingers before killing him. In exile other musicians such as Chile's Inti Illimani toured the world giving concerts

WRITING ON THE WALL   **103**

aimed at raising awareness and money for the solidarity movement. Safeguarded by exile and international fame, already-established writers responded with novels of dictatorship: Paraguay's Augusto Roa Bastos published *I The Supreme*, while García Márquez produced *Autumn of the Patriarch*.

For a decade, the Nicaraguan revolution of 1979 brought a chink of light to an otherwise sombre panorama. Poetry workshops sprang up in such unlikely places as the secret police and army barracks; a national literacy crusade brought the printed word for the first time to hundreds of thousands of peasants; an internationally acclaimed writer, Sergio Ramírez, became vice-president; state-sponsored musicians, dancers and circus performers sought to recover national traditions, and revolutionary murals adorned the walls of even the smallest village. In Ramírez' words: 'Once we lifted the yankee stone which weighed Nicaragua down, everything that was fundamental and authentic had to surface again: dances, songs, popular art and the country's true history.'

In the Southern Cone, the 1980s brought the military's slow retreat from power. In Argentina, war over the Falklands/Malvinas forced the military to treat youth as the saviours of the country, rather than potential delinquents. Radio stations were ordered to stop broadcasting music in English, giving 'national rock' access to the mainstream media for the first time. The military invited rock stars to take part in pro-war concerts, but instead an anti-war movement sprang up, whose anthem became León Gieco's song, '*Sólo le pido a Dios*':

> I only ask God
> not to make me indifferent to war
> It is a great monster that tramples on
> the poor innocence of the people

Following defeat in the Falklands, the end of the dictatorship led to a new cultural flowering in Argentine cinema. In general, however, the joy at the departure of the generals was tempered by the impact of the recession and the identity crisis of the left, leaving progressive musicians without the sense of grand purpose that marked the revolutionary sixties or the struggles against dictatorship in the 1970s. Salsa in the 1980s lost its political edge and retreated into the sentimentality of *salsa romántica*.

Latin America's literary establishment remains dominated by the grand old men of the 1960s boom, but new novelists and poets have also emerged. One of the most important developments has been the rise of a generation of women writers and poets, after centuries in which recognised writers were almost exclusively male. Authors such as Chile's Isabel Allende, Brazil's Clarice Lispector and Mexico's Elena Poniatowska and Laura Esquivel are gaining growing readerships both within Latin America and abroad. Allende's House of the Spirits became the first genuine bestseller by a woman in Latin American history.

Poniatowska has developed a style of documentary narrative to provide a 'people's eye view' of key moments in modern Mexican history, such as the social impact of the earthquake of 1985, and the 1968 Tlatelolco massacre of student protesters by the government. She has pioneered a form of writing in which middle-class women journalists and anthropologists work with working-class and peasant women to produce memorable life stories such as *Let Me Speak*, by Domitila Barrios de Chungara and Moema Viezzer, and *I, Rigoberta Menchú*, by Rigoberta Menchú and Elisabeth Burgos-Debray. In recent years Central America has also produced some renowned woman poets, notably Claribel Alegría (El Salvador) and Giaconda Belli (Nicaragua).

Interest in new Latin American writers has grown along with the booming interest in US-based latino writers such as Cristina García (*Dreaming in Cuban*), Julia Álvarez *(In the time of the Butterflies)* and Oscar Hijuelos *(Mambo Kings Play Songs of Love)* who have created a rich hybrid US/ Latino genre.

Through novels such as *Betrayed by Rita Hayworth*, and *Kiss of the Spider Woman*, Argentina's Manuel Puig has challenged the radical orthodoxy of the 1960s, with its scorn for Hollywood and cheap mass entertainment. Puig argues that writing off the cultural preferences of a large percentage of the population is an elitist mistake by intellectuals from the traditional left. Instead, they should be embracing mass culture. His characters belie the idea that Latin Americans are passive recipients of whatever the media throw at them; they are quite capable of indulging themselves with Hollywood fantasies while keeping a clear sense of their own identities. Puig also deals with issues of gender and sexuality in a way that has moved some women critics to describe him as the best creator of female characters in Latin American fiction.

Although the euphoria of the 1960s has been lost in decades of militarism and economic crisis, its cultural impact lives on in the quest for a truly Latin American identity. While Latin America continues to import its political and economic models from outside, often with disastrous results, the arts, especially music and literature, have always been more successful in finding words and rhythms that are authentically Latin American. If the region is to find its own way out of the recession and confusion of the late 20th century, its rich variety of cultural forms are bound to play a central role. García Márquez as always, is in the van, writing *The General in his Labyrinth* about Simón Bolívar in 1990. 'For me, what is fundamental is the ideology of Bolívar: the unity of Latin America,' he says, 'That is the only cause I'd die for.'

In his best-selling album *Buscando América* (Searching for America), Panama's salsa maestro Ruben Blades sums up the pressing challenges that lie ahead:

> I'm searching for America and I fear I won't find her
> ...I'm calling America but she doesn't reply
> those who fear truth have hidden her
> ...while there is no justice there can be no peace
> ...if the dream of one is the dream of all let's break the chains and
> begin to walk
> ...I'm calling you, America, our future awaits us
> before we all die, help me to find her.

The fat of the land. The Presidential Family, Fernando Botero

Chronology

1808-26	Latin American independence wars
1889	Brazil abolishes the monarchy and becomes a republic
1928	Caudillo General Plutarco Calles establishes the National Revolutionary Party (later the PRI) in power in Mexico; the PRI goes on to establish an effective one-party state
1930s	Urbanisation and industrialisation produce new political parties, led by populists
1946	Juan Domingo Perón elected president of Argentina
1958	The two main parties in both Venezuela and Colombia agree to share power in order to end decades of instability and military rule.
1964	Military coup in Brazil marks beginning of wave of military takeovers
1973	Salvador Allende, the world's first elected marxist president, murdered during the military coup which brings General Pinochet to power
1976	Argentina's military seize power
1982	Defeat in the Falklands/Malvinas war leads to return to democracy in Argentina
1989	Chile's Christian Democrats lead coalition which wins elections to end Pinochet presidency. General Stroessner ousted in Paraguay
1992	Brazil's Fernando Collor de Mello resigns presidency over corruption charges. Peru's Alberto Fujimori dissolves Congress to public acclaim
1994	Assassination of PRI presidential candidate precipitates political crisis
1997	Every Latin American country except Cuba ruled by elected leader

No Fit State

7

The State and Politics

Election time in the grey Chilean capital of Santiago and pictures of the candidates – forgettable grey men in black suits – look sternly out from the billboards like disapproving bank managers. One is the son of a former president, the other the nephew. To judge by the Chilean 1993 presidential campaign, politics in Latin America is even less eventful than in Britain or the US.

Appearances are deceptive. Only four years earlier, Chile had returned to democracy after 17 years of military dictatorship under the infamous General Augusto Pinochet. Within three months of overthrowing an elected leftist government in 1973, Pinochet's troops had killed some 1,500 people, and terrorised hundreds of thousands more in a war on their own people, yet by 1993 no soldier had been imprisoned and Pinochet remained head of the Armed Forces.

The twin threads of democracy and authoritarianism run through Latin America's history since independence, sometimes alternating between periods of democratic or dictatorial rule, at other times combining to produce hybrid forms of authoritarian democracy.

The authoritarian tradition stems from the conquest. The Spain from which Columbus set sail in 1492 was a militarised, crusading society, emerging victorious from a seven century battle with Islam and greedy for new conquests. Power lay with the Catholic monarchs, whose authority stemmed directly from God, as they ruled by 'divine right', in alliance with the Pope. As late as the 1970s, the Spanish dictator General Franco claimed to rule 'by the grace of God'. In their new colonies, the Spanish implanted a hierarchical system, enslaving the Indians. Ironically, the Indian empires they replaced in Mexico and the Andes were if anything even more authoritarian and centralised than the Spanish. Absolute power resided in the Aztec or Inca emperor (at the time of the Spaniards' arrival, Moctezuma II in Mexico and Atahualpa in Peru), allowing the Spaniards to defeat far more numerous rivals by first seizing the emperors, then replacing them at the top of the new social pyramid.

In Brazil, Portuguese rule was rather more lax. No gold or silver was discovered for the first two centuries, and Portugal concentrated on its other, more profitable ventures in the East Indies. Rather than develop an all-encompassing bureaucracy, it left the Brazilian colonists more to themselves, contenting itself with taxing Brazil's exports.

Independence came suddenly to Spanish America, and almost by accident. In 1808 Napoleon invaded Spain and installed his brother on the throne. Native-born *criollos*, already restive at Spain's insistence on monopolising foreign trade, seized the moment to declare independence. The monarch was

La Moneda, presidential palace in Santiago, Chile, burns under the air attack which began the military coup of September 1973. President Allende died during the assault.

now the enemy, and the American and French revolutions were still recent memories, so republicanism appeared the obvious alternative to many of the rebels (although some still supported an independent monarchy). As would come to be the case throughout the modern period, Latin Americans imported the latest political fashion from outside and attempted, unsuccessfully, to graft it onto their own traditions.

The greatest of Latin America's freedom fighters, Simón Bolívar, epitomised the process. His beliefs were a complex and often contradictory mixture of enlightenment-inspired republicanism and authoritarianism. Shortly before his death, disillusioned by his compatriots' lack of experience in government and the chaos unleashed by the independence wars, he wrote the Bolivian constitution. In it, Bolívar created a president-for-life, able to choose his own successor, thereby avoiding 'the changing administration caused by party government and the excitement which too frequent elections produce.'

Bolívar's dream of a United States of Latin America soon foundered on the rivalries and geographical and cultural differences which helped to divide up the region into today's republics. In the year of Bolívar's death, 'Great Colombia' disintegrated into Venezuela, Colombia and Ecuador; the former 'kingdom of Guatemala' splintered into the numerous feuding Central American republics. Each division took Latin America further from the path to prosperity and power followed by the USA to the north.

Republic after republic approved high-sounding democratic constitutions which had little connection with political and social reality. The wars against Spanish rule were won on the battlefield (see Chapter 8), and in the aftermath of independence, the economic elite of large landowners opted out and retired to their remote *haciendas*, leaving politics to the former military leaders, who became the feuding local strongmen, or *caudillos*, who have been a feature of Latin American political life ever since.

The caudillos were often charismatic, paternalist figures who became the real authority in many rural areas. As one Venezuelan caudillo wrote to Bolívar, 'the people bring me all their problems – how to build a house, whom to marry, how to settle a family dispute, and what seeds to plant'. In Latin America's rigidly stratified society, the military offered one of the few vehicles for ambition and social mobility, and caudillos and their personal retinues fought endless wars. Some of the strongmen managed to take over a whole country, such as Argentina's Juan Manuel de Rosas, or Mexico's Antonio López de Santa Anna, while others ruled over regional enclaves.In *One Hundred Years of Solitude*, Gabriel García Márquez portrays the life of a classic caudillo, Colonel Aureliano Buendía:

> Colonel Aureliano Buendía organised 32 armed uprisings and he lost them all. He had 17 male children by 17 different women and they were exterminated one after the other on a single night before the oldest one had reached the age of 35. He survived 14 attempts on his life, 73 ambushes, and a firing squad. He lived through a dose of strychnine in his coffee that was enough to kill a horse. He refused the Order of Merit which the President of the Republic awarded him. He rose to be Commander in Chief of the Revolutionary Forces.

Brazil, meanwhile, followed a different path. When Napoleon invaded, the British fleet shipped the Portuguese court *en masse* to exile in Rio de Janeiro. Portuguese rule had been less restrictive than that of the Spanish, producing less anti-royalist feeling, and in 1822, without violence or economic destruction, Brazil became an independent monarchy in 1822 under Emperor Dom Pedro I. Although Dom Pedro I faced a difficult few years, marked by political division, rebellions and the loss of what became Uruguay after a war with Argentina, his son, Dom Pedro II, succeeded in uniting the nation. He ruled for nearly fifty years, fending off the division, chaos and economic decline which afflicted the Spanish American colonies after independence. The Brazilian monarchy survived until 1889.

By the 1850s the caudillo period was coming to an end, as the economic elites emerged from relative seclusion to reimpose order. Modern nations started to emerge from the wreckage as British capital and technology flooded in, building railways, ports, and telegraph networks. Caudillos gave way to administrators, commercial agriculture expanded (often displacing Indian communities) and exports began to rise. By the 1880s, Latin America had become integrated into the world economy, setting the scene for a half century of economic boom, based on agro-exports.

Politics at this point was a preserve of the rich. This was the heyday of landowner rule, either running the government themselves, as in Argentina or Chile, or via the imposition of dictators in Mexico, Venezuela and Peru. Unlike the squabbling caudillos of the first half of the century, this new brand of dictator, exemplified by Mexico's Porfirio Díaz, were modernisers, intent on building up their nations through foreign investment and economic growth.

The key political issues of the time were reflected in the endless battles between Liberals and Conservatives. Although the ideological distinctions between them were frequently less important than the personal ambitions of their leaders, Conservatives tended to be pro-Church and supported a

Dom Pedro II

centralised system of government which favoured the big cities, while Liberals tended to be anti-clerical and federalist. As often as not, they conducted their discussion on the battlefield; 19th-century Colombia witnessed eight national civil wars, 14 regional civil wars and countless local disputes between the two parties.

Although many countries had universal male suffrage by the mid-19th century, the elite proved adept at preventing this from posing a threat to their rule. Using everything from ballot-box stuffing to free beer they managed to stifle political alternatives to elite rule. In the Andean countries the white elite, ever-fearful of Indian rebellion, made sure the vote went only to the literate, thereby excluding the indigenous majority from a say in government (in Peru, illiterates only got the vote in 1979). Since voting appeared unlikely to change anything, the electoral turnout across Latin America actually fell as the 19th century wore on. In Mexico and Argentina, despite universal male suffrage, only about five per cent of the adult male population bothered to vote. The landowners were quite happy to keep it that way.

Bringing out the vote became the speciality of a quintessential Latin American figure, the *cacique*. Originally the name for an Indian chief, the term came to mean a rural boss, an authoritative figure in traditional rural society who proved adept at drumming up support for his *patrón's* chosen party.

As long as Latin America remained a largely rural society, the caciques and other 'alchemists' (as government vote-riggers are known in Mexico) could ensure that politics stayed in the hands of the elite. But economic growth precipitated the destruction of the cosy, if exclusive, 19th-century political arrangement. Convinced by their own racism and the need for skilled labour that European blood was needed if their countries were to develop, governments in Argentina, Brazil and Chile encouraged mass immigration, predominantly from Southern Europe. With the immigrants came new and radical political influences, such as the anarchist trade unionists from Italy who founded the Argentine labour movement.

Immigration and growth produced an urban working class which proved both more articulate and far harder to control than the peasantry. Society was becoming more complex. The abyss separating the holders of political power from these new social forces grew ever wider. Something had to give, and in the end, as with independence, it took an event thousands of miles away to provide the catalyst for change. The Wall Street crash of 1929 and ensuing depression in the industrialised nations proved a major turning-point in Latin American history.

The Great Depression of the 1930s destroyed the world market for Latin America's commodity exports, bringing to an end the era of unquestioned dominance by the agro-exporting elite. The initial effect was a rash of military take-overs and a change in economic direction towards building up industry (see chapter 5). In the longer run, the new drive to industrialise created growing working and middle classes, laying the basis for a new kind of politics – populism. A new generation of political leaders came to the fore, bringing together workers and industrialists in an alliance that tried to bridge class barriers, often in opposition to the old guard of conservative landowners. Politics left the hacienda for ever, to find its new home in the bustling world of the city and the slum.

Populism was both popular and authoritarian – in the 1930s many of its leaders were military or ex-military men who drew inspiration from Hitler and Mussolini's rise to power. It was also fiercely nationalistic, condemning Latin America's traditional dependence on outside powers and often nationalising key foreign-owned industries, such as Mexican oil (1938) or the hugely popular purchase of the Argentine railways from Britain (1948). By bringing together both industrialists and workers in the same alliance, it was bound in the end to generate internal conflicts, although initially these were masked by the personal charisma of its leaders.

The great populists included Mexico's Lázaro Cárdenas, Getúlio Vargas in Brazil and Carlos Ibáñez in Chile, but the greatest of them all was Juan Domingo Perón, Argentina's beloved father-figure. Perón was elected in 1946, and Peronism has dominated Argentine politics ever since, despite Perón's death in 1974. Together with his wife Evita, he forged a personality cult, portraying himself as the heroic defender of the nation's *descamisados* (the shirtless ones), a man of the people who oversaw the growth of industry, redistribution of income, and the development of a welfare state. Evita's star quality allowed

Perón to woo another new political constituency – women, who won the right to vote in 1947.

Twenty years after his death, saint-like portraits of Juan and Evita still adorn walls in the shanty towns of Buenos Aires. In one of them, Ciudad Oculta, where cooking smells mix with the tang of eucalyptus leaves trampled with the rubbish into the muddy street, a mural of blond beautiful Evita looks out at the dark-skinned Paraguayan immigrant families. As one hard-bitten local activist, Juan Cymes, recalls: 'Evita was a goddess for me when I was a kid. I wrote to ask her to help some poor neighbours and she wrote back to me within a week!' Bearing the slogan 'Social Justice will be achieved inexorably, whatever the cost, whoever falls,' the freshly painted mural looks like publicity for this year's presidential candidate. Evita died of cancer in 1952, but her cult lives on. When the pop star Madonna went to Buenos Aires to film the musical of her life, outraged Argentines plastered the walls of the city with graffiti saying 'long live Evita, Madonna go home!'

Perón expounded the doctrine of *justicialismo* (social justice) which he saw as a third way between capitalism and communism in a world gripped by the deepening Cold War. The state replaced the caudillo as the all-powerful provider; it mediated in any dispute between different sectors of society, cared for the sick and elderly, as well as taking a commanding role in the economy via a burgeoning network of state-run industries. Perón's support rested on a highly organised and devoutly Peronist trade union movement, which became virtually an arm of government.

In 1955 Perón's conflicts with the military and the Church led to his overthrow and exile in Madrid. He returned only for a brief and chaotic

period as president from 1973-74. Nonetheless, despite his exile and death, and years of military prohibition and persecution, Peronism continues to dominate Argentine politics. When the Justicialista party lost the election in 1983 to Raúl Alfonsín's Radicals, it seemed the Peronists might be a dying force, yet in 1989 they returned in the shape of President Carlos Saúl Menem, a Peronist caudillo from the remote rural province of La Rioja. However, Menem promptly turned Peronism on its head by pursuing a radically anti-statist policy, privatising state industries and opening up the economy.

Juan Domingo Perón

Populism was more prominent in the larger countries, where industrialisation could take root. In the smaller, weaker economies of Central America and the Caribbean, a cruder solution emerged to the problems of economic collapse in the 1930s. In Nicaragua, El Salvador, Cuba and the Dominican Republic, military dictators took over. Men such as General Maximiliano Hernández in El Salvador or Nicaragua's Anastasio Somoza were willing to go to extreme lengths to stamp out unrest. After massacring 30,000 rebellious peasants in the *matanza* (massacre) of 1932, virtually wiping out El Salvador's Indian population, General Hernández explained in a radio broadcast, 'It is a greater crime to kill an ant than a man, because a man who dies is reincarnated, while an ant dies forever.' The Central American and Caribbean dictators remained in power for decades, stifling political modernisation and sowing the seeds for future revolutionary upheaval, including revolutions in Cuba (1959) and Nicaragua (1979) and a bloody guerrilla war in El Salvador in the 1980s. In the Dominican Republic, a US military intervention in 1965 helped prevent upheaval, installing another quintessential caudillo, Joaquín Balaguer, who proceeded to dominate the country's politics well into the 1990s.

Populist governments saw the state as the means to achieve development, by kick-starting the industrialisation of the economy. From the 1930s onwards, governments created hundreds of semi-independent agencies covering everything from state steel or oil companies, to agencies for agrarian reform or water supply. The state came to dominate the economy, employing almost the entire middle class and owning much of industry.

In the larger countries, notably Brazil, Argentina and Mexico, populism went hand in hand with corporatism – ruling parties set up and then controlled labour unions and other mass organisations of peasants and state employees. In return for the government improving wages and working conditions, these organisations had to sacrifice any pretence of independence. The unequal dialogue between state and mass organisation played the main role in controlling and channelling the demands of the new social groups, and legitimising the government in the eyes of the public. In contrast, elections often appeared marginal, marred by fraud or the huge inequality between the state/party machine and any opposition. Mass organisations worked to turn out the vote for the ruling party. Any individual or organisation that rebelled against this system could expect to be excluded from the state's bounty, hounded by the legal system and might face physical intimidation.

The strategy worked at first, as state intervention propelled economies into industrial growth. Booming economies and taxes on exports allowed governments to keep everybody happy, and when those were insufficient, governments overspent to buy off opposition at the expense of inflation.

The PRI

The most enduring of all the corporatist regimes is Mexico's aptly-named Institutional Revolutionary Party (PRI), a unique political animal born out of the chaos of the Mexican revolution of 1910-17. Through a combination of popular reforms, appeals to nationalism, coercion, corruption, and electoral fraud, the PRI has ruled Mexico since 1929, changing its name twice along the way, making Mexico the oldest one-party state in the world.

Although it is one of the most successful electoral fraudsters in the region, the PRI owes its longevity not to elections but to its control of an enormous and complex web of debts and obligations which reaches into every corner of Mexican society. Known to social scientists as clientilism, this network creates a vast system of personal allegiance, binding ordinary people to the party, and stifling the emergence of any significant opposition. By keeping in with the party, Mexicans can ensure everything from better rubbish collection to a new road for the neighbourhood, or a better job. Clientilism extends beyond the PRI to the whole of Mexican life; one study in the 1970s showed that 38 per cent of factory and office workers admitted obtaining their jobs through personal contacts.

When clientilism is not enough to prevent a threat to its power, the PRI is quite ready to use bribery and repression. But Mexico's relatively clean human rights record, compared to its more savage neighbouring regimes in Central America, attests to the PRI's skill in heading off opposition at an earlier stage; protesting student leaders are absorbed into the PRI bureaucracy before they can cause any trouble; trade union activists face the sack or exclusion from a PRI-dominated labour movement. Since the rule of law takes second place to personal loyalties, clientilist systems are also fertile breeding grounds for corruption, and in Mexico bribes are routine for everything from finding a parking space to winning a multi-million dollar government contract.

By the late 1990s, however, even the PRI's grip on power appeared to be weakening. The debt crisis of the 1980s and the rise of neoliberalism had seen the PRI reverse many of its earlier policies in a shift away from the pervasive state control of the economy towards the freer play of market forces. Until 1994, Presidents Miguel de la Madrid and Carlos Salinas tried to carry out economic reform without reforming the political system, but by the end of the Salinas period demands for political reform were growing and the incoming president, Ernesto Zedillo, pledged to turn Mexico into a liberal democracy, separating the PRI from the state apparatus.

The backlash was not long in coming. Cutting state spending as part of the neoliberal agenda inevitably reduces the government's ability to buy off the opposition, destroying the basis for its corporatist control of trade unions, peasant organisations and others. Separating state from party would spell disaster for the PRI, whose success relies on its ability to hand out state perks to its supporters. Political disasters such as the Zapatista guerrilla uprising and the assassination of the PRI's presidential candidate in 1994, a devaluation crisis in the same year, and a corruption scandal involving the Salinas clan have added to the impression that the once impregnable PRI is on the rocks. By late 1996 the party bureaucracy was in open revolt and it looked as though what the novelist Mario Vargas Llosa once named 'the perfect dictatorship' was finally on the way out.

Rise and Fall of Populism

Elsewhere, populism's star rose and fell with that of its economic brainchild, import substitution (see chapter 5). After notching up huge successes after the Second World War, import substitution started to run out of steam. By the 1960s, Latin American economies were slipping into crisis and the improbable alliance of industrialist and worker came apart in spectacular fashion. Moreover, economic growth and the rise of the middle class had further increased the number of social groups clamouring for a voice in running the country. When radical elements such as the student movement, were inspired by the Cuban revolution of 1959 to seek power through armed struggle, the generals decided that enough was enough. Military coups in Brazil (1964) and Argentina (1966) brought to power governments supported by a business sector determined to stamp out political opposition, crush the unions, reduce wages and give state-led development a new lease of life. They achieved it in Brazil, which entered an 'economic miracle' period of record growth from 1968-75.

The switch from civilian (if authoritarian) rule to military dictatorship was also helped by the international climate. After the Cuban revolution, the US and the Latin American military were determined to prevent revolution from spreading, and Washington was happy to support almost any military government that promised to crack down on leftism. There was also widespread support for military rule within Latin America, especially from the middle classes. Latin America's interwoven traditions of authoritarianism and democracy mean that many people do not see elections as the only legitimate route to power, and may well support a military government if they think it can impose order, or improve their economic situation.

The generals who seized power declared themselves to be 'above politics', disparaging all civilian politicians as corrupt incompetents. Instead, they saw the problems facing the continent as essentially technical, and cast themselves as 'iron surgeons, who would carry out prolonged and profound restructuring operations for which few suitable anaesthetics were available.' In the larger countries, the military ruled as an institution, seeking to avoid the temptations of caudillismo in Argentina by governing by committee – the *junta* – or in Brazil by rotating the presidency among the top generals.

The army's contempt embraced both politicians and the mass movement, as regimes sought to stamp out all political opposition or pressure which might interfere with what they saw as the efficient management of the economy. Although the Argentine and Brazilian regimes continued to pursue state-led development, they strengthened ties with multinational corporations, such as IBM, Volkswagen or Phillips, who built growing numbers of factories in the major economies of the region. Mexico, where state control of the labour movement was more deeply entrenched, weathered the period without requiring the kind of brutal crackdown seen further south.

The military's low opinion of politics did not include the state itself. It saw an efficient, well-managed state as essential to the achievement of national security and development, and if anything, increased the state's intrusion into every nook and cranny of society: in Argentina even the head of the national ballet was a military officer. Boosting state arms industries also proved popular with the generals. Only in Chile under General Pinochet, and to a lesser extent in Argentina after a coup in 1976, did military governments abandon state-led development in favour of a ferocious pursuit of the market. In the name of free trade and boosting competitiveness, both governments suddenly removed any protection to local industries, with the inevitable result that cheap imports flooded in, undercutting and bankrupting much of the industrial base so painstakingly assembled over the previous forty years.

The military's belief in its economic prowess proved seriously mistaken. Military governments showed themselves, if anything, to be even less competent than their predecessors, running up vast national debts during the free-spending 1970s, squandering resources on prestige megaprojects such as dams and nuclear power programmes and neglecting the nuts and bolts of long-term economic success, such as health and education.

In the longer run, the military's attempt to stamp out politics backfired. Banning political parties in countries such as Argentina, Chile and Uruguay created a political vacuum into which a new generation of grassroots movements grew, led by human rights and neighbourhood organisations. These were the first groups to fight back against military rule, becoming the catalyst for a broader opposition which brought about the military's eventual downfall. The new movements brought new sections of the population such as women and slum dwellers into politics, creating a richer, more pluralist spectrum of social organisations which augured well for the future.

The end of the military regimes came in different ways. In Argentina, the generals tried to divert attention from an economic crisis by invading the Falkland/Malvinas islands. Defeat in the ensuing war with Britain forced a humiliating withdrawal to the barracks. In Brazil, Uruguay and (later) Chile, the military managed to negotiate a controlled retreat, including pre-emptive laws granting them amnesty for their numerous abuses of human rights. These issues are more fully discussed in chapter 8.

Military rule was at its most stark in the southern cone countries of Argentina, Chile and Uruguay, along with Brazil. The development of the state elsewhere was more varied. In Venezuela and Mexico, the proceeds from oil exports helped governments to soften the impact of the crisis of state-led industrialisation, preventing the kind of political crisis which could have precipitated a military coup. Colombia pursued a more cautious role for

TABLE 6: PATTERNS OF CHANGE IN LATIN AMERICA

	Economic Development	Social Change	Typical Political Outcome
Phase 1 (1880-1900)	Initiation of export-import growth	Modernisation of elite, appearnace of commercial sector and new professionals	Oligarchic democracy or integrating dictatorship
Phase 1 (1900-1930)	Export-import expansion	Appearance of middle strata, beginnings of proletariat	Co-optative democracy
Phase 3 (1930-1960s)	Import-substituting industrialisation	Formation of entrepreneurial elite, strengthening of working class	Populism or co-optative democracy
Phase 4 (1960s to early 1980s)	Stagnation in import-substituting growth; some export-oriented growth in the 1970s	Sharpening of conflict, often class conflict	Bureaucratic authoritarian regime
Phase 5 (early 1980s to the present)	Scarcity of foreign exchange (worsened by foreign debt) leading to stagnation or recession	Increased mobilisation of middle and lower class groups	Incomplete electoral democracy (with military veto)

Source: Skidmore and Smith, Modern Latin America, p.62

the state, running up fewer debts and avoiding the worst of the collapse that afflicted the others. Paraguay looked more like Central America, as it languished under the rule of General Stroessner for 35 years from 1954. In Peru and Bolivia the recalcitrance of the landed elite blocked political change, eventually precipitating a revolution in Bolivia in 1952, and a modernising military take-over in Peru in 1968.

Life and Debt

The Latin American state entered the 1980s in bad shape. The debts accumulated by military and civilian governments alike during the final years of import substitution precipitated the debt crisis in 1982. Starting in Mexico but spreading across the continent, almost every Latin American government found itself bankrupt, forced to go, cap in hand, to the IMF. The quid pro quo for IMF help was radical economic surgery of the kind first attempted under General Pinochet in Chile in the 1970s, involving a massive cutback in the role of the state. Such policies won powerful supporters within the region too, as business and political elites concluded that the days of state-led development were over.

The political consequences of returning to elected governments at a time of economic recession have been complex. Despite massive recessions, economic crises and corruption scandals which in earlier decades would have had the generals champing at the bit, the military has mostly stayed in the barracks. Isolated bouts of sabre rattling when commanders have sent tanks onto the streets of Lima or Santiago have been easily seen off, not least because US support for military interference in politics largely ended with the fall of the Berlin Wall. In consequence, the 1980s and 1990s have been decades of unprecedented political stability under civilian governments. When Argentina's Raúl Alfonsín handed over the presidency to Carlos Menem in 1989, it was the first constitutional transfer between Argentine presidents of rival parties in the 20th century. One result has been a series of constitutional amendments to allow presidents such as Carlos Menem and Alberto Fujimori to run for a second (and in the case of Fujimori, a third) term in office. Up until the 1990s, most presidents had struggled to finish even one term in office without being forcibly ejected from the presidential palace. Now, other pretenders such as Brazil's Fernando Henrique Cardoso are lining up to ask for second terms.

In the 1990s, Latin American leaders have also shown a new-found vulnerability to public opinion and the law. Corruption scandals have seen national parliaments and public pressure combine to oust Brazil's Fernando Collor in 1992 and Venezuela's Carlos Andrés Pérez in 1993, while Colombia's Ernesto Samper barely managed to cling on to office in 1996 after his election campaign was accused of having received money from the drug cartels. In Ecuador, Abdalá Bucaram was driven from office in 1997 within six months of winning the presidency. Bucaram, who described himself as *El Loco* (the madman) managed to alienate both the poor (by introducing a savage austerity programme) and the business elite (by his corruption and unpresidential antics such as singing out of tune rock songs on stage, backed by mini-skirted dancing girls. In these countries, it would seem that the highly centralised presidential system has become somewhat more accountable to public and political pressure within the constitution.

Optimists see all this as evidence of a lasting transition to democracy, but there are also ample grounds for pessimism. The early hopes of a better life following a return to democracy in the 1980s swiftly foundered, as living standards dropped across the region. Many Latin Americans have become particularly disillusioned with professional politicians, although they no longer believe the army could run the country any better. In many countries the left too seems to have lost its self-belief and political appeal. The result has been a political vacuum into which has stepped a new breed of authoritarian populists.

Latin American constitutions have always been highly presidential, with presidents able to bypass Congress and rule by decree, or under states of emergency. Leaders such as Argentina's Carlos Menem have made enormous use of this executive power – Menem announced as many decrees during 1989-92 as were issued by all of his civilian predecessors since 1922 put together. Yet Menem has been a popular president, winning reelection in 1995. Presidents such as Menem or Mexico's Carlos Salinas have used their control of party machines, established in the previous period of populist government, to force through sweeping political and economic change, often at great political cost in terms of internal division and dissent within the

Peru's big brother

parties. Other 'neopopulists' have opted to go it alone, using TV to appeal directly to the electorate as they bypass national parliaments.

The most notable of the new wave of authoritarian presidents is Peru's Alberto Fujimori. Elected in 1990, Fujimori had little party support in Congress, and has shown little interest in building his Cambio 90 party into a serious political institution. In 1992, when opposition parties tried to block his programme, Fujimori dissolved Congress in a 'self-coup' and ruled by decree. Even after international pressure forced him to call fresh elections, one political opponent acidly observed, 'the only element of democracy in Peru today is the electoral process, which gives Peruvians the privilege of choosing a dictator every five years. Rule making is subsequently carried out in a vacuum, with the executive branch enacting new rules and regulations at a rate of 134,000 every five years (an average of 106 each working day) without any feedback from the population.'

Yet eighty per cent of Peruvians supported Fujimori's assault on the Congress, presumably sharing Fujimori's view at that time that, 'Democracy should no longer include political parties... Democracy is the will of the people: good administration, honesty and results.' Fujimori had tapped into popular discontent with professional politicians, widely seen as corrupt and incompetent. Once again, Latin America's twin traditions of authoritarianism and democracy have combined to produce phenomena which outsiders from Europe or North America can find baffling.

Fujimori presents himself as a political outsider, cultivating a man of the people image as he helicopters methodically from village to village, opening schools, handing out farm tools and listening to grievances in classic caudillo style. Even his Japanese origins have helped, distancing him from the traditional elite of white politicians such as his defeated rivals in 1990 and 1995 novelist Mario Vargas Llosa and former UN General Secretary Javier Pérez de Cuellar.

Through a combination of luck and diligence, Fujimori has remained extremely popular despite (or perhaps because of) his authoritarian style and poor record on human rights. His ferocious 'Fujishock' austerity programme has tamed Peru's hyperinflation, albeit at the cost of falling wages and growing poverty. Shortly after the self-coup, Peruvian security forces decapitated the Shining Path guerrilla movement by seizing its founder and leader, Abimael Guzmán. Portraying himself as the slayer of both inflation and political violence, Fujimori won a second term of office in 1995 and promptly changed the constitution again to allow him to run for a third term.

The new breed of 'anti-politicians' include more exotic political animals than Fujimori. Bogotá's mayor, and a possible future president, is Antanas Mockus, a bizarre philosopher-mathematician of Lithuanian extraction and former rector of the National University. Mockus was elected mayor of Bogotá after dropping his trousers before a group of barracking students, making the TV news and launching his political career. Mockus is anything but the grey man of traditional politics. He parades the city centre dressed as superman, employs mime artists to mimic misbehaving pedestrians and got married for the third time in an animal cage, with two Bengal tigers as witnesses, before leaving for the reception with his wife astride an elephant. Another colourful character is Venezuela's Irene Sáez, a former Miss Universe widely tipped as future presidential material.

Is Latin America democratic?

Foreign observers spend a great deal of time assessing Latin America's democratic credentials. Some concentrate on form, lauding regular elections, peaceful handovers of power, and the absence of military coups as proof of a lasting shift in the continent's politics. They also applaud the growing diversity and complexity of Latin America's social and political spectrum.

Sceptics, on the other hand, stress the lack of democratic content, pointing to the authoritarian style of many presidents, the prevalence of corruption, and the failure of legal systems to uphold the law. Party political systems are fragile and volatile. New parties rise and sink without trace at an increasing rate, while parliamentary politics is often chaotic and corrupt. Brazil has probably the most unstable party system in the region. During one term in office in the 1990s, 170 out of 513 members of the Lower House switched parties, some of them more than once – one did it seven times. Party loyalties are almost non-existent, a nightmare for any president and an almost certain guarantee of pork barrel politics, as political managers seek to buy the votes of deputies on key issues.

Other critics, especially in Brazil, stress the lack of true citizenship, believing that real democracy is impossible when rising inequality, crumbling social services, the crime wave, and police intimidation and immunity from prosecution are so widespread. A functioning democracy relies on a degree of social consensus; people have to accept the rules of the game and the legitimacy of the system. Yet according to Brazilian political scientist Paulo Sérgio Pinheiro, 'in almost all Latin American countries, the poor see the law as an instrument of oppression at the service of the wealthy and powerful.... According to Brazil's pastoral land commission, of the 1,730 killings of peasants, rural workers, trade union leaders, religious workers and lawyers between 1964-1992, only 30 had been brought to trial by 1992, and only 18 convictions achieved.' In Venezuela 18,800 of the country's 25,000 prisoners have not been sentenced, while 92 per cent of Venezuelans say justice does not apply equally to rich and poor, and 51 per cent say people should take the law into their own hands. This is hardly the basis for a functioning democracy, where disputes and conflicts can be settled through a judicial system which everyone believes in or at least accepts.

Commentators have always claimed that the latest Latin American trend was going to last for ever – in the 1950s the modernisers claimed that Latin America had finally made it onto the road to industrial development; in the 1960s the future was revolutionary after Cuba; in the 1970s and early 1980s, Latin America would forever remain grimly authoritarian. Each prediction was promptly disproved by events. Now foreign pundits and politicians alike once again affirm that Latin America is irreversibly democratic. Yet as we have seen, the undoubted advances in democratic government are deeply flawed.

Moreover, Latin America has to some extent achieved democracy by default: the Cold War has ended and for the time being Washington and foreign investors see democratic regimes as the best route to political stability (although happy to turn a blind eye to undemocratic practices in strategically important countries such as Mexico); the military has withdrawn to the barracks to lick its wounds after a disastrous performance in government; the left is still struggling to assimilate the fall of the Berlin Wall and is searching for a convincing alternative to neoliberalism. The latest generation of elected governments has yet to come under serious challenge. When they do, it seems a fair bet that the region's dual traditions of dictatorship and democracy will once again combine to confound the experts, throwing up a new role for the state.

Atlacatl brigade on anti-guerrilla sweep, El Salvador, 1982. The Atlacatl were
involved in some of the worst human rights abuses in the country's civil war.

Chronology

1808-26 Wars of independence free Spanish America from colonial rule

1939-45 Second World War establishes US as dominant military power in Latin America

1948 Costa Rica abolishes army

1949 Brazilian Higher War School founded, becoming central to spread of Cold-War national security doctrine

1959 Cuban revolution and ensuing support for other guerrilla movements seen by military as proof of international communist conspiracy

1964 Military seize power in Brazil and rule for 25 years

end 1976 At least two-thirds of people on mainland Latin America live under dictatorial rule

1982 Argentina loses South Atlantic war, and military government falls; senior officers subsequently imprisoned on human rights charges

1980s Civil wars in El Salvador and Guatemala marked by unprecedented human rights abuses by military. US backs Contras in proxy war against Sandinista government

1989 US invasion of Panama. Fall of Berlin Wall marks end of Cold War and difficult times ahead for military in Latin America

1990 Chile's General Pinochet becomes the last of the great military dictators to leave office

1992 Peace agreement in El Salvador following military stalemate between army and guerrillas. Military removed from politics

1994 US troops intervene to oust military government in Haiti

1996 Peace agreement in Guatemala. US pressure prevents military coup in Paraguay

Men at Arms 8

The Military

General Albano Harguindeguy sat on the sofa in his Buenos Aires flat. Now a retired Latin American patriarch, his genial back-slapping style must once have made him popular with his men. Over a Scotch he reflected on his period in office as Argentina's Minister of the Interior, priding himself on his grasp of world events. While his wife served pizza, he mused over what he would have done differently if he had the chance to be in government all over again. 'Not so many disappeared people – we should have used the law instead,' he concluded.

The bluff general in his cardigan and slippers was in charge of internal security during the worst years of the military junta which seized power in 1976. During the period of the 'dirty war', Harguindeguy's men took thousands of young men and women from their homes, often at night, and drove them away in the sinister unmarked Ford Falcons favoured by the security forces. Their relatives and friends never heard from them again, amidst rumours of torture cells, concentration camps and mass graves. After the military regime fell, the rumours proved to be true. The number of documented 'disappearances' exceeds 9,000, and the real number could be two or three times that amount.

Argentina's dark hours of fear and doubt have been repeated up and down Latin America. In *Mothers of the Disappeared*, by Jo Fisher, Aída de Suárez remembers how her son disappeared:

> On 2 December 1977 at four o'clock in the morning, twenty armed men broke into our house with rifles and pistols pointed at us. They were nervous. They opened and closed the cupboards, the fridge. They were looking for things, guns apparently. They took everything of any value they could carry, the few things of value that a working-class family has in their home, sentimental things. But that wasn't important to me. They could have taken everything, but my son, no. He was sitting on the bed, trying to get dressed. One man shouted, 'There's one in here!' and then two huge men with guns in their hands told me not to move. They asked only if he was Hugo Héctor Suárez and that he had to go with them.
>
> 'Who are you?', I screamed. 'We are the security forces.' They were in civilian suits but underneath they were wearing army fatigues and boots, and green bullet-proof vests, the colour of the army. So it was the army. I said, 'Why? My son has done nothing, he's not a criminal. Why have you come in like this, frightening the children with guns pointed at everyone?' – twenty armed men for a child of 21, an old woman like me, and two young children. 'We've come to take him away for questioning.'

Military ceremony, Buenos Aires, Argentina. The military form a separate caste in Argentine society, and have regularly seized power from civilian politicians.

'Why?' I asked and they pushed me and threw me against the wall. They took my son. That was the last time I saw him.

By the end of 1976 two-thirds of people on the Latin American mainland lived under dictatorial rule. Among the major countries, only Mexico, Venezuela, Colombia and Costa Rica had no general in the presidential palace. Pinochet, Stroessner, Videla; the continent became synonymous with vicious military dictators in sunglasses and the midnight knock on the door. As the 1980s passed, the generals began to return to the barracks, some in defeat and humiliation, others managing to retain a significant voice in politics. In March 1990, Chile's General Augusto Pinochet became the last of the great Latin American dictators to leave power when he reluctantly handed over the presidency to the elected Christian Democrat leader Patricio Aylwin. In many Latin American countries the military retained considerable power, and during the 1990s, military rumblings occurred in Haiti, Paraguay, Venezuela, Brazil and Chile, among others, but by early 1997, Fidel Castro's Cuban regime remained the last unelected government in the western hemisphere. In general, the military now finds itself with few friends, prey to budget cuts, public contempt and a profound identity crisis over its role in the post-Cold War world.

Military History

Unlike the UK or USA, where civilian political control over the armed forces has long been taken for granted, the military in Latin America has always been an independent political force. The nature of the Spanish conquest, led by soldiers who defeated the Aztec and Inca empires and were rewarded with land, slaves and booty, was in marked contrast to the methods and lifestyle of the civilian settlers who emigrated to start a new life in the US and Canada. When Spanish power collapsed, Latin America won its independence through the exploits of military heroes like Simón Bolívar (1783-1830) and José de San Martín (1778-1852). Today, the streets of every Latin American capital are littered with statues of heroic military figures on horseback, swords raised, and schoolchildren diligently learn the names of the military fathers of the nation.

Between 1808 and 1826, independence wars raged throughout Spanish America. Armed uprisings turned into liberation armies which marched across the continent in two great arcs: in the south, San Martín's Army of the Andes crossed the pampas from Buenos Aires, marched over the Andes into Chile and then moved up towards Peru. In the north, Bolívar's followers marched from Venezuela into Colombia and down to liberate Ecuador. The two armies converged on Peru, where they decisively defeated the remaining Spanish forces at the Battle of Ayacucho in 1824. In Mexico, violent social rebellion followed a course of its own. By 1826 Spain had lost everything except Cuba and Puerto Rico. Brazil declared its independence from Portugal in 1822, but in contrast to the republics of Spanish America, the new nation emerged with little violence as a monarchy ruled until 1889 by the emperors Pedro I and Pedro II, both members of the Portuguese royal family.

The independence armies were led by the small *criollo* class fighting to seize power from Spain, but otherwise intent on maintaining Latin America's social structures largely unchanged. 'Liberation' brought few benefits for the Indian population. Black slaves were, however, promised their freedom in exchange for fighting, and formed much of San Martín's army. Indians were press-ganged to fight by both sides. White leaders, whether royalist or republican, feared revolt by the blacks and Indians more than they feared each other – when the Spanish viceroy decided to abandon Lima in 1821, the terrified and hitherto royalist citizens asked San Martín for protection against a feared black uprising.

In the first decades after independence, the military often consisted of little more than armed members of the peasantry. Since the mid-19th century, however, a process of professionalisation has taken place, transforming the military from an irregular army in the hands of local chieftains into a sophisticated institution, while never removing its taste for occupying the presidential palace.

Professionalisation has involved building a national army with a proper career structure and a separate value system, encouraging its self-image as a caste apart from, and often superior to, the rest of society. Military schools and staff colleges were set up to forge young boys into tomorrow's generals. The schools take boys in their early teens and impose military discipline and values. A high percentage of the intake are sons of officers, which only increases the sense of separation from society. Once the boy has entered the military structure, he will often stay isolated from civilian society until he is a high-ranking officer – his life will revolve around the school and the barracks:

The isolation of the [Argentine] armed forces intensified over the course of the 20th century. Beginning in the 1920s, special neighbourhoods and clubs were constructed for officers and their families. These new institutions included free country clubs or *círculos* used for recreation, business functions and weddings of officers and their children. Paid for out of the military budget, these clubs – like the special apartment complexes erected near major military installations – accentuated the officers' ignorance of civilian values and aspirations. Usually only those with the rank of colonel or above could acquire their own apartments in civilian neighbourhoods. The virtual apartheid separating officers from both enlisted soldiers and civilians was epitomised in the rules governing elevators in military buildings: one set of lifts used by officers and another for civilians and lower-ranking soldiers.

Emilio Mignone, 'The Military: What is to be Done?', *NACLA Report on the Americas,* New York, July 1987

In the absence of combat experience, most Latin American armies place enormous importance on educational qualifications as the path to promotion. The standard of education in military schools is often higher than in civilian life, reinforcing the officers' sense of innate superiority.

Once the officers reach the rank of colonel, a new panorama opens. At this point they start to acquire significant political power, a coterie of civilian advisers, and contact with the civilian economic elites and overseas diplomats. In large economies like Brazil and Argentina, military officers are highly sought-after to sit on the boards of both state and private businesses, and opportunities for self enrichment begin to appear. In less sophisticated economies, officers must settle for more straightforward methods; in Paraguay General Stroessner kept his officers happy by cutting them in on the smuggling trade with Brazil; in Panama General Noriega bought his men's loyalty and silence by involving them in everything from protection rackets to prostitution; in El Salvador local commanders left soldiers killed in action on the battalion's books and pocketed their wages. As one army leader in the Mexican revolution of 1910 commented, 'there is no general who can withstand a bombardment of 50,000 pesos.'

From the early days of import substitution, some of the region's most developed armies began to assemble a military-industrial complex which gave them enormous economic muscle. In Brazil and Argentina, military conglomerates came to control everything from arms manufacture to petrochemicals. Brazil has even come to rival Israel as the Third World's foremost arms exporter, exporting US$1 billion of weaponry a year during the 1980s. In Chile, the Pinochet regime sang the virtues of privatisation, except when it came to the lucrative state copper company, which is still obliged to give ten per cent of its income directly to the armed forces. The military's growing economic power further strengthened its political autonomy from central government.

The social gulf between officers and men in Latin America's armies is exacerbated by the widespread use of conscription. Many of the young men who shivered in the Argentine trenches during the Falklands/Malvinas war of 1982 were conscripts with little interest in fighting. Non-commissioned officers, or young officers who have not yet acquired the privileges that go with senior rank, are traditionally a source of unrest within the military, often leading uprisings against the military hierarchy. These younger men often have more contact with society at large, and sometimes lead protests against unpopular economic measures, as in the case of Venezuela's Lt. Col. Hugo Chávez (see below).

THE SOLDIERS

The soldiers, *señor*,
are simple folk
peasants tied to the land
who lived in peace sowing their grain,
incapable of striking a bound man,
with innocence
hanging from their hands
like the white stars of morning.

The soldiers, señor, were born
without poison in their souls
or hatred in their eyes.
But one day
you sent your fierce overseers
to hunt peasants
and they rounded them up like beasts
herded into corrals
and began to strip them of their souls,
to make them believe
that the worker is their enemy,
that their country is its anthem and its flag,
the president
and his forty thieves,
the barracks and the generals.

And the soldier
got tough and hard
became a mere puppet
obeying orders
became accustomed
to gambling his life defending the faceless ones,
the shadowy criminal bureaucrats,
the revolting fair-haired people skulking
behind the large firms,
in the international agencies,
in that den by the name of the Pentagon.

The soldier, señor, sincerely believes
that he is doing the right thing,
not like yourself
playing at Pilate washing his hands.

Jaime Suárez Quemain, 'The Soldiers', *El Salvador: Poems of Rebellion*,
El Salvador Solidarity Campaign, London

The Spectre of Communism

Following the Second World War, Latin America's militaries increasingly adopted a Cold War ideology. This world view was refined at the military's staff colleges, where high-flying young officers were prepared for the high command. In Brazil, the military set up the Higher War School (*Escola Superior de Guerra*, ESG) in 1949, where young officers studied not only military tactics, but also politics, economics and sociology. From the outset, the ESG also recruited among the civilian elite – business leaders, top civil servants, politicians and judges who by 1966 comprised half the graduates. The ESG thus served both to train the future military top brass and establish firm links between them and Brazil's civilian rulers.

The ESG was instrumental in developing what became known as national security doctrine, an all-embracing viewpoint which saw the military as the guardians of order in the broadest sense, including economic development and the prevention of internal political or social divisions. The enemy of the continent's social order was the spectre of international communism, which was conducting a stealthy war of internal subversion against pro-western governments throughout Latin America.

National security doctrine became established as the linchpin of military thinking following the Cuban revolution of 1959, which the generals saw as proof of the international communist conspiracy. The doctrine provided the intellectual justification for the military to make the defeat of 'internal subversion' its top priority. Subversion was defined as anything which threatened the status quo – trade unionism, troublesome priests, peasant movements, socialist politics, or student protest. Since this was a 'Third World War' against the communist menace, human rights considerations and the rule of law became redundant, clearing the way for the atrocities, disappearances and bloodshed which followed.

Some of the wilder excesses of national security doctrine had a tragicomic air – in the late 1970s the Argentine junta reportedly burnt books on Cubism under the mistaken belief that they expounded the philosophy of Fidel Castro. Junta members were much given to describing themselves as the defenders of western Christian democracy despite their aversion to elections. The Argentine military's perception of what constituted a threat to western Christendom has always been broad; in the 1960s General Onganía defended the sanctity of the family by outlawing miniskirts.

Up until the Second World War, US influence was greatest in its traditional backyard of Central America and the Caribbean. In the early years of the century, Washington regularly sent in the marines to overthrow governments, before setting up client armies like General Somoza's National Guard in Nicaragua which enabled it to retreat to its bases in the Panama Canal Zone. Further south, in Brazil, Chile and Argentina, the German army had considerable influence in the early professionalisation of regular armies.

The Second World War destroyed Germany as a regional influence and established the US as the supreme foreign power throughout Latin America. US military missions spread across Latin America to supply and train the region's armies, in the process ensuring that future military leaderships would be firmly pro-US. As the Cold War gathered pace, US influence was crucial in forging national security doctrine.

In addition to sending military missions to the various countries, the US trained thousands of Latin American officers and future military leaders in

Joe Fish

Members of Guatemala's elite gather for cocktails on the Day of the Army.

the US or at the School of the Americas in the Panama Canal Zone, earning it the name 'School of the Dictators'. Pupils included Major Roberto d'Aubuisson, godfather of El Salvador's death squads, and the Panamanian dictator General Manuel Antonio Noriega. In 1996, the Pentagon provoked a scandal when it declassified documents showing that Spanish-language training manuals used at the school in the 1980s recommended to its Latin American trainees the torture of guerrillas, threats, bribery and blackmail.

As a result of President Carter's short-lived human rights policy in the 1970s, brutal military regimes in Latin America found their arms supplies from Washington reduced or cut off. Their response was to look elsewhere for suppliers and develop their own armaments industries. This undermined US supremacy in the region as arms suppliers from the UK, France, Italy, Germany, the Soviet Union and Israel broke into the market.

In 1981 President Reagan took office, determined to end Carter's human rights policy, which he blamed for the US 'losing' Nicaragua as a client state through the 1979 revolution. One of the key right-wing thinktanks behind Reagan's new policy, the Council for Inter-American Security, painted a lurid, and farcically incorrect, picture of the challenge facing the US in Latin America:

> World War III is almost over. The Soviet Union, operating under the cover of increasing nuclear superiority, is strangling the Western industrialised nations.... America is everywhere in retreat. The Caribbean, America's maritime crossroad and petroleum refining centre, is becoming a Marxist-Leninist lake.

President Reagan chose to 'draw the line against communism' in Central America and the Caribbean. US marines invaded Grenada in 1983 and overthrew its left-wing government, while in Nicaragua and El Salvador US strategists refined Vietnam-style counter-guerrilla tactics into a more general technique known as 'low intensity conflict'. This attempted to defeat the guerrilla movement in El Salvador and the Sandinista government in Nicaragua through the use of proxy armies in order to avoid the use of US troops which might lead to an anti-war backlash at home. In El Salvador the army was encouraged to 'win hearts and minds' among the peasantry, but at the same time had the conflicting objective of striking at anyone considered sympathetic to the guerrillas. In the end repression took precedence over reform. In Nicaragua the Contras played a significant part in the downfall of the left-wing Sandinista government by sabotaging the economy and forcing the government to divert scarce resources into defence.

Despite pouring US$6 billion in aid into El Salvador, the war ended in stalemate and a 1992 peace agreement which charply curtailed the military's power and made way for the guerrillas to re-enter civilian politics. In Nicaragua, Washington's war of attrition undermined public support for the Sandinistas, who were voted from office in 1990.

Relief at the end of the fighting was tempered by the problem of what to do with the newly unemployed soldiers from both sides. In El Salvador the UN accused the army of links to armed robbery and murder; in Guatemala the military is widely believed to be involved in crime rings which steal cars and run the drug trade; in Nicaragua, banditry has become endemic in the countryside. More generally, the militarisation of the 1980s has left the legacy of a more violent society, littered with left-over guns. As one former member of an elite Salvadoran anti-guerrilla battalion commented in an unguarded moment ,'I need to kill'. Having been fired from the army, and tormented by nightmares from his years behind guerrilla lines, the man was about to cross the US-Mexican border on his way to join a gang in Los Angeles, one small example of the violence sown by US anti-guerrilla tactics coming back to haunt it.

General Unrest

The quintessentially Latin American phenomenon of the military coup and military government long preceded the invention of national security doctrine, stretching back to the Spanish and Portuguese roots of the region's political systems. Prior to the Second World War, military interventions usually aimed to return power to the military's civilian allies, or took place in response to threats against the military as an institution, such as government attempts to interfere in the promotion system or cut the military budget. However, with national security doctrine came not only the notion that government was a legitimate role for the military, but that squabbling civilian politicians were often less fit to govern than well-educated military men with only their country's interests at heart. When the Brazilian military took power in 1964, even the US ambassador expected it to hand over power to a suitable civilian government within the year. Instead they ruled for two decades.

In most cases, military coups take place with the support of at least a section of the civilian political elite. In Chile Christian Democrat leader Patricio Aylwin openly supported the coup which brought General Pinochet to power in 1973, presumably hoping that once his socialist rival, President Salvador Allende, was removed, the army would then hand power to Aylwin's party before retiring to the barracks. Instead Pinochet kept power for himself and remained in the presidential palace for the next 17 years, until a chastened Aylwin led the campaign which secured his departure.

A RICH MAN'S COUP

The evening of that mild spring day, Tuesday 11 September, General Augusto Pinochet had been in power for a few hours. The guests were assembled in the main hall of the Hotel Carrera, a sumptuous room three storeys high...The new regime had decreed a curfew. The doors were barred.

People sat around on the sofas or at the little copper-topped tables. They talked animatedly, the suave men and the elegant ladies. They laughed and joked and drank noisily, the sound of their celebration bouncing and echoing off the shiny walls. Every so often there was an expectant hush when the television came up with a *bando*, some new message from the new masters of Chile. When it was ended there were cheers, more champagne corks popped and from ladies' slippers toasts were drunk to Pinochet and his brave companions.

In the corner the service door opened from time to time and groups of waiters peered timidly out. The juxtaposition of the stylish carousers and the apprehensive serving staff was dramatic and served like nothing else to bring home the social impact of the putsch above and beyond the patriotic and martial music that the radio and the television were broadcasting. The waiters and the rest of those below stairs knew what military rule was going to bring and they were afraid.

Hugh O'Shaughnessy, *Latin Americans*, London, 1988

The military's willingness to interfere, and civilian leaders' readiness to encourage it, destabilised democratic civilian politics by offering politicians a short-cut to power which seemed more seductive than the prospect of long years in opposition. Parties no longer needed to succeed by developing sound policies to win more support than their rivals, but could gain power by currying favour with the high command. The art of conspiracy became the successful politician's chief weapon.

In many third world countries the military has suffered severe damage from meddling in politics. Power politicises the military as an institution, opening the way to factional rivalries and threatening the vertical discipline on which armies depend. Yet Latin American armies have resisted the corrosive impact of military rule better than most. In Argentina the army has had to alternate periods of rule with periods back in the barracks, when it has licked its wounds and restored its cohesion by purging dissidents. Its continued survival has depended on its ability to give up power at the right time. Where armies have been totally destroyed by a revolution, as in Cuba or Nicaragua, it is partly because a military dictator refused to preserve the army as an institution by giving up power. The resulting collapse of the military then paved the way for a revolutionary victory.

Despite the prevalent image of the Latin American military dictator as a barbarian in dark glasses, military regimes have varied enormously in both ideology and structure.

In Peru and Panama, military leaders carried out reforms which gave out land to the poor and improved the lives of the workforce, while in Chile and Argentina they did the exact opposite. Generals Pinochet and Stroessner

INTERVIEW WITH GENERAL HARGUINDEGUY,
Minister of the Interior in the first Argentine military junta, 1976-81

Childhood

I come from an old cattle-ranching family. I went to school on our *estancia* with a private teacher along with the children of the farmhands. After four years they sent me to secondary school in Buenos Aires. The previous year the Argentine army had founded a new Military Institute, where young students could do their secondary studies at the same time as getting military instruction. Of the 280 kids who went that year, there were two future presidents – Alfonsín and Galtieri, two commanders-in-chief, ministers, brigadiers, admirals, generals, diplomats, surgeons, dentists.

The Communist Threat

We were being attacked, an attack that was just as dangerous as an attack from outside. If the Communist Party tried to take power in Britain and began to carry out attacks to annul democracy and the monarchy, if that group got to the stage when it overran the police, you too would send in the infantry to keep your way of life. Thanks to our intervention, Argentina remained a part of the free world. We didn't want another Cuba or Nicaragua in Argentina.

When a soldier is in combat, he thinks only of destroying the enemy. In every war there are excesses of all kinds. A bullet is a bullet. It kills or it doesn't kill. From the moment I sink a merchant ship with a torpedo; from the moment I bomb a city to rubble; from the moment I drop an atomic bomb on a city to make the enemy surrender unconditionally; from the moment that the resistance forces ambush the occupying forces, whether of left or right, they use any system or method and they don't take prisoners.

The Armed Forces in Power

We took power in 1976 because there was a political vacuum. Parliament was paralysed. I was a general in the first corps; many politicians came to see me, and I always said the same, 'Mr Deputy, Senator, doctor, engineer, I'd like to hear you explain how you're going to replace the president by constitutional means, and yet you come here asking for a military coup – I don't need politicians for that, I have the guns!'

The replacement of a constitutional government by the armed forces was never an overnight decision of six generals. There has never been a coup that did not have the support of a large number of civilians, and their political leadership. There's always a situation of conflict beforehand, where rival groups of civilians pressurise the army to intervene.

The impact of power on the army is negative – it loses its professionalism. While it remains in the professional sphere, everyone falls in behind decisions taken by the high command. The armed forces are monolithic, vertical and totalitarian – when a commander gives an order, no one argues, no one votes. When the army enters politics, you get failures, divisions, internal fights, loss of prestige, and an enormous erosion.

We suffered an enormous weakening in 1983, when the political failure of the last period of the government was combined with military defeat. We returned to the barracks ashamed, without prestige, defeated and divided. We even felt guilty for what had happened!

could have stepped out of the pages of Gabriel García Márquez' novel, *Autumn of the Patriarch*, whereas military regimes in Brazil, Argentina and Uruguay insisted on rotating the presidency to prevent any one officer acquiring absolute power. Increasingly, the military *junta* (committee) replaced the individual caudillo.

The Peruvian military developed a much more reform-oriented strain of national security doctrine than other Latin American armies. It believed that the Peruvian elite was blocking reforms which were essential to the nation's economic progress, creating the conditions for violent revolution. A 1963 document from the Peruvian Centre for Higher Military Studies commented:

> The sad and desperate truth is that in Peru, the real powers are not the Executive, the Legislative, the Judicial or the Electoral, but the large landowners, the exporters, the bankers and the American investors.

In 1968 General Juan Velasco seized power, promising sweeping reforms. Within months his government nationalised the property of the US transnational, International Petroleum Company, and began a radical land reform. These two measures marked the high point of military radicalism in Peru. Soon the government became engulfed in economic crisis and internal divisions, and just before Velasco's death in 1975, a conservative faction within the military seized power. However Velasco's reforms left a radically altered rural society, where the feudal powers of the *hacienda* owners had in many cases been destroyed for ever.

In 1992, a section of the Venezuelan military demonstrated a similar strand of left-wing nationalism when Lt. Col. Hugo Chávez led a military revolt by the 'Revolutionary Bolivarian Movement'. The uprising was swiftly crushed. leaving seventy dead, but not before Chávez's opposition to the government's economic austerity programme had turned him into a folk hero.

Yet most military regimes have been firmly on the right, following the example of Brazil, whose generals seized power in 1964 in an attempt to revitalise its economy, as import substitution was running out of steam. By cutting real wages (by 35-40 per cent in the first four years of the government), opening the economy to foreign investors and multinational companies, and investing massively in state companies and economic infrastructure, they succeeded in temporarily galvanising the Brazilian economy, before the debt crisis of the 1980s forced the military's long and orderly withdrawal from politics. Direct elections for a civilian president finally took place in 1989.

In Argentina, the army launched a coup in 1976 to overthrow the chaotic regime of Isabel Perón, which was collapsing beneath an economic crisis and guerrilla war. Several years of cruel army repression ensued, during which thousands of people disappeared. The junta pursued a free-market economic model, encouraging imports to compete with inefficient local industries. The result was massive capital flight and the collapse of much of Argentine industry. In 1982 President Leopoldo Galtieri tried to fend off rising protest at the economic crisis by launching an invasion of the disputed Falklands/Malvinas islands. The military's defeat led to a humiliating retreat from power and the jailing of the junta's main leaders.

In Chile, the most infamous of the region's military dictators, General Augusto Pinochet, overthrew the elected left-wing government of Salvador Allende in 1973, ending an unbroken period of 51 years of civilian rule. The coup began a traumatic period of repression and persecution as the military moved to stamp out all voices of protest. Pinochet pursued an aggressively monetarist free-market model, cutting subsidies and price controls, privatising state companies, allowing a flood of cheap imports which bankrupted local industries and encouraging different agro-exports to help reduce the country's dependence on copper.

Pinochet's rule began to unravel when street protests began in 1983. In 1988, he lost a plebiscite intended to consolidate his rule for a further eight years, and was forced to hold elections in December 1989, when his candidate was defeated by the opposition coalition.

A few countries in Latin America managed to buck the continental trend and avoid military dictatorships from the 1960s onwards. Foremost among them was Mexico, where the ruling Institutional Revolutionary Party (PRI) established control over the army in the early years of the Mexican revolution, and Venezuela, where after 1958 oil wealth enabled the Venezuelan elite to buy off a military which had previously been almost permanently resident at the presidential palace.

Costa Rica has succeeded in ridding itself of its military altogether. After a brief civil war in 1948, Costa Rica's rival political parties agreed to abolish the army. Free of the military burden, Costa Rica established a welfare state and now has a much higher standard of living than its Central American neighbours. In Bolivia the revolution of 1952 also radically weakened the army, but within four years the government had agreed to re-establish the armed forces as a condition for a vital US$25 million loan from the International Monetary Fund. By 1964 the generals were back in power.

Debt Crisis and the end of the Cold War

From the late 1970s, pressure began to grow on the military regimes to leave power. Arrogant generals who had scorned 'corrupt politicians' were humbled by economic failure, culminating in the region-wide debt crisis of the 1980s. Their passionate belief in the military's mission was also dashed, firstly by what they saw as Washington's treachery in supporting Britain against Argentina in the Falklands/Malvinas war of 1982, and then by the end of the Cold War. By the second half of the 1980s, it was becoming increasingly difficult to believe that communism posed a threat to Latin American societies. Furthermore, the decline and eventual disintegration of the Soviet Union prompted a profound change in US policy: Washington now gave top priority to political stability and pro-market policies in its relationship with the region, and concluded that elected government would prove more stable than dictatorship. The US would no longer support brutal military rulers simply because they were anti-communist. Washington showed its new resolve by pressurising the Salvadorean and Guatemalan militaries to accept deep cuts as part of the peace agreements that ended the civil wars in those countries in 1992 and 1996. The US also effectively abolished the armies of Panama and Haiti following its military occupations in 1989 and 1994. Latin America's growing integration into the global marketplace also gave increased power to foreign investors, who shared Washington's new perceptions.

One by one, the region's governments returned to civilian rule during the 1980s. Just as the nature of military regimes varied enormously between different Latin American countries, so did the way they handed over power to elected governments. In many cases, the outgoing military government tried to cover its retreat by passing legislation giving its officers immunity from prosecution over human rights violations. Success in achieving immunity depended on the degree of military unity during the withdrawal to the barracks and the pressure exerted by the civilian opposition. The regimes in Brazil and Uruguay both managed an orderly exit, not only acquiring immunity for crimes committed in government, but retaining considerable political power. Elsewhere, however, investigation and prosecution for past atrocities remains one of the main areas of civilian-military conflict everywhere from Chile to Honduras.

The Argentine military's humiliation in the Falklands/Malvinas war forced it into a humiliating flight from power, giving the incoming Alfonsín government the chance to waive immunity, and in 1985 five military leaders including President Videla were found guilty and given long prison sentences. Alfonsín thus achieved a Latin American first – never before had officers of a defeated military dictatorship been brought to trial. The trials were followed up with military spending cuts and a new law confining military activities solely to defending the nation's frontiers. Nationalist officers responded with a wave of military uprisings between 1987-90, which only ended when incoming president Carlos Menem amnestied the 300 jailed officers, and found new roles for the military in UN peacekeeping forces and 'civic action' programmes of public improvements.

The assault on military privilege has also been financial. Under pressure to cut spending from Washington, the IMF and the World Bank, governments have cut military budgets and privatised the military industries set up under import substitution. Across the region military spending per head of the population halved from 1985 to 1994.

Reviled by the public and former allies, confused over its role and facing falling wages, the military in many countries has entered a profound crisis of identity and morale. Where guerrilla insurgencies have continued to operate, in Colombia and Peru, joined in 1994 by Mexico following the Zapatista uprising, the military role has been clearer, if bloody. Elsewhere, less introspective officers have turned to crime, creating a military mafia involved in drugs, car theft rings, and kidnapping. Many of the army's more talented members have left. The small number of military thinkers that remains has struggled to define a new role which can restore its legitimacy with the general public and provide a renewed sense of purpose as an institution.

There have been many suggestions. Some governments have opted for civic action programmes to restore the army's reputation, covering everything from traditional road-building and teeth-pulling to more 1990s-style environmental campaigns such as cleaning up piles of rotting garbage in Lima, or soaping down oil-soaked penguins in Argentine Patagonia. Washington has prodded insistently for the military to take a higher profile in the fight against the narcotics trade but the military leadership fears that entering the 'war on drugs' opens the door to corruption, as soldiers on ever-lower wages are tempted by the vast wealth at the drug traffickers' disposal. Drug-related corruption is already on the increase in several Central American armies, while two former military leaders, Bolivia's General García Meza, and Panama's General Manuel Antonio Noriega, are currently serving long prison sentences for drug trafficking.

Policemen and Soldiers

In many Latin American countries part, if not all, of the police force comes under direct military command, further blurring the distinction between internal and external security which usually holds outside the region. Often, the two are simply lumped together as 'Security Forces'. In the aftermath of the Cold War, as the military has left the political arena and appeared to lose its sense of purpose, public attention has increasingly turned to the police forces, which are widely believed to be riddled with corruption, incompetent, and abusers of human rights.

In Brazil, so-called 'social cleansing' of street children and other 'undesirables' is carried out both by uniformed police officers, and by death squads, shadowy organisations with names like 'Black Hand' and 'Final Justice', themselves often made up of former or off-duty policemen. The police are particularly trigger happy in São Paulo, Brazil's largest city. There according to its own figures, the military police killed 1,470 civilians in 1992. By comparison, the notorious Los Angeles Police Department in the US notched up 69 killings in the same year. Although the police routinely claim that the deaths occur in shoot-outs with criminal gangs, not a single officer was killed in the first six months of that bloody year. Despite such evidence, police impunity from prosecution is near-total, with only the most high-profile cases going to trial, and then only after international pressure.

Corruption is deeply entrenched in the police system, with policemen expected to pay a 'quota' to their superior as they leave each shift. The pressure to bribe and extort is so intense that some policemen crack: in October 1995, a policeman had himself tied to a cross in the centre of Mexico City, with a sign at his feet saying, 'end the impunity, injustice and insecurity! Say no to police corruption.' The following year, the Mexican president put the army in charge of the police force in a desperate attempt to clean up its act.

Yet simply switching the army to carry out a police function often fails. Dealing with organised crime creates the same danger of corruption as joining in the drugs war, while letting soldiers loose on the streets can have bloody consequences. In many countries the army has been sent in to quell protests against economic austerity programmes, the most serious example being in the Venezuelan capital of Caracas in 1989, when troops shot anywhere from 300-1,500 people during street protests and looting. In 1994, when soldiers were sent into some of the most violent and crime-ridden favelas in Rio de Janeiro, initial public support swiftly evaporated as troops arrested people indiscriminately, accusations of torture and corruption mounted, and the operation failed to net a single important drug trafficker.

The Future

Are the general-presidents a thing of the past? In recent year there have been several military threats to constitutional rule, all of which have been put down with differing degrees of ease. In Haiti (1994) and Panama (1989), it took US troops. Elsewhere a combination of the military's political weakness and international pressure prevented General Oviedo from seizing power in Paraguay in 1996, or President Serrano from dissolving the Guatemalan Congress in 1993.

Yet focusing only on military government ignores its wider influence on politics. The Venezuelan uprisings of 1992 failed to take power, but succeeded

in reversing the cuts to the military budget – politicians are forced to listen to the army, especially on matters which directly concern it. When Peru's Alberto Fujimori dissolved Congress with military backing in 1992, he was, perhaps unwittingly, carrying out the generals' plan for civilian-military co-government drawn up several years earlier. According to a leaked military report entitled 'Moving Peru into the 21st century', 'those who decide where the vehicle of state should go in order to arrive at long-term national objectives will be the armed forces, which will use the best civilian drivers to steer the said vehicle.' Elsewhere, the military may not retain such a clear sense of direction, but it still enjoys considerable political influence.

Moreover, given the cyclical nature of military rule in Latin American history, it would be rash to write off the military for ever. Should the international climate change, and the military recover its self-belief, the tanks may once again rumble up to the doors of the palace, and the unmarked Ford Falcons return to prowl the streets of Buenos Aires.

Young radio operators of the FPL guerrillas, El Salvador, 1984. Throughout the 1980s women played an increasingly important role in guerrilla and non-violent movements for change.

Chronology

1910-17	Mexican revolution
1926	Augusto César Sandino returns to Nicaragua to begin a guerrilla war against occupying US forces
1959	Cuban revolution marks first successful guerrilla campaign and leads to wave of *foquista* guerrilla insurgencies throughout Latin America
1967	Death of Che Guevara in Bolivia
1968	Medellín conference of Latin American bishops galvanises the left by creating Base Christian Communities across the region
1970	Peru's Shining Path movement founded in remote Andean province
1979	Sandinista-led insurrection in Nicaragua becomes second guerrilla victory in the Americas
1979	Founding of Brazilian Workers' Party (PT), based on the support of the new 'social movements'
1980	Founding of Farabundo Marti National Liberation Front (FMLN) in El Salvador
.1988	PRI uses fraud to deprive left-wing FDN, led by Cuauhtémoc Cárdenas, of victory in Mexican presidential elections. Brazil's PT wins control of São Paulo and 35 other towns in municipal elections
1989	Brazil's PT narrowly misses winning presidency. Fall of Berlin Wall leads to identity crisis on left.
1990	Sandinistas voted from power in presidential elections. Uruguay's Frente Amplio wins Montevideo
1992	Peace agreement ends guerrilla war in El Salvador
1994	Zapatista uprising in Chiapas, Mexico

The Left

9

Guerrillas, Social Movements and the Struggle for Change

The first sign of the squatters is a huge red flag flapping above a depression in the hills a few hundred yards away. Across two barbed wire fences and an arid, sandy hillside lies the cluster of huts thrown up weeks ago by forty landless families. They have called the encampment 'Hope' (*Esperança*). Already the inhabitants are making the first improvements – tiles are starting to replace plastic sheets on the roofs of the huts, whose walls are made from branches tied together with twine. To provide safety in numbers, 500 people originally occupied the site. When ten armed policemen promptly arrived to evict them, the children stood in front with stones; behind them came the women and adolescents, followed by the men armed with their primitive farming tools. The policemen backed off without a fight, allowing the squatters to get on with planting their first crops of yams and fennel.

The red flag belongs to Brazil's Movement of Landless Workers, the MST. The MST leads landless peasants and the urban poor in well-organised invasions of waste land in the cities or uncultivated farmland elsewhere. Standing amidst newly-ploughed furrows thirsty for rain, one of the squatters explains: 'People came here for land. We weren't interested in riches – land created people and people must live from it. The owner says the land is his, but if he doesn't even farm it, how can that be?' As he talks, the skies open. Rain sheets across the grey fields and through the torn plastic roofs, onto the dripping but delighted farmers.

The MST is one of a number of organisations whose political activity, in this case over the explosive issue of land, takes place outside the channels of formal politics. Many of the new movements took off under military rule in the 1970s, when conventional opposition politics was suppressed. Today, in Latin America's shanty towns, women's organisations pressure local councils for food and milk for their children, and neighbourhood committees demand electricity or paved roads, while in the rural areas peasant organisations lobby for land reform or bank loans for their farms. In Peru, Colombia and Central America, human rights organisations demonstrate and protest about the 'disappearance' of their loved ones; in Brazil, radical Catholics run 'Base Christian Communities' to discuss the Bible and its message for the poor. What such a diverse range of organisations have in common is their use of direct action in order to improve their lives.

The best-known apostles of direct action are the guerrillas. In the 1970s no western student bedsit seemed complete without its poster of Che Guevara, with beret and beard, gazing mistily off into the middle distance. Che personified the myth of the guerrilla fighter, caricatured by Peruvian novelist Mario Vargas Llosa in *The Real Life of Alejandro Mayta*:

His beard had grown, he was thin, in his eyes there was an unconquerable resolve, and his fingers had grown calloused from squeezing the trigger, lighting fuses and throwing dynamite. Any sign of depression he might feel would disappear as soon as he saw how new militants joined every day, how the front widened, and how there, in the cities, the workers, servants, students and poor employees began understanding that the revolution was for them, belonged to them.

Today's guerrillas are heirs to a long Latin American tradition. In 19th-century Argentina the cowboy Montoneros of the pampas fought an unsuccessful civil war to free the interior from the stranglehold of Buenos Aires. Elsewhere, irregulars helped to win independence from Spain. As the century wore on, such exotic bands passed into folklore as they were replaced by regular standing armies.

The guerrilla tradition was rediscovered in the 1920s by Augusto César Sandino, the Nicaraguan rebel whose distinctive ten-gallon hat became the symbol of revolutionary Nicaragua. When US marines occupied Sandino's homeland in 1912, Sandino, who as a young man had worked in the Mexican oilfields and been influenced by the anti-yankee and socialist ideas of the Mexican revolution, returned to Nicaragua. With a band of 29 fighters, he began to harass the US forces. When conventional tactics led to a series of defeats, reducing his company to just six, he developed a new style of fighting which became the blueprint for guerrilla warfare. According to Sandino, guerrillas should:

• avoid set-piece confrontations where the enemy's superior firepower will give it an advantage;

• use hit-and-run tactics and surprise rather than defend fixed positions. The objective is not to seize and defend territory, but to make the costs of staying unacceptably high to the enemy;

• stay in small groups to avoid detection and increase mobility;

• rely on superior knowledge of the terrain and contacts with local people to outwit the enemy.

Sandino's movement gathered force, giving the Nicaraguan brief fame as a romantic hero at the head of 6,000 fighters. When the Kuomintang marched into Peking in 1928, they named a division after Sandino, and a thriving anti-war movement in the US sang his praises. For the first time, the US experienced the frustration of facing an enemy that wouldn't 'fight fair'. In the words of the writer and former Sandinista vice-president Sergio Ramírez:

The well-trained and elegantly uniformed yankee soldiers could find only one phrase to describe it: 'damned country'. Rains, mosquitoes, swamps, swollen rivers, wild animals, the horror of suddenly falling into an ambush, fevers, an always invisible enemy.

The words could just as well describe the US nightmare in Vietnam, and the US forces in Sandino's Nicaragua reacted in much the same way, venting their anger on civilians they suspected of supporting the guerrillas and thereby swelling the numbers of Sandino's supporters.

The day of triumph. After years fighting in the mountains, Sandinista guerrillas celebrate the overthrow of the Somoza dictatorship, Nicaragua, 1979.

In 1933 the US changed tactics, withdrawing from Nicaragua and setting up a National Guard which soon came under the control of Anastasio Somoza. Sandino's fight had always been primarily a nationalist one, so when the marines left he accepted partial disarmament and peace talks. In 1934 as Sandino and his generals were leaving a dinner in the presidential palace, they were ambushed and shot dead by Somoza's men.

The world forgot about Sandino, and the ensuing Somoza dictatorship did its utmost to wipe out his memory within Nicaragua, but his example inspired a group of radical students in the 1960s, who formed a new guerrilla band, the Sandinista National Liberation Front (FSLN), and took to the hills in Sandino's old strongholds. There they found many ageing Sandinistas willing to help them. One guerrilla leader, Omar Cabezas, recalls the time when a young Sandinista came for the first time to an old farmer's hut. 'See, I knew you'd come back,' the campesino said with a grin, 'I've got something you left behind last time.' He then dug up an Enfield rifle from the time of the marines, buried for fifty years since the days when Sandino roamed the mountains.

Castro, Cuba and Che

While Sandino's memory smouldered in the Nicaraguan hills, it was the Cuban revolution of 1959 which marked the start of the modern guerrilla era. Cuba under the Batista dictatorship combined misery in the countryside and urban slums with a millionaire's playground of casinos and brothels for US tourists and organised crime. Cuba's guerrilla war began in 1956 when Fidel Castro and 81 men, including the young Argentine Che Guevara, squeezed onto a motor launch with the unlikely name of *Granma* and set off from Mexico to invade Cuba. The mission was a disaster; Castro's 26 July Movement had already been infiltrated by Batista's secret service, and the

Cuban troops were waiting for them. Fewer than twenty survivors fled to the mountains of the Sierra Maestra to lick their wounds and begin a two-year guerrilla war. Batista's ferocity and intransigence fuelled peasant support for the guerrillas; in 1957 he attempted forcibly to relocate the rural population of the Sierra Maestra. By 1958 opposition political parties, landowners and businesses had joined in, while the guerrilla force had grown into a rebel army which was attacking the government forces on three separate fronts and was able to take and hold fixed positions. Castro mounted a nationwide offensive, during which Che Guevara's soldiers succeeded in splitting the country in two. Batista fled to the Dominican Republic in early 1959 and Fidel Castro swept into Havana.

Cuba had a huge impact on the thinking of the Latin American left, convincing it that revolution could be triggered in underdeveloped countries by *focos* (small nuclei) of guerrillas. Previously the Communist Party had dominated the debate, insisting that revolution could only be achieved once

BECAUSE I WANT PEACE

Because I want peace
and not war
because I don't want to see
hungry children
squalid women
men whose tongues
are silenced
I have to keep on fighting.
Because there are clandestine
cemeteries
and Squadrons of Death
drug-crazed killers
who torture
who maim
who assassinate
I want to keep on fighting.
Because on the peak
of Guazapa
my brothers peer out
from their bunkers
at three battalions
trained in Carolina
and Georgia
I have to keep on fighting.
Because from Huey
helicopters
expert pilots
wipe out villages
with napalm
poison the rivers
and burn the crops
that feed the people
I want to keep on fighting.
Because there are liberated
territories
where people
learn how to read
and the sick are cured
and the fruits of the soil
belong to all
I have to keep on fighting.
Because I want peace
and not war.

Claribel Alegría, *Poesía Viva*, translated by El Salvador Solidarity Campaign the 'objective conditions' were present. This entailed the creation of a 'bourgeois democracy' and the growth of an industrial proletariat which would then form the vanguard for a predominantly urban revolution.

There followed a wave of unsuccessful attempts to repeat the Cuban experience across Latin America. Many of the young men and women who took to the guerrilla's harsh life in the mountains did so because they had seen all peaceful means for bringing about change blocked by a combination of electoral fraud and physical repression. In El Salvador the military denied electoral victory to a reforming coalition of political parties in the 1972 and 1977 elections, thereby triggering a spiral of frustration and violence which was to plunge the country into a decade of horror during the 1980s.

The rise of guerrilla movements was partly driven by another social change: the extraordinary expansion of higher education in Latin America after 1960. In Mexico and Brazil, the student population increased fifteen-fold by 1980. Universities became centres of political and cultural ferment. The growing gulf between the expectations raised by education and the economy's inability to meet them turned the universities into prime recruiting grounds for future guerrilla leaders.

Guerrilla war, especially *foquismo*, suited student idealism and impatience in its offer of a short-cut to power. A few young heroes with sufficient courage and political clarity could go up into the mountains and lead the people to inevitable victory. For the region's angry and disenchanted middle-class youth, this was a far more exciting prospect than years of toil within the trade union and peasant movement.

Young radicals formed guerrilla groups in Brazil, Venezuela, the Dominican Republic, Colombia, Argentina, Peru, Bolivia, Guatemala and Nicaragua, all of which met with failure or were forced radically to rethink their tactics. A generation of young radicals, poets, students and peasant leaders lost their lives.

Guevara's own attempt to bring revolution to Bolivia in 1966 encapsulated many of the fatal errors of foquismo. Choosing Bolivia because it was the poorest country in Latin America and 'ripe for revolution', Guevara set off with a team of 16 Cubans and headed for a remote south-eastern province to set up their foco. The obstacles proved insuperable; although the guerrillas managed to recruit a few Bolivians, the leadership was entirely Cuban. As none of them could speak Guaraní, the local Indian language, local people viewed the outsiders with suspicion. Furthermore, the region they chose was more prosperous than surrounding regions, and was so cut off that it had almost no contact with the capital, La Paz, and therefore no one had suffered directly at the hands of central government.

With intensive counter-insurgency training from the US, the Bolivian army soon tracked down and defeated the isolated 'freedom fighters', and Guevara was shot. Following his death, foquismo came in for severe criticism, as new wars in Vietnam and later Nicaragua provided alternative models for guerrilla war.

The late 1960s and early 1970s saw a new phenomenon – urban guerrilla movements. In Argentina, the Montoneros named themselves after the horseback irregulars of the 19th century, while in Uruguay the Tupamaros took their name from Peru's 18th-century Indian rebel leader Túpac Amaru II. Similar movements sprang up in Brazil and Colombia. These groups concentrated on spectacular actions, described as 'armed propaganda', intended to win publicity and popular support. Some kidnapped prominent

> ### THE LONELINESS OF THE MOUNTAINS
>
> The hardest thing isn't the nightmare of the trail, or the horrible things about the mountains; it's not the torture of lack of food or having the enemy 'always on your track; it's not going around filthy and stinking, or being constantly wet. It's the loneliness. Nothing is as rough as the loneliness.
>
> Loneliness is starting to forget the sounds of cars, the longing at night for electric lights, the longing for colours. Longing for your favourite songs, longing for a woman, longing for sex. Longing to see your family, your mother, your brothers, your *compañeros* from school. Missing and wanting to see your teachers and the workers and the people in your neighbourhood; missing the city buses, the scorching city heat, the dust; not being able to go to the movies. You long for the company of all those things, but you can't have them; it's a loneliness forced on you against your will. You can't leave the guerrilla war. Because you've come to fight, which has been the great decision of your life.
>
> Eating is the main thing to look forward to, even though you know it's the same old shit: a handful of ground red corn with salt, a chunk of monkey meat with no seasoning at all, or three spoonfuls of plain cornmeal, or a teaspoon of powdered milk. And as hungry as you are, you have to go do political work with the campesinos. And you go, and get wet, and are shivering with cold and hunger, with no caresses, no laughter, nobody to hug and kiss, and the mud and the darkness of the night, and everybody by 7pm lying in their hammocks, each thinking his separate thoughts.
>
> Omar Cabezas, *Fire From the Mountain: the Making of a Sandinista*, London, 1985

politicians, ambassadors and businessmen. In Colombia the M-19 guerrilla group showed a keen sense of history by symbolically stealing the sword of independence hero Simón Bolívar. Such actions, however, won little lasting support and frequently led to severe repression at the hands of the military, who aimed far beyond the guerrillas to attack the whole popular movement. In Argentina, ninety per cent of the 5,000 Montoneros lost their lives. Such groups have been criticised for their lack of political direction and tendency to use methods little different from terrorism.

After the failure of the *foquistas* and the urban guerrilla movements, the armed left continued to seek the elusive magic formula which would enable it to overthrow the state. Learning from the US defeat at the hands of a guerrilla army in Vietnam, organisations such as the Popular Liberation Forces (FPL) in El Salvador embarked upon a strategy of 'prolonged popular war', involving a patient long-term programme of political work with the peasantry. As a result, guerrilla organisations became less dominated by students, and instead evolved into genuine peasant armies.

Other experiences enriched guerrilla thinking; the Nicaraguan revolution of 1979 showed the need for unity between different ideological currents on the left and demonstrated how a combination of rural guerrilla warfare and urban insurrection could produce a quick victory. In Peru, the Sendero Luminoso (Shining Path) showed that an authoritarian and violent movement

Andean village
wrecked by guerrillas
of Sendero Luminoso
in Latin America's
most brutal civil war,
Peru.

built around a god-like leader in Abimael Guzmán ('President Gonzalo') could win over the oppressed Indian communities of the Andes with a combination of intimidation and the promise of unheard-of security. Following Guzmán's capture in 1992, Sendero went into decline as a serious threat to the government. Yet President Fujimori's boasts of vanquishing the guerrillas were disproved when the tiny Túpac Amaru Revolutionary Movment (MRTA) group mounted a spectacular operation in the Japanese Ambassador's residence in Lima in 1996. Twenty MRTA guerrillas burst into an embassy cocktail party and took an initial four hundred hostages, a virtual Who's Who of Peruvian society, gaining world-wide media attention for their tiny band of fighters, which probably numbered less than one hundred throughout Peru.

The most important recent group, Mexico's Zapatista National Liberation Army (EZLN), is a less apocalyptic form of Indian rebellion than Shining Path. The Zapatistas burst onto the scene in spectacular fashion on New Year's day 1994, when 1,500-2,000 fighters simultaneously occupied four towns in the impoverished southern state of Chiapas. The action stands out as by far the largest inaugural operation by any guerrilla movement in Latin American history. Following the initial weeks of warfare, the Zapatistas holed up in their strongholds in the Lacandón jungle, conducting interminable and frustrating talks with the Mexican government and playing host to endless visits by the great and good of the European and US left, from Danièle Mitterrand to Oliver Stone.

The Zapatistas are governed by a council of representatives from the region's indigenous communities. Their main demands are for the defence of indigenous culture and peasant agriculture. The group seems largely confined to Chiapas, and most of their fighters are Indian, many speaking little or no Spanish, but the Zapatistas' most prominent leader is a *mestizo*, the charismatic 'Subcomandante Marcos', whose witty and biting communiqués and press interviews have made him a household name and Robin Hood figure in Mexico.

The Zapatistas disavow the guerrilla organisations' traditional aim of seizing state power. Instead, the EZLN explain that they see themselves as only one part of a broad-based effort to make Mexico's one party state more democratic.

Despite the idealism and courage of generations of guerrillas, the only two outright victories they have to show for forty years of fighting and bloodshed are Cuba and Nicaragua. In both instances, the brutality and intransigence of the previous regime had at least as much to do with eventual victory as the guerrillas themselves. In Nicaragua, the Sandinistas were toppled in 1990 with the aid of the Contras, themselves midway between a genuine guerrilla group and a band of hired thugs. By the end of 1996 Fidel Castro's regime also appeared in difficulties.

In Central America the guerrilla wars came to an end in the 1990s with negotiated peace agreements between government and guerrillas in El Salvador (1992) and Guatemala (1996). The Central American wars had been particularly bloody, as brutal counter-insurgency campaigns by the Guatemalan and Salvadorean armies accounted for 100,000 and 70,000 lives respectively, although such totals are only the roughest of estimates. The FMLN guerrillas' military strength in El Salvador enabled them to achieve greater concessions at the negotiating table, largely demilitarising the political system. Human rights abusers in the armed forces were purged (though not put on trial), the police were removed from army control, and the military establishment halved in size. Yet the unequal economic system which had prompted the guerrillas' uprising remained largely untouched and when the FMLN took part in elections in 1994, they lost heavily. In Guatemala, the guerrillas were much weaker, and so extracted fewer concessions from the government in return for laying down their arms.

A number of factors account for this dismal record of guerrilla achievement:

• The state and army invariably possess an overwhelming advantage in firepower, troops and logistical support.

• The difficulty of reconciling military and political work, both of which are needed for eventual victory. Military success requires a small tightly disciplined group, able to keep mobile, preferably in secret, not defending fixed positions. Political support requires steady contact with the 'masses', staying put to build up a relationship, and the ability to defend them against any ensuing attack by the army.

• The US has placed enormous importance on preventing first 'another Cuba' then 'another Nicaragua' in its hemisphere. Since Vietnam, the Pentagon has tried to develop effective counter-guerrilla strategies, which have come to be known as 'low intensity conflict'. These have combined elements of reform ('winning hearts and minds') with anti-guerrilla military tactics. Often counter-insurgency has involved severe repression of civilians judged sympathetic to the guerrillas, and Washington's readiness to support human rights abusers in El Salvador and Nicaragua has lost it many friends in the region.

Nicaragua and Cuba show that military victory only heralds the start of a revolution's problems. Both governments only managed to survive a US economic and political siege by turning to the Soviet Union for oil and other supplies. Radical governments in Bolivia (1952-6) and Chile (1970-73) which did not have Eastern bloc support soon fell or caved in to a combination of pressure from the US and local economic and military elites. Since the collapse of the USSR, Soviet aid is no longer an option. Instead, any future revolutionary government in Latin America will have to assuage historic US hostility to radical regimes or find another sponsor in Europe or Japan. Neither option looks likely as long as Latin America remains firmly in the US sphere of influence, although the end of the Cold War has seen slightly more tolerance in Washington. It is hard to imagine US troops during the Cold War invading a country to force a military government to restore the presidency to a radical priest, yet that is what they did with Jean-Bertrand Aristide in Haiti in 1994.

Trade Unions and Social Movements

Trade unions in Latin America occupy a very different place in society than in Europe or the US, since they represent that minority of workers who have stable jobs in the formal sector of the economy and are therefore relatively privileged compared to the mass of peasant farmers and the urban poor. In countries such as Mexico, Brazil and Argentina, most of the main trade unions were set up under corporatist governments during the early years of import substitution, and have never had any real degree of independence. Nevertheless, some trade unions have been at the forefront of the radical left. In Chile they were the first to take to the streets to begin the long campaign to topple General Pinochet, while in Brazil from 1978 a new independent union movement led the fight-back against the military dictatorship.

One side effect of structural adjustment and the debt crisis has been the reduction of corporatist regimes' ability to keep the unions on a tight leash. Austerity measures and falling wages have driven a wedge between the union membership and their pro-government leaderships in countries such as Argentina and Mexico, fuelling efforts in these countries to establish a new unionism independent of the state.

The last thirty years have seen a spectacular growth in so-called new social movements. At the heart of the phenomenon lies the work of the progressive Catholic Church, discussed in chapter 12, which through its 'Base Christian Communities' has formed generations of activists and leaders. Shanty town dwellers, women's groups, indigenous and environmental movements, and human rights organisations have joined radicalised trade unions and peasant associations to create a new form of grassroots democracy which involves large numbers of people who previously had little role in the party political process. Particular social movements such as the women's movement and shanty town organisations are discussed in more detail elsewhere in this book.

Although the social movements form a broad category, they have certain points in common:

• They are often based on a locality rather than a workplace, unlike traditional trade unions;

• They organise around specific and immediate demands, rather than wider appeals for structural change;

• They practise a much higher degree of internal democracy and show a far greater level of women's participation than either left-wing political parties or guerrilla groups;

• They generally demand improvements from the state rather than confront vested interest groups such as landowners, the military and big business.

So called 'catalyst' groups such as radical priests, social workers, non-governmental organisations (NGOs), feminist groups and political party activists often play an important role in helping to establish groups by encouraging organisation and discussion. The more traditional catalysts often found it hard to let the new groups take control:

Hands that rock the cradle. Women form the core of the new social movements which have sprung up all over Latin America. Demonstration in Mexico.

I still thank the church for having opened my eyes. Working with the mothers' clubs, I learned how important we women are and how important it was for us to get organised. We managed to set up dozens of mothers' clubs. The women were well organised, and were taking on all sorts of activities.

Then all of a sudden the church pulled the rug out from under us. It stopped the programme and took away all our funds. Why? They said there was no more money, but we don't think that's what happened. We think they were afraid of how far we'd gone. It was the church that first started organising us women. I'd never done anything before getting involved in the mothers' clubs. The church forged the path for us, but they wanted us to follow behind. And when we started to walk ahead of them, they decided that maybe organising the women wasn't such a good idea after all.

Elvia Alvarado, *Don't Be Afraid Gringo*, San Francisco, 1987

COOKING UP TROUBLE IN CHILE

Under the Pinochet dictatorship, Chilean women set up numerous self-help groups. Here, two founders of a Santiago soup kitchen explain the impact the work had on women's lives in their community:

'*Olga*: There were up to ten women cooking at any one time. There were women who'd never taken part in anything in the community before and they all loved it. They met other women and talked about their problems at home, they made new friends and women who'd spent years inside their houses got to know the community for the first time.

We also had regular meetings involving about fifty women, where we talked about the problems in Chile and about women's rights. There were women who arrived with black eyes, who'd lived with violence for a long time and who believed that you had to live all your life with a man however he treated you. I used to read a lot and I read a book once on women's rights which said you're not a slave or a piece of furniture. I'd tell the other women that it was our right to liberate ourselves from men and that we're not just here to sit in a chair and sew or look after the children, which is what the men want us to do. They used to laugh at me and say "what are you teaching us!"

Sara: Women are so worn out by housework and bringing up children that they don't have time for anything else; they feel isolated and alone. In the kitchens they begin to talk about their problems, while cooking, while they go out begging for food and everyone gets to know everyone else. They develop friendships and don't feel alone any more. Women talk to each other while they're cooking. If one has a black eye, they talk with other women and they begin to find the confidence to deal with their situation.'

Jo Fisher, *Out of the Shadows: Women, Resistance and Politics in South America*, London, 1993

The roots of the new generation of social movements lie in the period of military rule which began with the Brazilian coup of 1964. Politics as usual came to a stop in countries such as Chile, Argentina and Brazil, as the generals banned or severely curtailed the activities of political parties. Opponents of the government or those wishing to press for improvements to their lives had nowhere to go to channel their protest, and new single issue campaigns grew rapidly to fill the resulting political vacuum.

Other factors encouraged their growth. The period of military rule coincided with the rise of feminism in the industrialised countries and the sudden expansion of the student population within the region, which both provided activists and direction to the new movements. Military rule also coincided with the heyday of the radical Church, in the wake of the Medellín bishops' conference of 1968. The harsh economic programmes unleashed by some of the military governments, notably in Chile, made necessity a mother of political invention, as women set up soup kitchens to cope with the hunger that suddenly assailed the shanty towns.

Grassroots organisations such as Brazil's Cost of Living Movement or Argentina's Mothers of the Disappeared were instrumental in forcing the military to withdraw from power, but their victories in the early 1980s sometimes carried the seeds of future defeat. As dictatorship has given way to democracy, the new social movements have faced difficult choices about how to relate to the political parties and governments that have taken back political life from the protesters. Their central problem, according to the Mexican writer Jorge Castañeda, is that:

> Without participating in electoral competitions, they run the risk of being rendered marginal, forsaking significant opportunities to advance the aspirations of their members. But by participating, they are immediately subject to the contradictions of any electoral process: whom to vote for, whom to run, what to do if elected, how to govern. There is no solution to this dilemma.

Part of the problem lies in the very nature of social movements. Local needs and their solutions, such as land distribution or greater spending on social services, often require action by the national government. Recognising this, many social movements have attempted to link up their vast array of groups into broader regional and even national networks in order to lobby the government. In growing to such a size, however, they risk losing the internal democracy which distinguishes them from orthodox political parties. After decades of co-option and betrayal, social movements are understandably wary of giving power away even to elected leaders, and attempts at wider coalition building have often broken down or been hijacked by populists who promise the earth without ever being able to deliver.

In some countries, recession and structural adjustment have made survival so difficult and time-consuming for the poor, that many have had no energy left for activism. In Chile, adjustment has created an atomised society, where increased stress and individualism have damaged its traditionally strong and caring community life. 'Relationships are changing', says Betty Bizamar, a 26-year-old trade union leader. 'People use each other, spend less time with their family. All they talk about is money, things. True friendship is difficult now. You have to be a Quixote to be a union leader these days!'

In Brazil on the other hand, social movements have survived the transition to democracy rather better, building a strong, vibrant 'civil society' and forming the foundations of the region's most impressive left-wing party, the Workers' Party (PT). The PT was set up in 1979 under the military government by the social movements themselves, led by a new generation of radical trade unionists such as 1994's PT presidential candidate, Luís Inácio da Silva, known simply as Lula. The trade unionists came together with rural unions, radical Catholics, left-wing intellectuals, shanty town movements and a number of other currents to try and set up a party controlled by the membership which would avoid being absorbed into the Brazilian political establishment. In an astonishingly short time the PT became a major national force – Lula narrowly missed the presidency in the 1989 elections, and was overhauled at the last minute by Fernando Henrique Cardoso in 1994. At less exalted levels, it has won elections to mayor in several major cities, including São Paulo, and in 1994 won a good number of seats in both houses of Congress. Although the PT has suffered debilitating splits and arguments through its attempt to reconcile its diverse membership with internal openness and democracy, its successes and rapid rise to political maturity have given many social movements hope that they can build a national party which will remain true to its origins.

In Mexico, the Party of the Democratic Revolution (PRD), led by Cuauhtémoc Cárdenas, is a similar ramshackle coalition of fringe parties and social movements. The PRD was formally set up after Cárdenas missed coming to power in 1988 thanks to the most blatant of frauds by the ruling Institutional Revolutionary Party (PRI), which shut down the computers half way through the count. Since then, however, the PRD has struggled. In the 1994 election, it was easily defeated by the PRI, and came in third behind a pro-business party, the PAN.

Running for Office

Latin America's left has long had an ambivalent relationship to democracy. In the past, left activists derided 'bourgeois' democratic structures, portraying them as little more than a confidence trick by the elite, which did nothing to achieve real participation and empowerment for the region's poor majority. In recent years, however, many have changed their views and come to accept the virtues of elections. Activists who suffered repression and exile under military rule decided that formal democracy and the rule of law were not so bad after all, while the fall of the Berlin Wall and the collapse of state socialism in Eastern Europe convinced many doubters of the importance of accountability and democracy in ensuring that politicians remain in touch with the people.

Nicaragua under the Sandinista government (1979-90) encapsulated many of the arguments and dilemmas over the left's attitude to formal democracy. The Sandinistas came to power in 1979 as a small guerrilla organisation whose structure and ideas had been forged in the underground war against the Somoza dictatorship. Throughout the period of Sandinista rule, the party itself remained a small, vanguard organisation of hand-picked activists which sought to provide leadership for a wider popular movement.

At first the FSLN appeared to disparage electoral democracy, preferring more direct forms of participation. The party's leaders toured the country conducting face-to-face talks with peasants and workers to hear their complaints, and popular organisations such as trade unions, peasants and women's groups were given seats on a consultative Council of State, established to advise the FSLN in government. The party's cadres were told to act as the eyes and ears of the government, keeping it in touch with ordinary Nicaraguans.

Results were mixed. The emphasis on participation and organisation transformed a large part of Nicaraguan society. Many of the poor gained self-confidence as they learned to read and write and became involved in a myriad of 'mass organisations'. Since these organisations were largely controlled by the party, however, they were often forced to put party or national interests before those of their members. Participation dropped off as people became exhausted by endless meetings, the growing economic crisis and the rigours of the war against the US-backed Contra rebels.

In 1984 the FSLN held presidential elections to try and win international recognition as a legitimate government, but failed to convince Washington to stop funding the Contras. From 1984-90, the FSLN ruled Nicaragua in the dual role of a government that had been freely elected, but which also saw itself as a non-parliamentary vanguard party working directly with the mass organisations. Over time, its views changed. Instead of a tactical measure designed to forestall US pressure, elections became more central to Sandinista philosophy.

In February 1990 the FSLN was stunned when it lost the elections to Violeta Chamorro's UNO coalition, but passed the democratic test by accepting the result. The revolutionary vanguard had assumed the role of opposition in a party political system. Its credentials were further tested in 1996, when it again lost the elections, this time to right-wing populist Arnoldo Alemán.

With the exceptions of Chile (1970) and Nicaragua (1984), the left has won most of its victories at local government level, reflecting the dynamism and local nature of the social movements. Leftist local governments must work within severe constraints, since their budgets are normally determined by hostile national administrations. Even so, many have acquired a reputation for efficiency and honesty, and have introduced ground-breaking experiments in local democracy and accountability. In Peru the United Left's Alfonso Barrantes became mayor of Lima in 1983, and literally kept the poor alive with a free milk programme during a period of intense economic hardship. In Venezuela, the Causa R party has pioneered local democracy in the industrial city of Ciudad Guayana. In Brazil the Workers' Party (PT) won the giant city of São Paulo and 35 other major towns in November 1988. Although it lost São Paulo in 1994, it was reelected in several large cities such as Porto Alegre. In 1990 the Frente Amplio (Broad Front) broke Uruguay's two-party duopoly to take control of the capital city, Montevideo, and introduce innovative programmes to decentralise services and make them more accountable to residents. In 1994 the Frente won Montevideo with an increased vote and narrowly missed the presidency.

Does the Left have a future?

The collapse of state socialism in Eastern Europe has had a seismic impact on the left in Latin America. By the 1980s few left-wing leaders openly espoused the policies pursued by the Soviet Union or other Communist governments, but the Soviet model provided a reference point - the Latin American left defined itself by how it would differ from the Soviets, should it come to power. The end of communism seemed to reduce politics to a unipolar world politically and economically dominated by the US.

The Latin American left has been particularly damaged by the discrediting of state-led development, which has always formed a central part of its programme. Since the collapse of the Eastern bloc, the left finds itself rudderless, bereft of a Utopia with which to inspire its supporters. Until a coherent alternative vision emerges, its message will be made up of a combination of fierce critiques of the failings of neoliberalism, and an unfocused collection of ideas on what should replace it – decentralisation and more local participation in planning, a renewed role for a leaner, less corrupt state, support for the grassroots economy via credit to peasants and the urban informal sector.

As the end of the century approaches, guerrilla activity continues in Peru, Colombia and Mexico, and new uprisings and movements will undoubtedly emerge from time to time, but further revolutions along the lines of Cuba and Nicaragua seem improbable. Instead, guerrilla unrest will form part of the

LULA ON SOCIALISM

BK: Social democrats all over the world are saying that socialism is dead, that the left must give up the socialist utopia if it wants to have a real chance of being elected to power. A few *petistas*, such as José Genoíno, a one-time Maoist guerrilla, seem to accept this view. Others are sticking more firmly than ever to socialism. What do you think?

Lula: There are two opposing views in the Workers' Party. One, the more orthodox view, is that we should go on holding the same opinions as before as if nothing had happened at all in the world, and that we should even use the former socialist countries as models. The other view is simply that socialism is dead. Personally, I never supported what was called 'real socialism', that is, the socialism that existed in eastern Europe until 1990, so I have no reason now to wring my hands and say I got it wrong. In fact, I feel more socialist all the time. If you can accept the fact that eighty per cent of our wealth is concentrated in the hands of only twenty per cent of the population, while the other eighty per cent of Brazilians get only twenty per cent of the wealth, then you can support the capitalist system of production. But I don't accept it. People keep talking about the virtues of the capitalist system in Denmark, Germany, Switzerland, but they don't mention Brazil, India, Peru, Bolivia, Africa.

We must seek a model of society in which there is a fairer distribution of wealth. You don't even need to call it a socialist project; call it a Christian project, or an ethical project. Instead of socialism, call it the defence of human rights, or the defence of citizenship. For me, the label is unimportant; what matters is the content. In my view, the best way to increase people's awareness is not going into the street waving the banner of socialism, but by talking about the Constitution, the Children's Charter, or the Universal Charter of Human Rights, and asking people to fight for it. You get better results that way than with a general speech about the virtues of socialism.

BK: Some critics within the PT say the party should concentrate on educating workers and raising their awareness, instead of putting so much energy into winning seats in Congress or gaining control of local administrations. How do you react to this criticism?

Lula: It's illogical. Only by being elected to office can we have some influence over our political institutions, can we show that we are different – unless the idea is to raise mass awareness not in order to win elections, but to seize power. In that case we have a serious disagreement, because I think that the PT must seize power through democratic means. I've seen what a difference it makes for a town to have a PT administration. And the party immediately starts growing. It has a public image, takes part in the main political debates. This is good. We must never lose our links with the social movements, but it is extremely important to elect representatives at all levels, and for them to defend the interests of ordinary people.

BK: The Latin American left looks to the PT as its benchmark. How do you see the region's left at a time when neoliberalism still seems to be dominant?

Lula: The left is advancing in Latin America. There was an extraordinary advance in Uruguay in the recent elections. In Argentina the left opposition is growing. In Venezuela the social democrats won, but the left is playing an increasingly important role. In Mexico, new forms of opposition are emerging.

> These are big steps forward for the left. We must remember that until 1990
> the Latin American left didn't even meet to talk to each other. Today we are
> working out common policies; we have learned to accept our differences.
> The PT is playing a decisive role in this process, if only because it is the
> largest left-wing party in Latin America.
>
> Sue Branford and Bernardo Kucinski, *Carnival of the Oppressed*, 1995

general political instability which dogs the region, perhaps feeding in to a
broader left revival.

There are reasons to be optimistic about the prospects of such a revival.
The existence of the Soviet bloc was a burden, as well as a blessing. Now the
Latin American left is on its own, able to develop its own policies and build
its own future free from the distorting influence of the Cold War. Should it
take power, it may even find Washington less hostile to a progressive
government. Perhaps the greatest reason for optimism is the growing
recognition of the failure of the current model. Neoliberalism in the region
has not given people work; it has increased inequality, excluding the majority
of the population from effective citizenship, and is prone to recurring crises
and recessions. The 'objective conditions' for rebellion and change are if
anything, stronger than ever. In the words of Mexican crime writer and social
commentator Paco Ignacio Taibo II:

> The fact that the revolution is impossible does not make it morally less
> necessary, nor the reasons for revolt less urgent, even without an
> alternative. The PRI are still scum, and the country they propose is still a
> mixture of economic misery for many, social misery for the majority, and
> moral misery for all.

Women hoeing on squatted land, Honduras. Twenty women occupied the land and began to grow melons and corn.

Chronology

1930s on	Mechanisation of agriculture and growth of cities encourages young women to migrate from the countryside to the towns
1961	Paraguay becomes last Latin American country to give women the vote
1971	US Peace Corps expelled from Bolivia, accused of sterilising Indian women without their knowledge
1975-85	UN Decade for Women encourages some improved legislation on gender issues
1975	Cuban government passes law making childcare and housework equal responsibility of men and women
Late 1970s	Women in Brazil's Cost of Living Movement leads opposition to military rule
1976-83	Argentina's Mothers of the Disappeared challenge the military government; inspiring similar movements in Central America and the Andes
1979	Nicaraguan revolution: women head health ministry and police, and government bans use of women's bodies in advertising
1982 on	Debt crisis and structural adjustment make life harder for women
1990	Violeta Chamorro wins Nicaraguan presidential elections
1993	Proportion of female-headed households now stands at one in five across Latin America
1995	New quota rules in Argentina ensure that one in four congresspeople is a woman – one of the highest proportions in the world

Women's Work

Gender and Politics

10

Penha is an imposing figure, a big confident woman who has risen to become president of the Alagoa Grande Rural Workers' Union in Brazil's drought-prone and poverty-ridden Northeast. She recounts her life story, the words half lost in the drumming of a sudden downpour which turns the street into a river of rubbish from the nearby market. A broken home, starting work aged seven, a mother who died from TB when Penha was twelve, early marriage and struggling to feed her six children – the story of countless poor Latin American women. Then came transformation when she joined the union, inspired by a charismatic woman leader named Margarida Maria Alves. When Margarida was assassinated, probably by local landowners, Penha took over.

Earlier, out on her rounds, Pehna was trying to persuade an impoverished farming community to join the union. Pot-bellied children with skinny arms played at the feet of men and women as the banter and serious talk rolled easily along. Penha guided the conversation with a blend of authority, humour and kindness, letting others speak and enjoying the jokes, as the impromptu discussion developed into a full-blown community meeting about the causes of poverty in Brazil. As dusk fell, the meeting turned into music and dance, in honour of the visitors.

There are thousands of women like Penha up and down Latin America, inspirational grassroots activists breathing new vigour into the region's social and political life. Although generalisations are always dangerous in a continent with such a variety of cultures and lifestyles, there has been an undeniable transformation in women's lives over the last thirty years. In the past, descriptions of Latin American society have either ignored its women altogether or portrayed them as the submissive victims of a male-dominated order perpetuated by the Catholic Church. Women were shown as helpless figures, condemned to endless pregnancies which destroy their health and confine them to the house, subject to the burden of childcare and dependent on often unreliable and violent men. In the title of one book, they were 'the slaves of slaves'. But in recent years, as more women have gone out to do paid work, some, like Penha, have fought for recognition in male-dominated trades unions. Others, described in chapter 9, have built a new form of politics through the social movements, bypassing traditional political parties.

Women's lives and expectations may have changed, but so far there is little evidence of parallel developments among Latin American men. A dictionary translation of the Spanish word *macho* captures the essence of Latin American masculinity. Besides male and masculine, the word means tough, strong, stupid, big, huge, splendid, terrific and doubles as a slang term for a sledgehammer. *Machismo* is an extreme form of patriarchy, the social system of male dominance which exists through much of the world.

The Latin American variety has its roots in Mediterranean culture and the Catholic Church's contorted attitude towards women. As Virgin and Mother, Mary combines its impossible and contradictory ideals of Latin American womanhood. Machismo stresses the opposition between male and female; men are fearless, authoritarian, aggressive and promiscuous, while women are naturally submissive, dependent, quiet and devoted to the family and home. Machismo is often greater among the mestizo population, although Indian communities have their fair share of domestic violence, often linked to the men's prodigious consumption of alcohol, as an Indian woman from Chiapas in Mexico recalls:

Before, when I was poor, my first husband had to go away to work on the *hacienda*. I went with him, and stayed there for a few nights, but the men always got drunk because the *patrón* gave them money for booze. When he got drunk, he beat me a lot. I thought I would die from the blows. It was horrible. I would go back to our farm with my face all swollen, all beaten up. And I still had to look after the sheep, clean the house, go and cut wood, work on the maize patch, bring in the harvest. If I finished that, I had to sew, spin wool, weave. Like that, see, lots of work. Still, I was happy when I went home, because there were no more beatings. He gave me no food – no beans or meat. Just beatings. My life was very sad with the husband who went to the hacienda.
Guiomar Rovira, *Mujeres de Maíz*, Barcelona, 1996, author's translation

Women have their inferiority drummed into them from birth; in rural Peru the midwife receives a sheep for delivering a baby boy, while a girl merits only two chickens. Under the ideological barrage, women often internalise these ideas of femininity and submissiveness, giving rise to a female counterpart to machismo, known as *marianismo*, after the Virgin Mary. In some countries these traditional stereotypes have been overlaid by more modern versions of what constitutes the 'perfect woman'. In Argentina, girls as young as six or seven show signs of anorexia, part of a nation-wide obsession with thinness and the 'supermodel' look resulting in extraordinary levels of cosmetic surgery and eating disorders.

Latin America's most famous women have often filled these submissive and maternal roles. Evita Perón, a gifted politician and the darling of the Argentine masses, described her relationship with her husband as 'He the figure, I the shadow', while Violeta Chamorro became president of Nicaragua in 1990 by playing on her position as the widow of a national hero and presenting herself as the healing mother of the nation who could reconcile her divided children. Venezuela's obsession with beauty contests has spilt over into politics in the person of Irene Sáez, a former Miss Universe who was re-elected as mayor of the country's wealthiest suburb with an impressive 96 per cent of the vote. Sáez, who studied political science at the University of Central Venezuela, is widely considered the most popular politician in Venezuela, and a potential future presidential candidate.

Family Ties

Traditionally, girls are groomed from the cradle for their future role as wife and mother. Bolivian parents call their baby daughters *mamita* (little mother), and within a few years they can be seen hauling their baby brothers and

GROWING UP IN THE COUNTRYSIDE

I learnt early on what suffering meant. My father thought that women and girls were nothing. He used to say *mulher não é gente* (Women aren't people).

At home I was locked up. I wasn't allowed to have friends either, not even woman friends, and I was often beaten. I hated having been born a girl and envied my brothers like crazy.

Then there was the poverty. We often went hungry. My father had to sell our little plot of land, so we were tenants on a big landowner's *fazenda* (estate). Half of the harvest had to be handed over to the owner as rent. What was left wasn't enough for all of us. Two of the children didn't survive. Hunger and death are everyday occurrences for most of the families in our area.

I thought school was great fun, but after four years my father stopped me going any more. Sending girls to school was like casting pearls before swine, he said.

At 16 I thought I could escape from my father by getting married, so I married the first man who came along. But what I'd let myself in for was worse than I could ever have imagined. It was hell. You see, my husband was an oppressor too. He made me the slave he'd always wanted. I had one child after another, and I was either shut up at home with the babies or had to slog out in the fields.

I had my children, who I had to feed, on one side and a husband who only gave orders on the other. How I suffered!

The worst thing was when he used to hit the children and I wasn't allowed to intervene. He never once hit me, but the endless mental beatings that I had were far harder.

If ever I wanted to cry on my mother's shoulder, she used to say, 'Take it easy, daughter, don't get worked up about it. Women are born to suffer. And they have to obey their husbands – *mulher não é gente!*'

Caipora, *Women in Brazil*, London, 1993

sisters on their backs around the villages of the Andes. In rural Latin America, families usually have numerous children so that enough will survive high child death rates to work the family farm and to look after their parents in old age. For women this has led to the health problems associated with frequent pregnancies, compounded by malnourishment and poor or non-existent medical care. Large families lack even the most basic services such as running water, and need constantly to make do and mend. Together, these pressures create the archetypal Latin American mother who never rests: cooking, cleaning, changing nappies, looking after children with frequent illnesses, queuing for scarce food, mending clothes or making food to sell outside the home consume every waking hour. In rural areas fetching water or firewood and the long haul to sell left-over produce in the local market impose further strains on women's workload.

My day begins at four in the morning, especially when my *compañero* is on the first shift. I prepare his breakfast. Then I have to prepare the *salteñas* [small meat pies], because I make about one hundred salteñas every day and I sell them in the street. I do this in order to make up for what my husband's wage doesn't cover in terms of necessities. The night before, we prepare the dough and at four in the morning I make the salteñas while I feed the kids. The kids help me: they peel potatoes and carrots and make the dough.

Then the ones that go to school in the morning have to get ready, while I wash the clothes I left soaking overnight. At eight I go out to sell. The kids that go to school in the afternoon help me. We have to go to the company store and bring home the basics. And in the store there are immensely long queues and you have to wait there until eleven in order to stock up. You have to queue up for meat, for vegetables, for oil. So it's just one line after another. Since everything's in a different place, that's how it has to be. So all the time I'm selling salteñas, I line up to buy my supplies at the store. I run up to the counter to get the things and the kids sell. Then the kids line up and I sell. That's how we do it.

Domitila Barrios de Chungara, *Let Me Speak*, New York, 1978

The size of the average family has dropped at a startling rate over the last forty years. In the 1950s, the average Latin American woman had six children. Now that figure has almost halved. The causes of such a rapid fall in childbearing include the more widespread availability of contraception, the spread in girls' education, and the rate of urbanisation. In the shanty towns, large families can be a liability: women have to go out to work as maids or in the markets and since they have left their families in the countryside, there is often no one at home to look after the children.

Diversity has increased both within and between countries. Poor countries such as Bolivia, Haiti and Nicaragua still have large families, while Argentina, Cuba and Chile more closely resemble 'northern' family models. Within each country, family size depends greatly on income and women's education: poor, uneducated women have much larger families than better-off or more educated women.

In recent years there has been a sharp increase in the number of female-headed households, which now stands at over twenty per cent in most countries. These are often among the poorest families, with women forced to perform a gruelling combination of housework and wage-earning, often in the informal sector, to keep their children from starvation.

In the last thirty years, contraception has become more widely available. In the 1980s the number of couples using contraception varied widely from 23 per cent in Guatemala to 70 per cent in Costa Rica. The commonest form of contraception is female sterilisation, followed by the Pill. Nevertheless, the issue remains far more controversial than in the US or Western Europe. Not only is the Catholic Church hostile to all forms of contraception, but the health problems provoked by the often unsupervised use of the Pill, IUDs and injectables such as Depo Provera have created widespread suspicion. Contraception is anathema to many Latin American men, who see their wives' regular pregnancies as proof of their virility. In only four per cent of couples do men take responsibility for contraception via condoms or sterilisation.

In some cases, foreign agencies have been implicated in sterilising women without fully informing them of the consequences. Such incidents led to the expulsion of the US Peace Corps from Peru and Bolivia in the 1970s.

Sean Sprague/Panos

One consequence of suspicion, ignorance and the shortage of contraceptives is a high abortion rate. Except for Cuba, abortion on request is illegal in all Latin American countries, forcing women unable to afford a medically safe abortion to resort to back-street practitioners or their own efforts. Botched abortion is the greatest killer of women of child-bearing age. By one estimate, there are four million abortions performed every year in the region, one for every three live births. Not surprisingly, in view of its more liberal legislation, Cuba has one of the lowest maternal death rates in the region.

Family planning adviser explains the use of the Pill at a public washhouse, Guatemalaa.

Although huge numbers of women undergo abortions, it remains a taboo subject, as a woman from a Chilean shanty town explains:

Women don't want to talk about abortion because it's against the teachings of the Church and also because it's against the law, but nearly all women have them. The difference is that the women from the *poblaciones* use a knitting needle, parsley twigs or rubber tubes and many end up in hospital or die, while the middle class go to a clinic and walk home afterwards. When we go to the hospital with haemorrhages the doctors slap our faces; they send their wives to the best clinics but they slap the faces of poor women.

Literacy plays a vital role in empowering women, making it easier for them to find better-paid work, and to wade through the avalanche of printed information resulting from almost any contact with the state. Research by the World Bank and others suggests that women's education is also the single biggest factor in determining family size – the more years of schooling a woman has, the fewer children she ends up with. Illiteracy is higher among women than men in every Latin American country, in some cases reaching ninety per cent among elderly women. The figure for both sexes is higher in

GAYS IN LATIN AMERICA

Attitudes and legislation over homosexuality vary enormously across the continent. Latin American machismo appears to have a complex relationship to homosexuality and finds lesbianism incomprehensible. Countries such as Colombia and Peru have a tradition of transvestite homosexuality stretching back to pre-Columbian times, while studies from Nicaragua and Cuba suggest that heterosexual men break no taboos by having sex with other men, provided they are the dominant partner. Social stigma is reserved for those who behave in an 'unmanly' effeminate way, but even then, there is little of the kind of rabid 'queer-bashing' found in the US or Europe. Perhaps because of the lower level of discrimination, gays in Latin America do not always identify themselves exclusively in terms of their sexuality, and the gay pride movement is much weaker than in the North.

In many countries homosexuality is not specifically outlawed, but more general laws such as 'offences against morality' are used to harass gays and lesbians. Cuba under Fidel Castro has come in for severe criticism over its treatment of gay men, in particular those with HIV and AIDS. In the mid-1980s, the Cuban government was condemned for its initially draconian policy of locking up HIV-positive people in state sanitoria, sometimes against their will. Closer examination, however, revealed a complex situation: the policy of quarantining patients was the state's normal reaction to previous epidemics such as dengue and African swine fever; the quarantine policy was only possible in the first place because the Cuban health service had the capacity to implement it – in other countries in Latin America, AIDS patients receive little or no state support. In any case, by the early 1990s, the policy had been substantially liberalised with most patients free to leave the sanitoria on home visits and about three in four seropositives transferred to an outpatient system.

rural than in urban areas, since schools are often scarce, and parents may need the children to work on the farm. Many families prefer to keep girls at home to help with the household tasks and learn how to keep house, while believing that boys must study to prepare themselves for the outside world. However, the situation is improving rapidly due to the massive expansion in primary education, which has absorbed an extra two million children a year since 1950, even during the recession-hit 1980s.

Among the middle classes, the situation is already very different. By the 1980s, almost half of students in higher education were women, although a large number of them were concentrated in the traditional female spheres of teaching and health care.

The ideology of machismo has influenced legislation affecting women. In most countries adultery is only sufficient grounds for divorce if committed by the wife, while divorce is only available in exceptional cases in countries such as Argentina, Brazil and Colombia. Under El Salvador's Penal Code, a married woman is liable to a jail sentence of six months to two years if she is found guilty of 'carnal access to any man other than her husband', yet the husband is only breaking the law if he *keeps* his mistress, and thereby fails to meet his family obligations. In Brazil until recently, one law required a woman to have explicit permission from her husband before going out to work. Such double standards were condemned three hundred years ago by Sor Juana Inés de la Cruz, a Mexican nun-cum-poet who has become a feminist icon in modern Mexico:

Ignorant men who accuse
Women wrongly
Without seeing that you cause
The very thing you condemn.

Whose is the greater guilt
In a sinful passion,
She who falls to his lure
Or he who, fallen, lures her?

Or which is more rightly reproached
Although both are guilty
She who sins for pay
Or he who pays for the sin?

Thanks to the work of women's lobby groups and the UN Decade for Women (1975-85) many governments have improved their legislation and established agencies to promote the status of women and ensure equal rights. Yet despite such paper safeguards, social attitudes and the implementation of equal rights laws lag far behind. Statutory rights on maternity benefits or equal pay are frequently ignored by both employers and male-oriented Ministries of Labour, and legislation often appears irrelevant to the poor. Most women work in the unregulated informal sector and so do not have even a theoretical right to maternity benefits. Since formal marriage is the exception among poor families, the niceties of divorce law hold little meaning.

Working for Wages

The number of women in the economically active population more than tripled between 1960 and 1990. In most countries about half of women over 15 now work for money, the proportion being highest among 25-34 year olds. Even these figures are underestimates, as women often do not see themselves as wage earners when asked during household surveys, even though they may bring in money from selling food or taking in washing.

Despite this rise in numbers, the kinds of jobs have changed little, with a strong emphasis on 'women's work' which merely extends their caring role in the home. Fewer women work in rural areas than in towns and cities, where as many as half the women employed are domestic servants, most of them young unskilled migrants from the countryside who average only three years of school education. The other main categories of paid women's work are the informal sector (market women, street sellers), caring professions, such as teaching and nursing, and office work. Women's participation in agriculture and manufacturing actually fell between 1960-80, as mechanisation reduced the proportion of unskilled jobs traditionally performed by women, although it has picked up in recent years in the new export crops such as fruit and flowers which have been promoted under structural adjustment programmes.

In manufacturing women are concentrated in industries such as textiles, clothing and the booming *maquiladora* assembly plants in northern Mexico and the Caribbean basin. Besides being segregated by job, women also earn twenty to forty per cent less than men, even though their educational qualifications for comparable jobs are generally higher.

The Domestic Worker

Usually young unskilled migrants from the countryside, servants are among the most exploited and invisible of the region's women. Ignorant of their rights or life in the city, and isolated in their employer's house, they are on virtual 24 hour standby, and vulnerable to verbal, sexual and physical abuse by their employers. Young girls emotionally dependent on their employers often absorb their values, feeling self-loathing and contempt for their own families and backgrounds, especially in countries where the employers are white, and the servants Indian:

> The old lady explained everything to me, and little by little she made me aware of my class, using words like 'Indians' and 'Yokels' and saying 'You shouldn't be like that, you're going to get civilised here.'
>
> When you hear it that often you end up being ashamed and uncomfortable about your own class and finally you find yourself supporting the class of your boss. I thought she loved me because she told me: 'I love you like a daughter; here you have everything.' And I accepted it all.
>
> The truth is that the bosses use us even through love. Without realising, we end up loving them and so we say, 'Ay, my señora is good, she loves me a lot.' We look after her things as though they were our own, and after a while you start identifying totally with her mentality.
>
> Ana María Condori, *Mi Despertar*, La Paz, 1988, author's translation

The Street Seller

Market women and street sellers are perhaps the most conspicuous of Latin American women workers, lining the streets of major cities with stalls offering home-made cakes, imported toiletries, vegetables or soft drinks. Their numbers have been swollen by the impact of structural adjustment over the last 15 years. By the early 1990s, there was one street vendor for every three houses in the Bolivian capital of La Paz. Market women's daily contact with the public and unscrupulous wholesalers has made them a self-confident and fiercely individualistic group. As Anita, a 28-year old Nicaraguan market woman, explains:

> I'm better off working in the market. If I don't want to sell, I don't have to. I can go home whenever I want to, we can bring our children to work and no one bosses you about and tells you when to come and when to leave. I don't want to work for a boss again.

Maquiladoras

Since the mid-1960s, Mexican industry has been transformed by the growth of *maquiladora* plants along its northern border with the US. Others have sprouted elsewhere in Central America and the Caribbean. These factories, largely owned by US, Japanese and other foreign electronics or textile companies, use cheap local labour to assemble products for export to the US. In the Caribbean, women are also used to perform cut-price data processing for US companies. About sixty per cent of maquiladora employees are women, usually single and in their late teens or early twenties. Young women are ideal because, in the words of one plant manager, 'they are willing to accept lower wages', and 'girls are educated to obey at home. It is easier to get their confidence... they are loyal to the company.'

Martina, like many working-class Mexican women, has a hard exterior, a tough skin of nonchalance until you get to know her. She has worked in various maquilas in Ciudad Acuña but dislikes them intensely. Last Monday she started at a Korean-owned maquiladora called Kim Toys, where the employees sew small cheap stuffed animals to go inside the ironclaw machines in the American chain of Pizza Huts across the border.

'It's the worst place I've ever worked in,' she says, while making supper. 'Rundown and dirty. And no air conditioning, just a couple of old fans in the whole place. It was so hot. Everybody just sat there sweating so much it looked as if someone had come in and thrown a bucket of water over them. I saw one supervisor get mad at a woman for taking too long in the bathroom. "Five minutes," he was saying. "All you've got is five minutes." She went back to her sewing machine and was crying.' Martina decided it wasn't worth US$30 a week and quit after just one day.

Augusta Dwyer, *On the Line: Life on the US-Mexican Border*, London, 1994

Women's growing role in the workforce has brought them mixed blessings. Although paid jobs have often increased women's economic independence and self-confidence, there has been no compensating reduction in housework, with the result that working women are expected to perform what is known as a 'double shift'. A study of women in Chile during the early 1980s showed that working women did an average 12-hour day, seven days a week, between workplace and home. When women did manage to reduce their housework, it was by employing poor women as domestic servants – men did no more housework than before, despite the decline in their role as breadwinner. For any macho man, scrubbing floors or cooking is the ultimate shame. In Cuba, where women's participation in the paid workforce has grown rapidly over the last twenty years, one writer noted that although male Communist Party militants may offer to do the washing, they insist their wives hang it out to dry so that the neighbours won't find out!

Life is if anything even harder for peasant women in rural areas, whose duties include childcare, maintaining the home, and a number of specialised jobs on the farm. Often women tend the animals and a small vegetable plot, while the men look after the main food crops. Housework in peasant farms can be far more time-consuming than in the cities, since women may have to carry water over long distances, collect firewood, and make long trips to markets in nearby villages.

As commercial agriculture has encroached on the traditional peasant farms, this pattern has been disrupted. Peasant farms have been squeezed by large landowners and by subdivision between members of each new generation, so that they are rarely productive enough to maintain a family. This forces their owners to find work on the big commercial farms. Men's greater access

THE PRICE OF ADJUSTMENT

The tiny adobe house is crammed with gnarled *pailliris* (mining women) in patched shawls and battered felt hats whose calloused hands work breaking up rocks on the surface in search of scraps of tin ore. Outside, the scene is one of high altitude poverty, all greys and browns in the thin air. The paths between the miners' huts are strewn with plastic bags and human excrement, dried black in the unforgiving *altiplano* sun. Rising beyond the squalid settlement, the barren hills and grey slagheaps of the tin mines complete the bleak panorama. The litany of poor women's woes begins, gathering momentum as it goes:

'Before, it was not too bad, but now we never have a good month. We're mainly widows or abandoned. My husband left to look for work and never came back. Now I have to look after four kids – I can't pay for their schoolbooks and clothes. I've been doing this work for seven years now and my lungs are finished. I've vomited blood for weeks at a time and still had to keep working.

In the old days, women used to stay at home because the men had work. Now, with the recession, we've had to go out to work. Many of our children have been abandoned. Their fathers have left and there's no love left in us when we get home late from work. We leave food for them, they play in the streets – there are always accidents, and no doctors. I feel like a slave in my own country – we get up at 4am and at 11 at night we are still mending and patching.'

The speaker, Josefina Muruchi, breaks down in a coughing fit. Suddenly, in a mixture of Spanish and Quechua, all the other women burst into speech, unleashing a torrent of pain and suffering. In the gloom, most of the women are sobbing.

'This is *doloroso* for us. We have nothing. Nothing. Only coca [a stimulant leaf chewed to suppress hunger] to keep us going. It's the children, we want them to study, but they're so malnourished and the price of tin is so low. Our kids say "mami, I want to help" and don't do their homework, but then they fail their exams and have to repeat the year and the teachers are always asking for money and we haven't got it and because our children are so ashamed they drop out of school. If I start vomiting blood again, what's going to happen to my children?'

Duncan Green, *Silent Revolution: The Rise of Market Economics in Latin America*, London 1995

---

to education and training has meant that they take the permanent jobs on new mechanised farms, and women have been relegated to temporary work at harvest time.

With food in short supply, parents favour boys to stay and eventually inherit the farm, and many young girls are packed off to the city as domestic servants. As a result, young women have outnumbered men in the exodus to the cities which has marked the last fifty years of Latin American history.

Women still supply most of the workers in a number of labour-intensive export industries. They pick coffee, tobacco or cotton, and produce new export crops such as strawberries in Mexico or peanuts in Brazil. In Colombia the women weed, fumigate, pick and package carnations for Europe's florists, suffering frequent respiratory problems and miscarriages from the pesticides to which they are constantly exposed.

Latin America's agrarian reform processes, (see chapter 2), have largely failed to benefit women, their apparent 'gender blindness' masking discrimination in favour of men. Most reforms hand out land to individuals identified as 'heads of household', by custom a man, except for widows and single mothers. Instead of being treated as producers in their own right, peasant women are seen as the equivalent of urban housewives and hence as dependents. In traditional Andean culture, farms are owned equally by husband and wife, so the new reforms marked a step backwards for women. In most cases the reforms helped permanent workers, rather than seasonal workers. When General Velasco expropriated Peru's cotton plantations in the late 1960s, women represented forty per cent of their seasonal workforce, but held few permanent jobs. The reform gave the plantations to their permanent workers organised into co-operatives, and as a result women made up only two per cent of members on the new cotton co-operatives. In Chile and Venezuela, agrarian reform laws specifically decreed that land given out under the reform should be passed to the beneficiary's sons when he died.

Structural Adjustment

The debt crisis which began in 1982, and the ensuing process of structural adjustment, has hit women hardest. As employers shed jobs, they have preferred to sack women, since they are not seen as breadwinners and are generally under-represented in trade unions. Public spending cuts have targeted 'female' professions in health and education, and the limited choice of jobs open to women has made it hard for them to find other employment. Poor women have increasingly turned to the informal sector and part-time work to make ends meet.

In their role as mothers, women have been hit by price rises in basic foods as subsidies are cut, making it harder to feed a family. As education and health budgets have been cut, mothers have had to find increasing sums for school notebooks or medicines. Clothes must be endlessly patched when there is no money to buy replacements. All these tasks add to the growing burden of keeping the family afloat. The stress of family life has also led to increased cases of alcohol abuse among men, leaving women to face the frequent domestic violence and family breakdown which follow. As one Bolivian miner says:

In my work I am happy. I joke with my compañeros, I work in peace. And then I come home and I see my wife and children undernourished, poorly clothed. It is then that I have a sense of the problems in my life and I get filled with rage.

Women in Politics

Driven in part by a need to unite to confront the economic crisis of recent years, growing numbers of women have begun to participate directly in political life. In the new social movements such as Mothers' Clubs, Base Christian Communities and neighbourhood associations, women have built

TABLE 7: DATE OF WOMEN'S SUFFRAGE IN THE AMERICAS

Country	Date
United States	1920
Ecuador	1929
Brazil	1932
Uruguay	1932
El Salvador	1939
Guatemala	1945
Panama	1945
Argentina	1947
Venezuela	1947
Chile	1949
Costa Rica	1949
Bolivia	1952
Mexico	1953
Honduras	1955
Nicaragua	1955
Peru	1955
Colombia	1957
Paraguay	1961

Source: J Nash and H Safa, *Sex and Class in Latin America*, New York, 1980

a bridge between the traditionally female world of home and family, and the predominantly male sphere of political activism.

Before the social movements appeared, women were largely excluded from political life. Although a small suffrage movement of largely middle-class women had won the vote in the whole of Latin America by 1961, this did not lead to the expected upsurge in political participation.

In Argentina, Juan and Evita Perón mobilised women as their footsoldiers in the Peronist Women's Party, led by Evita. Yet despite some progressive legislation, the 'father and mother of the nation' never challenged the ideal of wifely submission displayed by Evita herself. The Peronists introduced women's suffrage in 1947 and gave children born out of marriage equal rights before the law. In 1955 Perón's decision to legalise divorce alienated the Catholic Church and helped bring brought about his downfall at the hands of the military.

Elsewhere, few women have reached the leadership of political parties and trade unions. In 1995, Argentina led the way, with women comprising 25 per cent of congressional representatives. The relatively high proportion, on a par with Norway and Iceland, was due to a quota rule which forced parties to include female candidates at the top of their ballots, increasing their representation nine-fold in the 1995 elections. Even in cases where women are politically active at the grassroots level, for example in textile workers' unions, they thin out rapidly further up the union hierarchy.

During the left-wing Popular Unity government of Salvador Allende in Chile, women divided along class lines; middle-class women organised 'marches of the empty pots' to protest at food shortages and economic chaos, while women in the shanty towns worked in support of the Allende

Eduardo Longoni

government. In Chile and elsewhere, many left-wing men have been suspicious of an independent women's movement, arguing that it would prove to be a right-wing defender of the status quo, but also unwilling to give up their own privileged status in the home. As Yanci, an activist in El Salvador's women's movement comments: 'In all the key moments of our history, women have always participated, but we have been anonymous. Women have made the coffee so the compañeros could think better. Women cook while the men take the important decisions!'

Unlike the traditional left, which has often ignored women in its political programmes, the right and the military regimes of the 1970s and 1980s stressed the importance of the family, paying homage to the traditional Latin American icon of the long-suffering mother. The names of right-wing pro-military organisations such as Argentina's 'Tradition, Family and Property' encapsulated the conservative Catholic message. Such an ideology recognised and applauded women only as long as they remained safely in the 'female sphere'. When women dared to trespass into public politics, the military's chivalry proved short-lived. In Argentina, thirty per cent of those 'disappeared' by the military were women. The traumatised mothers of disappeared children, meeting on their fruitless round of the different military barracks in search of news, came together to form the Mothers and Grandmothers of the Plaza de Mayo. Every Thursday under the military government, a small but indomitable band of women wearing white headscarves walked silently around the Plaza de Mayo in front of the Presidential Palace in Buenos Aires, their placards carrying old, fading photographs of their children. As one mother described it, 'from washing, ironing and cooking we went out on to the streets to fight for the lives of our children.' The human rights movement they created grew to play a crucial role first in forcing the generals to hand power over to an elected government, and then in putting the military's leaders in jail for killing their children.

Lone voices. Mothers of the Plaza de Mayo confront police, Buenos Aires, Argentina.

The Mothers of the Disappeared were able to protest because they did so *as mothers*, effectively preventing the military from using outright repression as they did against virtually all other protest movements. By using the generals' own ideology against them, the women of the Plaza de Mayo opened up the first possibilities of public resistance, which grew into the mass protest movement that helped remove the military from power.

Military rule forced women to take to the public arena to defend their families in many other countries. In Brazil, opposition to the military took off in the late 1970s with the Cost of Living Movement, made up of women protesting at the suffering being inflicted on poor families by the military's economic policies. In Peru and Colombia, organisations of mothers and relatives of the disappeared have yet to obtain answers from a military that kills their sons and daughters with virtual impunity. In each case the crushing of traditional political parties has enabled women's organisations to expand into the political vacuum, sowing the seeds of the region's new social movements.

The grassroots women's organisations have had a difficult relationship with Latin American feminism. The military period coincided with the rise of feminism in the North, and many returning exiles in the 1980s brought with them feminist ideas from their experiences in London, Paris or New York. However, they did not find it easy to combine their new beliefs with political activism in the shanty towns, as two working-class activists from Chile recall:

We were always very wary that we would lose our independence if we let middle-class women in. The difference is that we work with our class identity and middle-class feminism doesn't, they work only with gender. They say women's problems are common to all women. We have things in common with middle-class women but we also have other problems that middle-class women don't have, like the housing shortage, debt problems, unemployment, and we're not going to advance as women if the two things aren't closely linked.

Gender discrimination may be the same but the class situation is different. Working-class culture is more rigid – we've got more brakes. Perhaps because of the influence of religion and perhaps because we've got less choice – we haven't got the economic freedom to do what we want.

Feminism of the upper class or middle class is a long way from our feminism. We've tried to work with middle-class feminists but they talk about a different world from ours. For example, they did a workshop where they told us we've got to value ourselves, stop serving the biggest steak to the men. Of course poor women like us aren't very familiar with steaks!

Once we went to a feminist meeting where they told us we should watch blue films to improve our sex lives. That was very shocking to our women. We've been to their women's centres because they have the resources to offer legal advice or psychologists for battered women. It's another world, all carpeted, with pictures on the wall, everything brand new. We felt uncomfortable. The only time we'd been in houses like that was as domestic servants. We are the ones these women use as their servants.
Quoted in Jo Fisher, *Out of the Shadows; Women, Resistance and Politics in South America*, London, 1993

The nature and tactics of the new social movements reflect their predominantly female origin. Stressing the need for internal democracy, social movements aim to improve local communities, usually by putting pressure on local or national governments. They fiercely defend their independence from political parties or the state, both male-dominated. Many of their demands reflect women's immediate needs: campaigns for day nurseries for working women, for better health care or street lighting, running water or electricity are often seen by the women involved as extensions of the struggles they face as wives and mothers. On occasion, the movements' strengths have also proved to be their weaknesses. Once immediate demands have been achieved, for example, the local authority has agreed to put in street lighting, the movement often disintegrates.

After the return to civilian government in Argentina, the Mothers of the Disappeared found it hard to maintain the unity and determination they showed under military rule. New governments often stole the clothes of the women's movement, passing laws to outlaw domestic violence, creating a national women's office in Chile, or setting up women's police stations in the case of Brazil. New laws and constitutions did not always translate into changes in real life, but the women's movement has found it hard to move from opposition to the new perilous new world of co-option and engagement with professional politicians. Nevertheless, the experience of meeting other women and organising successful campaigns has transformed many women's lives and could lay the foundations of a new and democratic politics for the future.

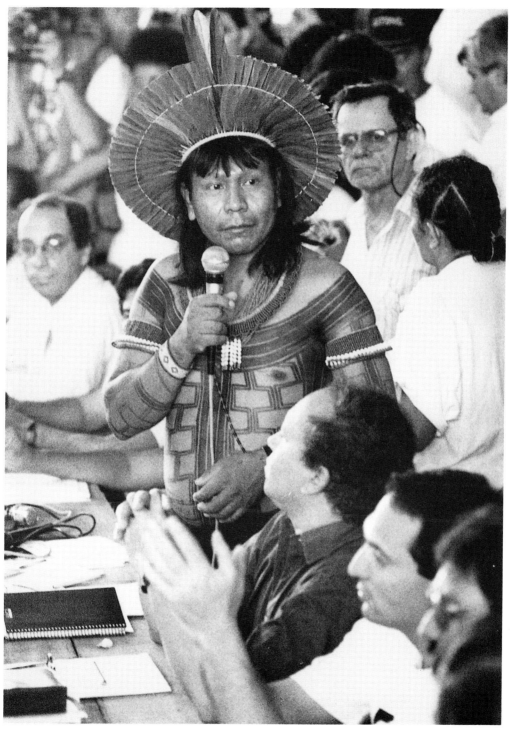

Susan Cunningham/Panos

Kayapó leader Bep Koroti Payakan Kayapó protests against the building of the Altamira dam on Kayapó territory in Amazonia, Brazil.

Chronology

Circa 30,000BC	First people reach the Americas across the Bering Straits from Asia
1492	Columbus arrives in the Americas, to be met by friendly Arawak Indians
1519	Cortés invades Mexico with 600 men
1535	Pizarro completes conquest of Inca empire
	mid-16th century. Arawak population of the Caribbean extinct within fifty years of Columbus' arrival
1781	Túpac Amaru lays seige to Cusco, the former Inca capital, in Indian rebellion. Amaru captured and executed
1960s	Officials of Brazil's government agency for Indians use poison, machine guns and disease to 'clear' land for large landowners
1982-83	400 Indian villages destroyed, 40,000 killed in counter-insurgency operations in Guatemala
1992	Indigenous groups throughout the Americas condemn the official celebrations of the quincentenary of Columbus' arrival in the Americas. Rigoberta Menchú wins Nobel Peace Prize
1994	Mayan Indians rebel in the Zapatista uprising of Chiapas, Mexico. In Ecuador, Indian organisations cut off cities in protest at economic structural adjustment measures.
1996	Guatemalan government signs indigenous rights accord with URNG guerrillas

Race Against Time   11

Indigenous Peoples

Cape Sunday (Cabo Domingo) is a lonely place. Low, dark hills under an enormous sky sink towards the ocean at the southern tip of the Americas. At this spot one Sunday in the 1920s a German landowner held a banquet for the local Yaganes Indians. When they were drunk, his hidden henchmen opened fire with a machine gun. The Yaganes died because, unaccustomed to the concept of private property, they had killed and eaten the landowner's sheep. The Indians of Tierra del Fuego were an almost stone-age people dressed in skins and using flint hand-tools. When the whites started to colonise the region in the 1880s, the various tribes soon succumbed to disease and slaughter. Today only a few impoverished old folk remain of the people whose permanent camp fires gave Tierra del Fuego (Land of Fire) its name.

Several thousand miles north, Ecuador came to a grinding halt for two full weeks in June 1994, when indigenous organisations rose up against the government. They were protesting against a new agrarian law, part of the government's economic structural adjustment programme, which would eliminate the Indians' traditional communal lands, converting them into private property open to market forces. Indian organisations believed that this would mean the eventual loss of their land to wealthy non-indigenous farmers, and responded with road blocks, rallies and protest marches. Ecuador's trade unions backed them by calling a general strike. In parts of the Ecuadorean Amazon, indigenous communities broadened the focus of the unrest by taking over oil wells to protest against the privatisation of the state oil company.

The government tried to crack down, sending in the army, but after four people had been killed, it finally had to back down and renegotiated the agrarian reform law with the indigenous organisations. The victory was unprecedented in the history of Ecuador's Indians.

The Ecuadorean movement's dynamism belies the conventional western image of fatalistic Indians calmly awaiting extinction. Latin America's history is full of the uprisings and resistance of native peoples, whose civilisations were in many ways far in advance of Europe's at the time of the conquest.

The Americas' original inhabitants came from Asia, crossing the Bering Straits about 30,000 years ago and migrating slowly south until every part of the continent was populated, albeit thinly, with Indian groups. The original migrants were hunter-gatherers, and groups like the Yaganes changed little over the millennia. Elsewhere, however, Indian groups developed agriculture about 5,000 years ago. Once settled on the land, they swiftly built the highly complex and cultured civilisations which dazzled the first European visitors.

The Mayas were a nation of astronomers and architects, already in decline before the Spaniards came. They were brilliant mathematicians, developing the concept of zero long before any other civilisation, and making astronomical calculations of astonishing accuracy. Their ornate temples are still being rescued from the jungles of Central America, and it is not yet clear what caused the Mayan empire to go into a sudden decline around 1000 AD.

The Incas covered the largest area of any of the pre-Columbian empires, spanning present-day Peru, Ecuador, Bolivia and parts of Colombia, Chile, Argentina and Brazil. Their extraordinary level of social organisation can still be seen in the mammoth stone buildings of Cusco and Machu Picchu and the remains of agricultural terracing that line many Andean valleys, often still being farmed by the Incas' descendants.

The Aztecs, at their height when Cortés and his band of *conquistadores* arrived in Mexico, lived on a permanent war footing. In their capital city of Tenochtitlan, site of today's Mexico City, they sacrificed up to 20,000 prisoners of war in a single day to the gods of war, rain and harvest. Their empire was built on a constant thirst for booty and fresh sacrifices, and the Spanish proved skilful in using the subject tribes' hatred of the Aztecs in their overthrow.

Despite their vast numerical superiority (Cortés invaded Mexico with just 600 men against an Aztec empire with a population of five to seven million), the mighty Indian empires crumbled before the Spanish. In part, the conquistadores' success came from their superior technology: they used armour, horses, cannon and muskets against Indian soldiers armed with spears and arrows. Their greatest allies were the microbes that they brought with them from Spain. Diseases such as smallpox and influenza, previously unknown in the Americas, wiped out millions of Indians, fatally weakening indigenous societies before the Spanish attack. The Spanish also proved adept at playing off rival Indian peoples against each other and at capitalising on the Inca and Aztec empires' extreme dependence on a single emperor. Both Cortés in Mexico and Pizarro in Peru first took the emperor prisoner then murdered them, leaving the empires leaderless before the Spanish onslaught.

TABLE 8: ESTIMATED INDIGENOUS POPULATION OF
AMERICA AT THE TIME OF EUROPEAN CONTACT

	Estimated population (million)	% of total
North America	4.4	7.7
Mexico	21.4	37.3
Central America	5.65	9.9
Caribbean	5.85	10.2
Andes	11.5	20.1
Lowland South America	8.5	14.8
Total	57.3	100.0

Source: William M Denevan (ed), *The Native Population of the Americas in 1492*, University of Wisconsin Press, 1976.

Once the centre had been removed, the Spanish viceroys replaced the emperors as the supreme authority and the former empires fell into their hands. Where Indian groups were less advanced and centralised, the Spanish encountered much greater difficulties. In southern Chile and Argentina the native Mapuche peoples successfully resisted the colonial forces, finally losing their fight to the new Chilean and Argentine armies following Latin America's independence from Spain. As always, the victors wrote the history books, and Argentine schoolchildren now learn the names of the heroes of the 'War of the South', a 19th-century campaign to exterminate the Indians, during which soldiers were paid a reward for each pair of Indian testicles they brought in to their commanders. The extermination of the Indians opened up the south of Argentina for sheep and cattle ranching.

A further legacy of the conquest was the misnomer, 'Indian', dating from Columbus' first landfall in the Americas, when thanks to a miscalculation of the circumference of the globe, he was convinced he had reached Asia. In the furore surrounding the Columbus quincentenary in 1992, many indigenous Latin Americans not only rejected the term 'Indian', which in Spanish carries distinctly derogatory overtones, but even objected to the words 'Latin American'. The region's native peoples pointed out that they are not in any sense Latin, and object to being called American, since the term stems from the name of another European explorer, Amerigo Vespucci.

Military victory marked the beginning of a process of extermination. Within a century of the conquest, as much as ninety per cent of Latin America's Indian population were wiped out in what became known as 'the Great Dying'. In the Caribbean, the Arawak peoples who first greeted Columbus with delight soon rued the day they had paddled their canoes out to his ships, bearing gifts for the exhausted sailors. Enslaved to the Spanish lust for gold, those who survived smallpox, influenza, measles and the other new diseases

Women at Sololá market, Guatemala. Guatemala and Bolivia are the only countries in Latin America with majority Indian populations.

committed mass suicide by poisoning and hanging. Mothers even slaughtered their new-born babies to prevent them being enslaved by the Spanish. Within 25 years of Columbus' arrival, only 3,000 Arawaks remained of an original population of 600,000, and by the mid-16th century they were extinct. Five centuries later, the youth of Brazil's Kaiowa Indians met the same threat in the same way. In 1990 alone, twenty boys and girls from the threatened tribe, all aged between 13 and 18, killed themselves by hanging or poisoning. Thirty others tried but were saved. On February 3, 1991, 15-year old Maura Ramírez hung herself from a tree. Her mother said, 'She was sad. She dreamt Helena was calling her.' Helena, Maura's elder sister, had committed suicide three months earlier. Psychologists blamed the deaths on the dislocation caused by going away to work on the sugar plantations.

Although more Indians fell victim to the diseases introduced by the Spanish and Portuguese than died in the mines, plantations or battlefields, the level of economic exploitation and misery inflicted by the Europeans was at least partially responsible for making the Indians so vulnerable to illness. Millions were literally worked to death.

The colonial authorities adopted various systems for exacting tribute and labour from their Indian 'vassals'. During the initial period the *encomienda* system rewarded Spanish officers and favourites with whole Indian communities. In return for supposedly bringing their allocated Indians to Christianity, the *encomenderos* were authorised to demand tribute and unpaid labour. In the densely populated regions of Mexico and the Andes, this left Indian villages more or less intact. In more sparsely peopled regions, the encomienda system degenerated into raiding parties to abduct slaves.

In the Andes an adapted version of this scheme, known as the *mita*, persisted through to independence, while in Mexico and Central America, the authorities preferred a 'free' labour force. European writers and theologians put forward a variety of ideological justifications to show that the natural inferiority of the Indians made their enslavement both necessary and an act of mercy.

As the centuries passed, racial boundaries became blurred. Since men far outnumbered women in the European colonial communities, Indian women were frequently obliged to have sex by their owners and the subsequent intermingling of blood created a growing mixed-race population, known as *mestizos*. Other Indians abandoned their traditional dress and learned Spanish, often moving to the cities. Over time, cultural criteria, rather than physical characteristics, became the means of identifying ethnic background. An 'Indian' wore non-European dress and spoke little or no Spanish, whereas a 'mestizo' adopted both the white language and western dress. In the coastal regions of Latin America, Indians were swiftly wiped out on the plantations and were replaced with African slaves who added a further ingredient to the continent's racial mix. By the time independence came in 1825, 12 per cent of Latin Americans were black, 28 per cent were mestizo, and only 42 per cent remained Indian. The remaining 18 per cent were white.

Statistics are even more unreliable than in the case of Indians, but by one calculation, the current black population of Latin America (i.e. excluding the English-speaking Caribbean, US and Canada) lies somewhere between 31 million and 90 million, probably exceeding the number of Indians. The largest black population by far is in Brazil (9 to 53 million), followed by Colombia, Haiti and Cuba. Although slavery was abolished in 1888, Afro-Brazilians remain at the bottom of the social pyramid, often living in shanty towns, with minimal power or representation in national political life.

The independence wars of the early 19th century were largely a dispute between the local *criollo* ruling class of whites born in Latin America, and the Spanish. Little changed for the continent's indigenous peoples. For blacks on the other hand, many of whom fought in the liberation armies, victory over the Spanish paved the way for the abolition of slavery. The 19th century brought further encroachments on the Indians' traditional communal lands as liberal administrations in many countries made it illegal to hold land in common and insisted on private ownership. The Indians' traditional collectivism was anathema to governments trying to introduce notions of private property and individual enterprise, although their cohesion as communities made them better able to resist. The new legislation paved the way for large landowners to move in and buy or seize Indian lands for new crops such as coffee.

Modern Indians

The continent's Indian survivors now make up five per cent of its total population and fall into two distinct groups. The first, and by far the largest, is that of the highland Indians, descendants of the Inca, Aztec and Mayan empires. The second are the lowland Indians, largely confined to the Amazon basin and Central America. In both Guatemala and Bolivia, over half the population is Indian, while the largest numbers live in Peru and Mexico. Although highland Indians number some 22 million, lowland Indians do not exceed 1 million, of whom about a quarter live in Brazil, with smaller numbers in the other countries of the Amazon basin: Venezuela, Colombia, Ecuador, Peru, Bolivia and the Guyanas. Isolated groups of lowland Indians also survive in the Central American countries of Panama, Nicaragua and Honduras.

When not tied to the *haciendas* of the big landowners, highland Indian communities farm the land in much the same way as they did five centuries ago. They grow the traditional crops – maize, beans and squash in Mexico, potatoes and maize in the Andes, using mainly the simple technology of the digging stick and hoe. Communities are tightly-knit, and members are

INDIAN IDENTITY

Our parents tell us: 'Children, the earth is the mother of man, because she gives him food.' This is especially true for us whose life is based on the crops we grow. Our people eat maize, beans and plants. We can't eat ham, or cheese, or things made by machines. So we think of the earth as the mother of man, and our parents teach us to respect the earth. We must only harm the earth when we are in need. This is why, before we sow our maize, we have to ask the earth's permission.

By accepting the Catholic religion, we didn't accept a condition, or abandon our culture. It was more like another way of expressing ourselves. It's like expressing ourselves through a tree, for example; we believe that a tree is a being, a part of nature, and that a tree has its image, its representation, its *nahual*, to channel our feelings to the one God. That is the way we Indians conceive it. Catholic Action is like another element which can merge with the elements which already exist within Indian culture. And it confirms our belief that, yes, there is a God, and, yes, there is a father for all of us. And yet it is something we think of as being only for what happens up there. As far as the earth is concerned, we must go on worshipping through our own intermediaries, just as we have always done, through all the elements found in nature.

When we evoke the colour of the sun, it's like evoking all the elements which go to make up our life. The sun as the channel to the one God, receives the plea from his children that they should never violate the rights of all the other beings which surround them. This is how we renew our prayer which says that men, the children of the one God, must respect the life of the trees, the birds, the animals around us. We must respect the life of every single one of them. We must respect the life, the purity, the sacredness, which is water. We must respect the one God, the heart of the sky, which is the sun. We must not do evil while the sun shines upon his children. This is a promise.

I, Rigoberta Menchú, Elisabeth Burgos Debray (ed), London, 1984

encouraged not to sell land to outsiders and to marry within the village. Although their lifestyles are often romanticised by outsiders, Indian farming communities lead harsh lives, suffering the high levels of infant mortality and insecurity common to all peasant farmers.

Where they have managed to retain a level of independence, such communities frequently enjoy a rich cultural life. In Guatemala, each highland village has its own distinctive costume, with unique designs passed on from mother to daughter for generations. Many traditional practices have survived the efforts of the colonial authorities. Faith healers combine herbal medicine and magic, and the religion of the European invaders has been fused with its predecessors into an original form of 'folk Catholicism'. Communities attach great importance to ritual cycles involving saints' days, feast days and ceremonies such as baptism, marriage and funerals.

In the course of this century modern influences have gradually encroached upon this traditional pattern. Improved roads have increased trading and

A healer practising a ritual, Peru.

involvement in the money economy; improved education and contact with the outside world mean that most Indians now speak Spanish; and growing numbers of Protestant missionaries have both converted Indian groups and persuaded them to abandon their traditional customs. The old ways persist most stubbornly in Guatemala, where many speakers of the country's 21 Indian languages still know no more than a few words of Spanish. In most areas men are assimilated into non-Indian ways faster than women, who have become the custodians of traditional culture. Men have more contact with the money economy through wage labour, and women less frequently go to school, where Spanish is often the only permitted language.

Another major cause of what is known as 'acculturation', the Indians' loss of their traditional culture, is urbanisation. The exodus to the cities brings contact with poor mestizos and Indians from other communities, and Spanish frequently becomes the common language. The disruption of the move can leave few vestiges of traditional culture intact.

War and repression also accelerate the process. In Guatemala, a ferocious army counter-insurgency campaign in the Indian highlands since the early 1980s left 40,000 dead and over 400 Indian villages destroyed. Many more Indians fled their villages to seek refuge in the cities, where they sought anonymity by abandoning their traditional dress and customs. Over a million people were displaced from their homes in what bordered on a race war against the Indians. In the mid-1980s one Guatemalan President warned 'we must get rid of the words "indigenous" and "Indian".' Peru's civil war between the Sendero Luminoso guerrillas and the army has also driven many Indian families into the swelling shanty towns around Lima.

Violent racism persists in most countries with a significant Indian population. In Guatemala the enormous divide between poor, non-Spanish speaking Indians and wealthy white landowners and entrepreneurs closely

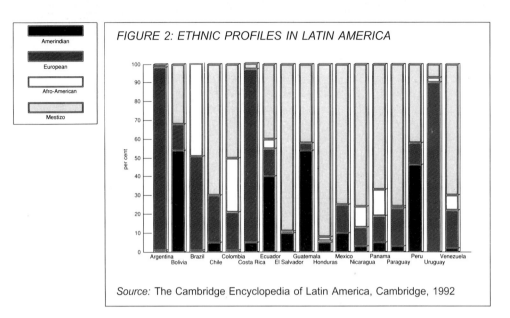

FIGURE 2: ETHNIC PROFILES IN LATIN AMERICA

Amerindian

European

Afro-American

Mestizo

Source: The Cambridge Encyclopedia of Latin America, Cambridge, 1992

resembles apartheid. When Indian activist Rigoberta Menchú won the Nobel Peace Prize in 1992, wealthy Guatemalans were torn between national pride and race hatred, and were heard to joke that at last Barbie had found a maid.

Lowland Indians

No one sells his own son or his mother, because he loves them. In the same way, it is an absurd idea for an Indian to sell his land. We can't change our feelings for our land, which is where our ancestors are buried.
Taxáua Indian, Brazil

In contrast to the highland Indians' stable agriculture based on herding and crop rotation, lowland Indians usually practise mobile slash-and-burn forms of farming, combined with fishing and hunting. Both groups, however, share an overwhelming and mystical bond with the land. Lowland Indians, like those of the highlands, have strong religious traditions in which worship of aspects of the natural world is mediated through shamans who speak to the deities in a trance.

Lowland Indians traditionally live more communally than highlanders, often in communal houses, known as *malocas*, which can hold several hundred people. Malocas have been criticised by Protestant missionaries for encouraging promiscuity and in many cases have been abandoned in favour of family houses. Many hundreds of different language groups exist, some comprising only a few dozen speakers.

Whereas highland Indians have been in contact with whites virtually since the first days of the conquest, lowland Indians have frequently lived in inaccessible areas, especially those in the Amazon basin, which outsiders have only recently penetrated. There are still believed to be a few groups, numbering perhaps a few thousand, of 'uncontacted' Indians in the area. When contact does occur, it is frequently as disastrous for the Indians as it was in the 16th century, leading to epidemics of disease and violent

confrontations with settlers, such as those that have recently befallen the Yanomami Indians.

Lowland Indians have suffered the same 'curse of wealth' as their highland relatives. In the rubber boom at the end of the 19th century, unscrupulous rubber companies trapped and enslaved large numbers of Indian tribes as latex collectors. In the Putumayo region of Colombia, 40,000 Indians were killed by these rubber barons between 1886 and 1919. After rubber came African palm, cattle and oil, each new commodity penetrating fresh areas of the forest and absorbing or driving out the local Indian groups. In the 1990s, Indians in the Ecuadorean Amazon have started to fight back against the oil companies whose drilling is destroying their forest ecosystem (see chapter 3).

The other main source of encroachment on Indian lands has been the colonisation programmes, either spontaneous or government-run, through which landless peasants have moved into the forest, cutting down the trees to make way for food crops. This has provoked frequent armed conflict between peasants and Indians.

Government attitudes to the lowland Indians have alternated between cynical disregard and a desire to 'integrate' the Indians into national life, a process anthropologists condemn as 'ethnocide'. One Brazilian government official proudly described his policy to a visiting journalist:

> We resettle them as quickly as possible in new villages and then remove the children and begin to educate them. We give them the benefit of our medicine and our education, and, once they are completely integrated citizens like you and me and the Minister here, we let them go out into the world.

Yanomami Indians, Amazonia, on the border between Brazil and Venezuela. The Yanomami are Amazonia's largest tribal group, but are declining rapidly as gold prospectors and roads invade their territory, spreading diseases and disrupting communities.

DEBT BONDAGE IN COLOMBIA

We called all the Indians together, along with their families, in a ravine or at the mouth of a river and there, in the presence of the Indian authorities, we advanced them: one shirt, one machete, some knives to make the cuts [in the rubber trees], a belt so that they didn't fall out of the trees, and of course, any goods they wanted. Throughout the year, we advanced them anything they, or their women, asked for. The women were their ruin and our business, because they fancied everything. Vanity does not respect colour, nor age, nor sex. They wanted combs, perfumes, mirrors and coloured beads, cloth and more cloth, high-heeled shoes and ribbons for their hair. The men asked for drink, Italian sweets and German radios. They liked music and partying.

Every day around 4pm the line of Indians would arrive with the latex, which was weighed on scales and then each Indian's amount was entered in a book. The scales didn't measure the true weight, and the amount we wrote in the book wasn't the amount on the scales. The [German missionary] did a lot of damage because she taught the 'cousins' figures and they began to cause trouble the whole time. When they got unhappy, they'd run away. So we had to invent the pass – no boss would give them an advance if the Indians couldn't show a pass signed by their previous boss to prove that they had paid off their debts. Some Indians managed to pay off their debts, and even earned some money on top, but others didn't. Everything depended on their boss. Some bosses fiddled the books so they never managed to pay it off. But others were very humane and only wrote down what the Indian asked for.

Alfredo Molano, *Aguas Arriba*, Bogotá, 1990, author's translation

Once out in the world, 'integrated' Indians often end up on the social scrapheap, surviving as beggars or prostitutes on the fringes of the frontier boom-towns of the Amazon. Sometimes the ethnocide was more deliberate. In Brazil in the early 1960s, a government enquiry found that corrupt officials of its own Indian agency had connived with local landowners to massacre entire tribes using dynamite, machine guns and poisoned sugar. Other investigations showed that tribes in the Mato Grosso had been deliberately infected with smallpox, influenza, tuberculosis and measles.

Rebellion and Resistance

The slow genocide of the Indian nations provoked fierce resistance. In some cases, as in the Caribbean or Brazil, Indian groups opted for mass suicide rather than bow to the dictates of the whites. Many others retreated into the most inaccessible areas of the continent to escape the burden of constant tributes and forced labour. Some took up arms against the Spanish authorities, the most famous being Peru's Túpac Amaru, the most recent the Mayan Zapatista uprising in southern Mexico. Yet neither Indian revolts nor independence succeeded in re-establishing Indian self-rule. In the endless cycle of revolt and defeat, the Indians learned the wisdom of the advice given by Quintín Lame, a Colombian Indian revolutionary leader: 'Do not

THE LAST INCA: TÚPAC AMARU II

In 1781 Túpac Amaru laid siege to Cusco. This mestizo chief, a direct descendant of the Inca emperors, headed the broadest of messianic revolutionary movements. The rebellion broke out in Tinta province, which had been almost depopulated by enforced service in the Cerro Rico mines. Mounted on his white horse, Túpac Amaru entered the plaza of Tungasuca and announced to the sound of drums and *pututus* [conch-shell trumpets] that he had condemned the royal *Corregidor*, Antonio Juan de Arriaga, to the gallows and put an end to the Potosí mita. A few days later Túpac issued a decree liberating the slaves. He abolished all taxes and forced labour in all forms. The Indians rallied by the thousands to the forces of the 'father of all the poor and all the wretched and helpless.' He moved against Cusco at the head of his *guerrilleros*, promising that all who died while under his orders in this war would return to life to enjoy the happiness and wealth the invaders had wrested from them. Victories and defeat followed; in the end, betrayed and captured by one of his own chiefs, Túpac was handed over in chains to the royalists. The Examiner Areche entered his cell to demand, in exchange for promises, the names of his rebel accomplices. Túpac Amaru replied scornfully, 'There are no accomplices here except you and I. You as oppressor, I as liberator, deserve to die.'

Túpac was tortured, along with his wife, his children and his chief aides, in Cusco's Plaza del Wacaypata. His tongue was cut out; his arms and legs were tied to four horses with the intention of quartering him, but his body would not break; he was finally beheaded at the foot of the gallows. His head was sent to Tinta, one arm to Tungasuca and the other to Carabaya, one leg to Santa Rosa and the other to Livitaca.

Eduardo Galeano, *Open Veins of Latin America*, New York, 1973

believe in the friendship of the white man or the mestizo; distrust gifts and flattery; never consult a white lawyer; do not allow yourself to be hoodwinked by the chattering politicians of any party.'

Elsewhere, Indian resistance to oppression was more subtle, but no less stubborn.

In those days we dressed in dark colours decorated with flowers, black *awayos*. We always wore dark blue. But we had to put on coloured clothes because the landowner scolded us: 'How long are you going to continue going around in black, when will you change?!' The foremen would go from house to house and whip those wearing dark blue skirts and destroy the tubs used for dying. But we carried on wearing our clothes. That landowner is dead now. The foremen would beat us up and say furiously: 'Damn you, don't you have ears?' We would escape to some corners of the river and change our clothes: the dark skirt that we had on underneath we put on top and the other underneath it.

Andean Oral History Workshop, 'Indigenous Women and Community Resistance: History and Memory', Elizabeth Jelin (ed), *Women and Social Change in Latin America*, London, 1990

TRADITION AND CONFLICT

The civilised people invade, kill our children. We have no support. People let cattle loose all over the land of the Indians. The oldest shamans are dying off. The young ones don't have the knowledge that the old ones had. ...The Xerentes have feasts and dances – the feasts of yam, of honey, of the cutting of hair. They have their own language. When they return from hunting, they don't rest immediately, but wait for the old shaman. Then they relax slowly, while the shaman sings and prays to God.

When a son is born, they go on a diet. The father doesn't eat manioc flour. He doesn't kill snakes. He doesn't collect feathers. Only after spreading honey on his face does he eat honey. When someone dies, he weeps.

When the Indian is about to travel, people join with him and sing and cry with him. When he returns, there is another feast of joy – because he went and he returned. When the moon is beautiful everyone sings. They sing with bowed heads. Only the chief looks at the moon.

Every full moon they sing and celebrate. But ever since civilisation came, they have suffered tremendously. Flu, which they never had in the past, has appeared. The shamans are no longer able to carry out cures. Tuberculosis is what most effects the Xerente today....They used to take medicines from the forest, but there is nothing to deal with the sicknesses of the civilised people. They tried medicines from the forest, but they don't help. They asked the priest to get them some medicine for the sicknesses of the civilised people, and now they are a bit better. This year there was no big sickness.

Indian spokesman in Sue Branford and Oriel Glock, *The Last Frontier*, London, 1985

The key battleground has been over culture, in particular religion and language, which are central to indigenous identity. 'Religion is a Spanish word. For us, the Mayan priests pass down culture, not religion,' explains Justina, a Guatemalan indigenous activist. Through the centuries, Indians have proved extraordinarily able to adapt to outside pressure while safeguarding the essential aspects of their cultural identity. This stubborn, silent refusal to give in explains the reputation for passivity which the Indians acquired in the eyes of outsiders, and goes back to the earliest days of the conquest. In 1534 Mancu Inca Yupanki, an Inca leader, told his followers:

Give the outward appearance of complying with their demands. Give them a little tribute, because if you don't give it they will take it from you by force.... I know that some day, by force or deceit, they will make you worship what they worship, and when that happens, when you can resist no longer, do it in front of them, but do not forget your ceremonies... reveal just what you have to and keep the rest hidden.

Through this combination of both passive and violent resistance, Latin America's Indian peoples have achieved their most remarkable victory – survival. In the face of five centuries of a military, epidemic, cultural and economic onslaught, the Indians have survived, and are now increasing in

Sebastian Turpo/Ayaviri/TAFOS/Panos

numbers. However, most remain outsiders in their own lands, condemned to poverty, racism and persecution.

Wedding arch and procession, Peru. Ceremonies and rituals form a central part of the Indian calendar.

The last thirty years have seen attempts to build a politics based on the indigenous peoples' growing sense of identity and self-confidence, producing an upsurge in Indian resistance. Among highland groups, Indians have organised peasant associations and taken up arms to become involved in civil wars in Mexico, Guatemala and Peru, while in the lowland areas a plethora of Indian organisations has sprung up, demanding land and help from the government, and defending themselves against the invasions of agribusiness, mining companies and poor peasant colonisers. Lowland Indians have achieved a political impact out of all proportion to their numbers: 'Five centuries of contact has produced only marginalisation, exploitation and misery for our highland colleagues. We're not volunteering for the same,' says Evaristo Nugkuag, an Aguaruna leader from lowland Peru.

Mario Juruna, the first Indian to become a deputy in Brazil's parliament, made his people's demands quite clear:

Indian wealth lies in customs and communal traditions and land which is sacred. Indians can and want to choose their own road, and this road is not civilisation made by whites... Indian civilisation is more human. We do not want paternalistic protection from whites. Indians today...want political power.

Indian organisations typically rely on individual communities as their basic building blocks. Federations of communities then grow to cover an area, in some cases combining to form regional and even national confederations. Cross border co-operation took off in the Indian campaign over the 500th anniversary of Columbus' first voyage to the Americas in 1992. The anti-Columbus campaign reached its peak in October 1991, when 500 Indian delegates from every corner of the Americas met in Guatemala. A year later their campaign received international recognition when Rigoberta Menchú,

In the main church in Guatemala's lakeside town of Santiago Atitlán, a tomb commemorates the life of Father Stanley Rother, a priest from Oklahoma assassinated by the army in 1981. Rother was killed for his outspoken defence of Santiago's 40,000 Indian community at a time when the army was rampaging through Guatemala's Indian highlands. Around the memorial, which contains the priest's heart and a phial of his blood, hundreds of crude paper crosses are stuck to the wall. Each carries the hand-written name of a villager: blue paper for those killed, yellow for the wounded, pink for the disappeared. Freshly cut branches of pine decorate the tomb, filling the gloom with a resinous scent.

In Guatemala, the paper crosses make Atitlán unique. Nowhere else can people so publicly commemorate their dead. The people of Atitlán earned that right on a bloody night in December 1990, hours after drunken soldiers had harassed townsfolk in one of many such incidents. This time, however, something snapped. 'They had violated our rights for eleven years. That night we rose up when a brother asked for help,' says Francisco Coquix Coché, a community leader. 'When we rang the church bell, everyone came out. It was life or death. It was a decision.'

Summoned by the bells, several thousand angry but unarmed Indians set off to protest at the army encampment on the outskirts of town. They were met with machine gun fire which killed 13 villagers, including a nine-year-old boy. Santiago's leaders stormed off to Guatemala City, alerted the international press and managed to corner President Vinicio Cerezo, forcing him to sign an agreement to demilitarise the town. The returning leaders were met by the townsfolk as they walked into town, and when they read out the letter, 'the people fell on their knees and praised God', says Francisco.

Today Cerezo's letter to the villagers is literally carved in stone; a six-foot high marble and stone replica stands by the dusty road, opposite 13 rough wooden crosses which mark the spots where the villagers fell. Green young coffee bushes now grow where the army encampment once stood.

Duncan Green, *Guatemala: Burden of Paradise*, London, 1992

a young woman leader from Guatemala, received the Nobel Peace Prize. Many observers now see the Columbus campaign as a watershed for the indigenous movement, a view which seemed confirmed when the Indians of southern Mexico and Ecuador rose in revolt in 1994.

Several problems have dogged these attempts at organisation. The first has been the difficulty of building alliances between different indigenous groups and between highland and lowland Indians. But even more thorny has been the problem of the relationship between Indian and non-Indian organisations. Indian organisations are often justifiably suspicious of non-Indian political parties and peasant organisations, fearing that they see the world purely in terms of class divisions, and fail to recognise and respect the Indians' right to be culturally distinct.

Conflicts between Indians and poor colonists can further sour the relationship between Indians and peasants. In Bolivia, one Indian woman gave voice to the extreme 'indigenist' position: 'To the Indian, the Spaniard is only a tenant. And we have to hit him, complain about him and tell him to leave, because we are the owners and we are going to return.'

Despite these obstacles, the political strength of Indian organisation has grown steadily in recent years, forcing parties, social movements and governments alike to take their demands seriously. Some of the greatest recent advances have been in Bolivia, where a leading Indian activist, Víctor Hugo Cárdenas, became vice-president in 1993. When the president left on a foreign visit, Cárdenas formally assumed the presidency, making him the first Indian to hold that office in Latin America since Benito Juárez in Mexico in the 19th century.

In Brazil and Colombia new constitutions now enshrine a number of indigenous rights. In Mexico, the Zapatistas signed an indigenous rights accord with the government which recognises the 'autonomy' of Mexico's ten million Indians, and their rights to multilingual education and 'adequate' political representation. But the accord did not touch on the economic issues at the heart of the Zapatista uprising, such as control of natural resources and land redistribution. In Guatemala the government signed a similar accord with the URNG guerrillas prior to the peace agreement of 1996. Such paper guarantees do not always translate into real improvements on the ground, but they provide a rallying point for the indigenous movement.

For the optimists, the Indians are on the way back. Many in the Andes are convinced that the *pachakut'i*, literally the 'balance upheaval' that legends and oral history have prophesied for centuries, has finally arrived, heralding an Indian cultural and political renaissance which will transform Latin America. They point to the resurgence in Indian identity and organisation as evidence.

Pessimists see the tide moving in the other direction and blame the region's new-found obsession with structural adjustment. With its focus on individualism and the market, neoliberalism stands diametrically opposed to the indigenous traditions of community, subsistence agriculture and reciprocal aid. In the spring of 1993 the annual congress of Mexico's *brujos* or shamans, passed a resolution condemning the North American Free Trade Agreement (NAFTA), saying it would 'bring a cultural invasion that could adulterate the roots of our knowledge.'

The pessimists may yet be proved wrong. Indians in Latin America have showed extraordinary tenacity in surviving five centuries of cultural, political and economic assault by outsiders.

Joe Fish

Indian preacher, Guatemala.

Chronology

1494	In the Treaty of Tordesillas the Vatican divides up the New World between Spain and Portugal
1826 on	Independence leaders sign concordats with the Vatican, maintaining Catholicism as the state religion
1926-29	Mexican Church suspends public worship to protest at state harassment. Ninety priests executed during the Cristero rebellion.
1962-65	Second Vatican Council commits the Church to work for human rights, justice and freedom.
1960s on	Born-again Protestant churches begin to expand rapidly throughout Latin America
1968	Meeting of the Latin American bishops in Medellín, Colombia adopts a 'preferential option for the poor.'
1978	Pope John Paul II becomes Pope and leads conservative offensive within Church against 'liberation theology'
1980	Assassination of Archbishop Oscar Romero of San Salvador
1982	General Efraín Ríos Montt seizes power in Guatemala, becoming the region's first evangelical dictator
1989	Army assassinates six Jesuit priests in El Salvador, leading to the withdrawal of US support for the military and the end of the civil war
1991	Guatemala's Jorge Serrano becomes the region's first elected evangelical president
1996	Estimated number of Protestants rises to 60 million from 5 million in 1970

Thy Kingdom Come 12

The Church

In the main square in front of Guatemala's national palace, a paunchy preacher in a shiny new bomber jacket is haranguing the crowd. Grinning with tension, as he shouts into a fat blue microphone, he talks of drought, disease and salvation, exhorting them to praise the Lord. An 'Alleluia' rises from the largely female audience. The preacher is an Evangelical Protestant, and he is standing outside the capital city's Roman Catholic cathedral. Inside, everything is cool and white after the dust and heat of the square. The smell of candle-wax fills the air as a queue of Indian worshippers of all ages stand in line, waiting to pray to and kiss the wounds of a dark-skinned statue of Christ, his legs worn shiny from the stroking of thousands of hands. Catholicism has the cathedral, but the Evangelical preacher has the crowds. The crusading zeal of the Evangelicals is winning millions of new converts every year, threatening a new Reformation in Latin America. Even so, 42 per cent of the world's Catholics live in Latin America, a figure expected to rise to half by the next century.

In Guatemala, as in most of Latin America, old belief systems are breaking down, producing a kind of religious supermarket where worshippers shop around between Catholicism and the different Evangelical churches. But there are other, more exotic offerings on the shelves: in the church of a lakeside town in the Indian highlands, the townsfolk, both Protestant and Catholic, worship Maximón, an enigmatic Mayan combination of St Peter and Judas, with a taste for cigars and liquor. In Brazil, African spiritist religions such as Candomblé and Umbanda, which arrived with slavery, are also doing battle for the souls of the poor.

Christopher Columbus had a triple purpose when he set sail for what he imagined to be Asia in 1492. In the words of Bernal Díaz del Castillo, a comrade of Hernan Cortés in the conquest of Mexico, Columbus and the *conquistadores* who followed went 'to serve God and His Majesty and also to get riches.' In the year that Columbus 'discovered' America, the Spanish led by Ferdinand and Isabella finally drove the last Muslim king out of Granada, bringing to an end the seven-century war to expel the Moors from Spanish soil. That same year, a royal decree expelled all Jews from Spain. With Spain united, the Vatican, at that time under Spanish control, looked to the Americas as the next great crusade. Two years after Columbus landed, the Pope decreed in the Treaty of Tordesillas that Spain and Portugal could divide up the New World, with a mission to evangelise the heathen.

Despite well-intentioned efforts by the Crown and the Church to restrain the worst excesses of the colonists, evangelisation took second place to the mass-extermination of the Indians through disease and slavery. When Columbus despatched 500 Indian slaves back to Spain, he commented in his diary, 'Let us in the name of the Holy Trinity go on sending all the slaves that can be sold.' Under the *encomienda* system, Spanish officers were granted large numbers of Indian labourers, in return for bringing them to Christ. It is not clear how many were successfully converted before dying in the mines or on the *haciendas*.

From the start, there were dissident friars who protested at the treatment of the Indians. Just 19 years after Columbus first landed, a Dominican named Antonio de Montesinos on the island of Hispaniola (today the Dominican Republic), outraged his Christmas congregation with his questions: 'by what right do you keep these Indians in such a cruel and horrible servitude?...you kill them with your desire to extract and acquire gold every day.. Are these not men? Have they not rational souls? Are you not bound to love them as you love yourselves?' Five centuries on, many Church workers are still asking the same questions of Latin America's rulers.

The sermon changed the life of one young landowner in Montesinos' congregation, a man by the name of Bartolomé de las Casas. Shortly afterwards, las Casas gave up 'his' Indians and travelled to Spain to begin a lifetime's crusade to persuade the Spanish Crown to end the extermination of the continent's native peoples. First as a Dominican friar, then as a bishop, las Casas became the Indians' foremost defender, and his book *A Short Account of the Destruction of the Indies* gives a graphic portrayal of their suffering under the conquistadores. In one famous debate in 1550, the 76-year old bishop took on the leading Spanish scholar of his day, Juan Ginés de Sepúlveda, to argue that the enslavement of the Indians was theologically unacceptable, and that Indian civilisation was in many ways superior to that of the Europeans.

Not only the Dominicans, but also the Franciscans and the Jesuits brought with them a more enlightened version of Christianity. In the early 17th century the Jesuits set up vast 'reductions' covering much of Paraguay, where Guaraní Indians could live and work safe from the depredations of Portuguese slavers. In these sanctuaries, the Indians developed their skills in working metal, stone and wood to levels of artistry matching anything in Europe. In the end, however, the burgeoning Brazilian state drove out the Jesuits and the Indians were captured.

From its earliest days in Latin America, the Roman Catholic Church supported the colonial authorities, in return for being made the official religion and receiving the tithe – a levy on all wealth generated in the Indies. In consequence, an increasingly complacent and materialist priesthood lost touch with the poor. In 1748, one report to the Spanish king commented:

> it seems relevant to mention here what a priest from the province of Quito told us, during his visitation of this parish, in which – between feasts and memorial services for the dead – he received each year over 200 sheep, 6000 poultry, 4000 Indian pigs and 50,000 eggs. Nor is his parish one of the more lucrative ones.

The independence wars of the early 19th century threatened this cosy relationship and split the Church between pro- and anti-Spanish factions. Usually the upper echelons of the Church supported the old ways, while local priests like Miguel Hidalgo and José María Morelos in Mexico went as far as taking up arms in the independence cause. Both were captured and

executed. Despite these schisms, independence leaders subsequently swore allegiance to Rome, and soon came to a series of agreements with the Vatican which maintained Catholicism as the state religion.

Religious procession, Peru.

Later in the century, the Church paid the price for backing the most backward sections of the elite, usually via the Conservative parties, when Liberal reformers severed the Church-state relationship in Ecuador, Brazil, Cuba, Honduras, Nicaragua, Panama, Chile and Mexico. Liberal governments limited Church control over education and confiscated its property. The countries where the Church was disestablished later became the most fertile ground for the growth of the radical Catholic Church and the Evangelical Protestants. Anti-clericalism reached its height in post-revolutionary Mexico, where the tensions between Church and state following the Mexican revolution of 1910-17 led the Church to suspend public worship for three years from 1926-29. Ninety priests were executed during the ensuing Cristero rebellion of Church militants, whose name came from their battle cry '*Viva Cristo rey*' ('Long live Christ the King'). A wartime speech by one Mexican general, J.B. Vargas, encapsulated the virulence of anti-clerical feeling:

It is enough to have some idea of the terrible history of the Inquisition for one to realise that priests and cassocks reek of prostitution and crime. Confession is an industry invented to seduce maidens, to win over Catholic ladies and transform fathers and husbands into chaste replicas of Saint Joseph... The Pope is a crafty foreigner who accumulates wealth in collaboration with the exploiting Friars who swindle the foolish people for the benefit of a country quite other than their own ... Nowadays, if Jesus Christ were to come down, the first thing he would do would be to hang them like rabid dogs.

The rebellion ended when the government backed down and allowed limited autonomy for the Church, though with greatly reduced influence.

While Roman Catholicism remained essentially European at the top, cultural cross-fertilisation was occurring at a local level. From the earliest days of the conquest, many traditional Indian beliefs and practices were incorporated into a 'folk Catholicism', where Catholic saints rubbed shoulders with Andean gods on the niches and altars. In Bolivia's historic mining town of Potosí, the wild baroque carvings of the San Francisco Church look distinctly pagan. Bare-breasted goddesses are interwoven with the ubiquitous symbols of sun and moon, while at the very top of the building, an Inca warrior looks out sternly over the city. A minute, red-cheeked Indian boy explains, 'we built this for ourselves when we Indians weren't allowed in the Cathedral.' Folk Catholicism has come in for particular criticism by the Evangelicals, who see it as even more pagan than the pure Roman version. 'We take the cross up to see our crops grow', says an Indian peasant woman in Peru's Sacred Valley, 'That's our belief. We worship the Catholic religion. Mother Earth (*pachamama*) as well. Only the Catholics still believe in Mother Earth and the Cross. The other religions, the Evangelicals, don't worship these any more.'

The Modern Church

The social turmoil of the 1930s, with broader suffrage, the beginnings of urbanisation and the rise of mass politics in the cities, brought home the growing irrelevance of the Church's traditional allies, the Conservative parties and land-owning elites. The Vatican began to wake up to the disastrous condition of its Latin American operation. Grown fat and lazy through its links to the rich, the Church had only the shallowest roots among the poor majority with which to confront a new era of change and mass involvement in politics. Paradoxically, in a continent where the overwhelming majority declared themselves Catholic, few went to church and the ratio of priests to parishioners was far lower than elsewhere in the Vatican's empire.

The Church embarked on a crusade, loosely termed Catholic Action, to organise its lay members and extend its influence within groups such as students, peasants, women, workers and the middle classes. The new emphasis was on social issues, and the movement grew with the emergence of Christian Democrat parties after the Second World War. Church leaders saw such organisations as a bulwark against the expansion of communism, and religious organisations in the US contributed funds and personnel as the Cold War gathered momentum in the 1950s. Yet, although the Church acquired renewed political influence, it failed to increase significantly the numbers of active worshippers and reduce its social isolation. In the 1960s only twenty per cent of baptised Catholics regularly attended mass, compared with eighty per cent in Poland or Ireland; there was only one priest for every 5,700 believers compared to a ratio of 1:830 in the US. In addition, the first signs of the imminent explosion of Protestant Evangelism were beginning to alarm the bishops.

As the 1960s wore on, events threatened to overtake the Vatican. The Cuban revolution in 1959 and the failure of Christian Democrat governments to deliver reforms led to the radicalisation of many grass-roots Church workers and activists. Many student sections split off from the Christian Democrat parties to found guerrilla organisations. In Colombia, a radical young priest,

Camilo Torres, took up arms to fight with the National Liberation Army (ELN), declaring, 'the Catholic who is not a revolutionary is living in mortal sin.' Torres died in a shoot-out with the army in 1966.

The speed of events gave an added urgency to the Second Vatican Council, a massive shake-up ordered by Pope John XXIII to drag Roman Catholicism into the modern era. In four years of meetings with 2,500 bishops from around the world, the Vatican charted a new direction. It changed its vertical chain of command for a looser structure based on consultation with local churches, and redirected its attention to the material world, especially emphasising issues like human rights, justice and freedom. The Church had a duty to pass moral judgements on the state when it contravened basic human rights.

Vatican II, as it became known, had a seismic effect on the Latin American Church, leading in 1968 to the meeting of Latin American bishops in Medellín, Colombia. Medellín took the Latin American Church far beyond Vatican II. In a new doctrine which became known as liberation theology, it identified unjust social structures with sin, and came close to justifying guerrilla warfare as a response to 'institutionalised violence':

> One cannot help seeing that in many parts of Latin America there is a situation of institutionalised violence, because the actual structures violate fundamental rights and this situation demands global changes of a bold, urgent and deeply new kind. We should not be surprised that 'the temptation for violence' arises in Latin America.

The bishops then went on to establish a new organisational model to implement these revolutionary new ideas. They suggested the setting up of Base Christian Communities (CEBs), grassroots groups of working-class or peasant Catholics who would study and reflect on the Bible and use it as a basis for action. This pastoral expression of liberation theology was called the 'preferential option for the poor'.

Medellín was a political and theological explosion. The Church abandoned nearly five centuries of largely cosy cohabitation with Latin America's elites in favour of an active commitment to the poor and oppressed. The picture varied enormously between countries; in Chile the Catholic Church became a centre of opposition to the Pinochet dictatorship, and through its *Vicaría de la Solidaridad* played a vital role in documenting and publicising the army's violation of human rights. Radicals also gained substantial influence in Brazil and Central America, whereas the Colombian and Argentine Churches remained true to their conservative past. The CEBs became a crucible for a process known as *conscientización*, whereby the poor became conscious of injustice and organised to change their lives. As one Salvadorean peasant leader recalls, many went on to lead social movements or even guerrilla organisations:

> What made me first join the farmworkers' union was when I compared the conditions we were living in with those that I saw in the Scriptures; the situation of the Israelites for example...where Moses had to struggle to take them out of Egypt to the Promised Land...then I compared it with the situation of slavery in which we were living. Our struggle is the same: Moses and his people had to cross the desert, as we are crossing one right now, and for me, I find that we are crossing a desert full of a thousand hardships, of hunger, misery and exploitation.
> Jenny Pearce, *Promised Land*, London, 1986

THE GOD OF THE POOR

You are the God of the poor,
a human and a simple God.
The God who sweats in the street,
the God of the withered face.
That's why I speak to you,
just like my people speak,
because you are the worker God,
the labouring Christ.

From the *Misa Campesina* (Peasant Mass) by Nicaraguan singer Carlos Mejía Godoy

CEBs treated the Bible as a manual for action. The story of Jesus throwing out the money-lenders acquired enormous political impact when brought up to date through a CEB Bible study group. The groups also had a democratising effect, since the shortage of priests meant that many groups were led by local lay catechists, both men and women, many of whom went on to become popular leaders in their own right. One of them was Rigoberta Menchú, a Guatemalan Indian woman who became a peasant leader and went on to win the Nobel Peace Prize in 1992. In her autobiography, *I, Rigoberta Menchú*, she describes the impact of becoming a catechist:

When I first became a catechist, I thought that there was a God and that we had to serve him. I thought that God was up there and that he had a kingdom for the poor. But we realised that it is not God's will that we should live in suffering, that God did not give us that destiny, but that men on earth have imposed this suffering, poverty, misery and discrimination on us.

CEBs took firmest root in Brazil, where they were instrumental in starting the protest movement which helped drive the military government from power in 1985. They also formed an essential part of the social movements which went on to challenge for power through the Workers' Party (PT). They played a vital role in Central America, where the radical Church supported the insurrection which overthrew the Somoza dictatorship in Nicaragua and then supplied three priest-ministers to the Sandinista government. In El Salvador, the CEBs were at the forefront of the protest movement which ended in a bloodbath in the early 1980s and a prolonged civil war.

Yet the Church paid a high price for its 'option for the poor'. Within the Church hierarchy, conservative bishops began to backtrack on the Medellín commitments almost as soon as the conference was over. Their efforts were greatly helped by the appointment of a fiercely anti-Communist Polish Pope, John Paul II, in 1978. An increasingly acrimonious dispute between radicals and conservatives threatened to divide the Church from top to bottom.

The new radical Church also became a target for repression. 'Be a patriot, kill a priest,' ran one death squad slogan in El Salvador in the late 1970s. Although dozens of clerics were killed, the most celebrated being Archbishop Romero and four North American nuns killed in El Salvador in 1980, an even

greater slaughter awaited the lay preachers, who died in their hundreds. As a result, the Salvadorean CEB movement was devastated.

Option for the poor. Open air mass in the Peruvian Andes.

By the mid-1980s, doubts were starting to surface among radical Catholics about the effectiveness of the CEBs. Field research revealed that most CEB members were not the poorest of the poor, but had steady jobs, and that many were much less socially active than had been imagined. Other studies suggested that the numbers had been greatly exaggerated – instead of the two million active CEB members routinely claimed for Brazil in the mid-1980s, 250,000 seems a more realistic estimate. In Latin America as a whole, CEBs only existed in a maximum of ten per cent of parishes, and even there such communities were small islands in a sea of Catholics whom the Church scarcely touched.

The research also showed that, far from representing a lasting transfer of power from the Church hierarchy to the laity, successful CEBs were heavily dependent on the goodwill of sympathetic bishops, the active involvement of priests and nuns at local level, and on funding from a range of foreign (usually European) church and development agencies.

Partly, the CEBs were a victim of their own success in forging generations of leaders for the new grassroots social movements. As those movements took off, many of the most dynamic CEB leaders went with them. In Brazil, large numbers of the best CEB activists devoted themselves to building up the Workers' Party, while in Nicaragua, the Sandinista revolution similarly sapped the strength of a hitherto dynamic CEB movement.

In the 1990s, the end of the Cold War freed the Catholic hierarchy from anti-Communist preoccupations, enabling it to take on many demands formerly put forward by the progressive Church, particularly in response to the social impact of neoliberal structural adjustment programmes. In 1995, Latin America's bishops concluded, 'We cannot remain indifferent to the extreme

poverty, growing unemployment, uncontainable violence and corruption
and impunity that sink millions of families in anguish and pain.' They then
attacked neoliberalism for glorifying 'market forces and the power of money.'
But by then, the grassroots movement which might have given teeth to such
statements was in decline.

A New Reformation

One of the principal causes of the disillusionment with the CEBs was the
meteoric rise of the Pentecostal Protestant Churches over the same period.
'Evangelicals', as they are commonly called in Latin America, are born-again
Christians committed to converting others to their own brand of Christianity.
Evangelical services typically involve rhythmic clapping, chanting and
swaying, leading to a cathartic mass euphoria. The most dynamic strain of
Evangelism in Latin America is the Pentecostal movement, which believes
that true Christians are taken over by the Holy Spirit during religious
gatherings, culminating in speaking in tongues and faith healing. The name
comes from a biblical reference to the 'Day of the Pentecost' (a Jewish holiday),

when Jesus' disciples were visited by the Holy Spirit and received the 'gift of tongues' to enable them to preach and evangelise in other languages.

The tide of Pentecostalism has rapidly swamped the traditional Protestant Churches of Latin America, such as the Lutherans and Presbyterians. These are small groups generally set up by immigrants from northern Europe, and have largely middle-class congregations. In 1936, Pentecostals represented just two per cent of Central American Protestants; by 1996 the figure was closer to ninety per cent.

With the exception of the Assemblies of God, which have at least seven million worshippers in Brazil alone, the Evangelical movement in Latin America is divided up into innumerable separate Churches, disparagingly labelled 'sects' by their opponents. Often these are the personal vehicle of a single pastor. When a congregation grows, it will often splinter into new Churches. Although this reduces the coherence and influence of the movement as a

A modern martyr. Ninth anniversary of the murder of Archbishop Oscar Arnulfo Romero. He was assassinated for calling on the Salvadorean army to disobey orders and end the repression of their own people.

whole, it means that Evangelical Churches remain rooted in their communities. Pastors display a zeal rarely encountered in their Catholic counterparts. In the middle of a war zone in Nicaragua in the 1980s, Evangelical pastors could be found three days from the nearest road, walking between peasant huts in search of converts. The Catholic Church was nowhere to be seen.

The social message of the Evangelicals is one of individualism, hard work and sobriety. Evangelical pastors are fiercely hostile to collective organisations such as trade unions. Critics, especially radical Catholics, have accused them of encouraging political passivity which only benefits the powerful and denies the poor the ability to organise to improve their lot. Evangelicals respond that their focus on immediate steps such as giving up drink and working hard actually has more impact than the search for long-term social change. The proof is that Evangelical Churches are far more popular than the Catholics among the poorest communities. As one famously barbed quote from a Brazilian Baptist pastor put it, 'The Catholic Church opted for the poor, but the poor opted for the Evangelicals.'

In any case, Evangelicals believe that true salvation lies in an individual's relationship to God, and, as one Costa Rican group sings, 'I've got nothing in this world, but a mansion in the next.' Carlos Chávez, a 46-year old follower of the Elim Church in San Salvador, explains: 'The Lord changes the Evangelical's life. He makes him more patient, more passive, more humble, more loving, more centred in what he does.' Carlos showed a typically Evangelical view of El Salvador's bloody civil war:

The war is the fulfilment of the prophesies – the Lord told his disciples there would be wars, plagues, famines and earthquakes, and these would be signs of his coming. As Evangelicals, the war doesn't torment us, it brings us joy, because it's a sign that Jesus is coming soon. We don't intervene in the conflict. What we do is pray to God that things should change. Today God's people don't struggle with arms, but with prayer.

Sean Sprague/Panos

Protestant evangelical preacher, Guatemala. The rise of Pentecostal Protestant groups is on the verge of creating a Latin American reformation.

This essentially conservative message contrasts with the more progressive doctrines gradually being adopted by many of the traditional Protestant Churches. Grouped together in the Latin American Council of Churches (CLAI), these groups have built ecumenical links with the more radical Catholic Church, although not endorsing the full content of liberation theology. CLAI has attempted to turn Protestant attention to issues such as the drug war and the debt crisis, but remains a small voice with very limited influence within the Pentecostal movement.

The Evangelical Churches have numerous advantages over their rivals. Worshippers have direct contact with their preacher – in 1987 in Nicaragua there was one Protestant pastor for every 92 worshippers, while there was only one priest or nun for every 3,190 Catholics. Furthermore, the preacher is much more likely to be from their own community than is the case with white, and frequently foreign, priests. Protestant preachers are adept at appealing both to the spiritual and practical needs of their flock – Jesus acts as marriage counsellor, employment agency and alcoholics anonymous group rolled into one, while church services provide song, dance, cathartic possession and the odd miracle thrown in. With its emphasis on testimony and participation, Pentecostalism empowers and involves the poor far more than difficult study classes on the causes of poverty, as well as being more fun. Ironically, Pentecostalism turns out to be in some ways more of a symbolic subversion of the traditional social order than the nominally radical Catholicism of the CEBs.

Protestant preachers and TV broadcasts tap into the anxieties of life in modern Latin America – health, jobs, crime and family breakdown. Many authors connect the rise of Protestantism to urbanisation. Peasant migration to the cities severs an individual's links to the community, resulting in isolation and confusion. In such circumstances, Evangelism can offer both a supportive community and a strong sense of purpose and identity. The emphasis on sobriety is particularly attractive to many women whose partners have alcohol problems.

Compared to the music, dance and participation of the Pentecostals, the traditional Catholic Church can seem stultifying:

My grandmother did the circuit of each saint, repeating 'forgive my sins'. I imitated everything she did, I knelt, I repeated 'forgive me, forgive me'. I had no idea what it was all about. You had to keep quiet, look at the saints without saying anything to them, pray, light candles and you can't even cough. When you left, you felt like you were emerging from a cellar, because the churches are huge, dark and full of relics and echoes. The Catholic Church made me very upset. In the Baptists we can talk normally, it is more communicative. If you want you can express all your feelings. All that stuff about imitating the prayers of the priest just seemed stupid to me.
Ana María Condori, *Mi Despertar*, La Paz, 1988, author's translation

The most recent, and fastest-growing Pentecostal churches have abandoned the more austere side of Protestantism, absorbing the icons of popular religiosity that were often dropped by embarrassed Catholic priests in the aftermath of Medellín. Especially in Brazil, the use of faith healing, magic, holy water, song, dance and possession shows the Pentecostals' readiness to adopt the trappings of the Afro-Brazilian religions, even as they vilify them as devil worship. To the outsider, Bishop Macedo's exorcist priests bear a remarkable resemblance to their counterparts in Candomblé. African religions and Evangelicals are often in conflict for the same constituencies, yet increasingly share similar methods. In Honduras, Evangelicals have made inroads among the black garifuna community on the Atlantic coast, urging them to abandon their traditional *dugú* religion. But the converts find the Evangelical services familiar. 'I used to dance for the world, now I can do it for the Lord,' explains one teenager.

In countries with large black communities, African spiritist religions are on the rise, despite the efforts of the Evangelicals. Edilson is a *paí de santo*, or Candomblé priest in Brazil's black capital of Salvador, centre of the former

TABLE 9: ESTIMATED NUMBERS OF PROTESTANTS IN LATIN AMERICA

Country	% Protestant
Chile	29
Guatemala	25
El Salvador	25
Brazil	22
Nicaragua	21
Panama	12
Honduras	11
Costa Rica	10
Dominican Republic	9
Mexico	8
Bolivia	7
Argentina	5
Venezuela	5
Peru	4
Colombia	3
Ecuador	3
Paraguay	3
Cuba	2
Uruguay	2
Latin America	14

Source: Rapidas, October 1995

slave trade. He operates from his house in a well-established favela, with two rooms devoted to Candomblé, a fascinating hybrid of African and Catholic influences. In the first room, Christ and the saints hang alongside Candomblé's African gods, or *orixás*, faceless figures of beaten copper. A set of conga drums and a large urn of holy water also stand by ready for ceremonies which combine drumming, drinking and possession by any one of the pantheon of orixás. In the second room, known as the 'room of the slave', Edilson intones a prayer in the African Yoruba language before entering to sprinkle cane spirit, or *cachaça*, over the altar and light a candle. 'People come to purify themselves when they're sick or have spiritual problems,' he explains. 'The Evangelicals are always speaking against us,' he adds, 'but the Catholics are more ready to coexist - many people here have two religions.'

Figures on the Protestant explosion should always be treated with caution. The Protestant Churches often exaggerate, while the Catholic Church suffers an equal tendency to minimise them. However, many sources accept that in the last three decades the number of Protestants in Latin America has risen twelve-fold to sixty million. Although sixty million people only represents about 14 per cent of the total population, and most of the rest describe themselves as Roman Catholics, virtually all Protestants are active churchgoers, whereas the rate among Catholics may be as low as 15 per cent. In terms of active participation, Protestants may already outnumber Catholics in several countries, leading to predictions that Latin America is ripe for Reformation.

A further source of confusion over the figures is the growing fluidity of people's religious affiliations. One recent study in Costa Rica showed that there were almost as many ex-Evangelicals as current ones. Two thirds of those leaving returned to the Catholic Church. Others happily shopped around, worshipping at both Catholic and Protestant Churches during the course of a week, as well as moving regularly between different Pentecostal denominations.

Evangelicals in Politics

Although the growth of the Evangelical Churches has fed on social chaos, suffering and the divisions within the Catholic Church, other influences have attracted severe criticism from progressives of both Catholic and Protestant backgrounds. The Latin American Evangelical movement is partly financed and heavily influenced by right-wing Evangelical groups in the US, which have sent thousands of missionaries, run aid projects which also serve as recruitment drives, and trained new generations of local pastors to spread the word. 'Televangelical' preachers like Jimmy Swaggart and Pat Robertson are household names in many Latin American nations, where the resources of the multi-million dollar Bible Belt TV and radio chains buy hours of airtime. A new breed of US-based Spanish-speaking 'super preachers' like Luis Palau and Alberto Mottesi has now joined their ranks.

One key organisation in the Evangelical crusade is the Wycliffe Bible Translators (WBT), also known as the Summer Institute of Linguistics. WBT has translated the Bible into dozens of Indian languages and trained local pastors to preach from it. An analysis by anthropologists of one of their dictionaries for the Tzotzil people of Mayan descent showed that the WBT had failed to translate political words such as 'class', 'community' or 'exploitation' despite their existence in both languages, while their examples of contexts for other words were politically loaded. They included:

Right: Man has a right to punish his children when they behave poorly
Boss: The boss is good. He treats us well and pays us a good wage.

The link between the US fundamentalist New Right and Latin America's Evangelicals has been strongest in Central America. Believers from the southern states of the US raised millions of dollars for Guatemala when General Ríos Montt seized power in 1982 to become Latin America's first Evangelical dictator. The New Right became an apologist for the Guatemalan regime as Ríos Montt launched a counter-insurgency campaign which killed thousands of civilians and wiped out whole Indian communities. Ríos Montt was a member of the El Verbo (The Word) Church, a mission of the California-based Gospel Outreach. In a video distributed by the California Verbo community, US missionary Ronny Gilmore revealed a chilling side to his work with the Guatemalan army:

One soldier in particular was an Evangelical and he said that he didn't know if God could forgive him because he had taken children and their mothers and put them into a house and then set them on fire, under orders from the captain. I shared with him God's love for him and told him that he could be forgiven.

Although some radical Catholics claim the Evangelical movement is entirely funded and controlled by Washington, many local churches have few ties to the US and the astonishing speed of their expansion shows that they meet a real spiritual and social need in the region.

The Pentecostal Church itself has so far shown little interest in politics, with some isolated exceptions to both left and right. It is undoubtedly a genuine Church of the poor, far more so than its Catholic rival, and it could undergo the same kind of radical political conversion as occurred within the Roman Catholic Church in the 1960s. There are a few signs of changes of this kind. In Chiapas, where Protestants have suffered violence and expulsion from indigenous communities at the hands of local bosses of the ruling PRI, Evangelicals came out in support of the Zapatista uprising, while there are some high-ranking Evangelicals in the Workers' Party, such as Benedita da Silva, Brazil's first black woman senator.

In general, however, the Evangelical Churches have shown little interest in turning their new popularity into political strength at national level. The main exceptions have been in Guatemala, which has provided both Latin America's first Pentecostal dictator (General Ríos Montt (1982-83)) and president (Jorge Serrano, although he was forced into exile after trying to seize dictatorial powers in 1993). Even there, however, the fragmented and apolitical nature of the Pentecostals means that the Catholic Church remains a much more coherent and powerful political force.

Conclusion

L atin America is in ferment. The signs of modernity and change are everywhere: TV and public transport have transformed the lifestyles and aspirations of all but the most isolated communities; the sharp hustling world of the city has replaced the slow seasonal cycle of rural life. Politically, the region's depressing round of dictatorship and democracy has been replaced by an unprecedented degree of political stability and civilian government. A Catholic continent is going through a breakneck process of conversion to Pentecostal Protestantism.

But scratch the surface, and there is ample evidence of continuity beneath the froth of change. Old evils persist as Latin America's system of economic apartheid, an unbridgeable gap between rich and poor, has been strengthened even further in recent years. A battery of external influences, from the IMF to the Northern governments and international capital markets, is forcing the region to adopt unregulated 'savage capitalism', an implausible remedy for the continent's social and economic ills. The region's authoritarian traditions are evident in the style of 'exclusionary democracy' which has characterised the region's return to elected government.

Other continuities provide more grounds for optimism. Latin America's extraordinary ability to absorb and transform outside influences remains undimmed. Ever since the conquest, foreign invasions, be they cultural, political or religious, have been steadily 'Latin Americanised' into distinctive syntheses of traditional and modern. Brazilians joke that their country is 'the land of the future', and always will be. The same is true of all Latin America, whose political and economic systems have squandered the region's vast wealth and human potential. Those systems must change if Latin America is to struggle free from five centuries of want and waste. With governments and the right held hostage by market economics' seemingly invincible power, the left looks like the only hope for change, yet the traditional political left is still reeling from the multiple blows of guerrilla failure, and the collapse of central economic planning, both in Latin America and the Communist bloc. Its fortunes will depend on finding a new sense of direction to replace old and discredited doctrines.

The most likely source of such a new direction stems from what Latin Americans call 'social effervescence', the ever-widening range of grassroots community groups which are struggling for immediate improvements to their lives. The range of new players is impressive – women's organisations, shanty-town movements, peasant groups, Indian federations, trade unions, environmental movements. Despite numerous obstacles, these might form the building blocks for a new left revival. Already, city-wide movements are winning municipal elections and introducing policies of local democracy and accountability which look radically different from those of the old left. This burgeoning political pluralism with its promise of empowerment offers the greatest grounds for optimism that Latin America's centuries of inequality and injustice may yet be overcome.

Further Reading

Chapter 1: The Commodity Trade
John Crabtree, Gavan Duffy and Jenny Pearce, *The Great Tin Crash: Bolivia and the World Tin Market*, Latin America Bureau, London, 1987
Eduardo Galeano, *Open Veins of Latin America*, Monthly Review Press, New York, 1973
Gordon MacMillan, *At the End of the Rainbow? Gold, Land and People in the Brazilian Amazon*, Earthscan, London, 1995
James Painter, *Bolivia and Coca: A Study in Dependency*, Lynne Rienner Publishers, Boulder CO, 1994
Nick Rowling, *Commodities: How the World Was Taken to Market*, Free Association Books, London, 1987

Chapter 2: Land Ownership, Power and Conflict
Tom Barry, *Roots of Rebellion: Land and Hunger in Central America*, South End Press, Boston, 1987
Sue Branford & Oriel Glock, *The Last Frontier: Fighting Over Land in the Amazon*, Zed Books, London, 1985
Roger Burbach and Patricia Flynn, *Agribusiness in the Americas*, Monthly Review Press, New York, 1980
Joseph Collins, *Nicaragua: What Difference Could a Revolution Make?: Food and Farming in the New Nicaragua*, Food First, Oakland CA, 1985
Alan Gilbert, *Latin America*, Routledge, London, 1990
William C. Thiesenhusen, *Broken Promises: Agrarian Reform and the Latin American Campesino*, Westview, Boulder CO, 1995

Chapter 3: The Environment
Marcus Colchester, *Guyana: Fragile Frontier: Miners, Loggers and Forest Peoples*, Latin America Bureau, London, 1997
Helen Collinson (ed), *Green Guerrillas: Environmental Conflicts and Initiatives in Latin America and the Caribbean*, Latin America Bureau, London, 1996
Susanna Hecht and Alexander Cockburn, *The Fate of the Forest: Developers, Destroyers and Defenders of the Amazon*, Penguin, London, 1990
Chico Mendes, *Fight for the Forest: Chico Mendes in His Own Words (second edition)*, Latin America Bureau, London, 1992
Bill Weinberg, *War on the Land: Ecology and Politics in Central America*, Zed Books, London, 1991

Chapter 4: Migration and Life in the City
Alan Gilbert, *The Latin American City*, Latin America Bureau, London, 1994
Duncan Green, *Hidden Lives: Voices of Children in Latin America and the Caribbean*, Latin America Bureau, London, 1997
Carolina Maria de Jesus, *Beyond All Pity: The Diary of Carolina Maria de Jesus*, Earthscan Publications, London, 1990

J.J. Thomas, *Surviving in the City: The Urban Informal Sector in Latin America*, Pluto Press, London, 1995

Peter Ward, *Mexico City*, Belhaven Press, London, 1990

Hernando de Soto, *The Other Path*, IB Tauris, London, 1989

Environment and Urbanization, biannual magazine, International Institute for Environment and Development, London

Chapter 5: Industrialisation, the Debt Crisis and Neoliberalism

Victor Bulmer Thomas, *The Economic History of Latin America since Independence*, Cambridge University Press, Cambridge, 1994

Eliana Cardoso and Ann Helwege, *Latin America's Economy: Diversity, Trends and Conflicts*, MIT, Cambridge MA, 1992

Joseph Collins and John Lear, *Chile's Free Market Miracle: A Second Look*, Food First, Oakland CA, 1995

Duncan Green, *Silent Revolution: The Rise of Market Economics in Latin America*, Latin America Bureau, London, 1995

Fred Rosen & Deidre McFadyen (eds), *Free Trade and Economic Restructuring in Latin America*, Monthly Review Press, New York, 1995

Chapter 6: Culture, Identity and Politics

Hernando Calvo Ospina, *Salsa: Havana Heat, Bronx Beat*, Latin America Bureau, London, 1995

Gabriel García Márquez, *One Hundred Years of Solitude*, Picador, London, 1978

Alma Guillermoprieto, *Samba*, Bloomsbury, London, 1990

John King, *Magical Reels: A History of Cinema in Latin America*, Verso, London, 1990

Peter Manuel, *Caribbean Currents: Caribbean Music from Rumba to Reggae*, Temple University Press, Philadelphia, 1995

William Rowe and Vivian Schelling, *Memory and Modernity: Popular Culture in Latin America*, Verso, London, 1991

Chapter 7: The State and Politics

Tessa Cubitt, *Latin American Society* (second edition), Longman, London, 1995

Oxford Analytica, *Latin America in Perspective*, Houghton Mifflin, Boston MA, 1991

Thomas E. Skidmore and Peter H. Smith, *Modern Latin America* (Third Edition), Oxford University Press, Oxford, 1992

Howard J. Wiarda and Harvey F. Kline, *Latin American Politics and Development* (Fourth Edition), Westview Press, Boulder CO, 1996

Chapter 8: The Military

Pamela Constable and Arturo Valenzuela, *A Nation of Enemies: Chile Under Pinochet*, W.W. Norton and Co., New York, 1991

Ronaldo Munck, *Latin America: The Transition to Democracy*, Zed Books, London, 1989

George Philip, *The Military in South American Politics*, Croom Helm, London, 1985

Chapter 9: Guerrillas, Social Movements and the Struggle for Change

Jon Lee Anderson, *Che Guevara: A Revolutionary Life*, Grove Press, New York, 1997

Sue Branford and Bernardo Kucinski, *Brazil: Carnival of the Oppressed. Lula and the Brazilian Workers' Party*, Latin America Bureau, London, 1995

Jorge Castañeda, *Utopia Unarmed: The Latin American Left After the Cold War*, Vintage Books, New York, 1994

Omar Cabezas, *Fire from the Mountain: The Making of a Sandinista*, Plume, New York, 1985

José Ignacio López Vigil, *Rebel Radio: The Story of El Salvador's Radio Venceremos*, Latin America Bureau, London, 1995

Jenny Pearce, *Promised Land: Peasant Rebellion in Chalatenango, El Salvador*, Latin America Bureau, London, 1986

Report on the Americas, bimonthly magazine, NACLA, New York

Chapter 10: Gender and Politics

Caipora, *Women in Brazil*, Latin America Bureau, London, 1993

Gaby Küppers (ed), *Compañeras: Voices from the Latin American Women's Movement*, Latin America Bureau, London, 1994

Jo Fisher, *Out of the Shadows: Women, Resistance and Politics in South America*, Latin America Bureau, London, 1993

Elizabeth Jelin (ed), *Women and Social Change in Latin America*, Zed Books, London, 1990

Ian Lumsden, *Machos, Maricones and Gays in Cuba: Cuba and Homosexuality*, Temple University Press, Philadelphia, 1996

Nancy Scheper-Hughes, *Death Without Weeping: The Violence of Everyday Life in Brazil*, University of California Press, Berkeley CA, 1992

Chapter 11: Indigenous Peoples

Elisabeth Burgos-Debray (ed), *I...Rigoberta Menchú: An Indian Woman in Guatemala*, Verso, London, 1984

Bartolomé de las Casas, *In Defense of the Indians*, De Kalb, Illinois, 1974

Minority Rights Group, *No Longer Invisible: Afro-Latin Americans Today*, MRG, London, 1995

Phillip Wearne, *Return of the Indian: Conquest and Revival in the Americas*, Latin America Bureau, London, 1996

Chapter 12: The Church

Phillip Berryman, *Religion in the Megacity: Catholic and Protestant Portraits from Latin America*, Orbis Books, New York 1996

John Burdick, *Looking for God in Brazil: The Progressive Catholic Church in Urban Brazil's Religious Arena*, University of California Press, Berkeley CA, 1993

Virginia Garrard-Burnett and David Stoll (eds), *Rethinking Protestantism in Latin America*, Temple University Press, Philadelphia, 1993

David Martin, *Tongues of Fire: The Explosion of Protestantism in Latin America*, Blackwell, Oxford, 1990

Index

Other books by Duncan Green

Hidden Lives
Voices of Children in Latin America and the Caribbean

In **Hidden Lives**, Duncan Green talks to children across the continent, at work and at play, on the streets and in their homes. He interviews teachers, welfare workers and parents. The result is an evocative mosaic of impressions, children's words and background narrative; a powerful and revealing insight into the lives of Latin America's children.

Based on first-hand research in Brazil, Jamaica, Peru, Colombia, Honduras and Nicaragua, **Hidden Lives** covers key issues facing children growing up in a turbulent continent. It challenges conventional wisdom on third world children, showing, for example, how those campaigning to abolish child labour often ignore children's own desires to work. It reveals how street children often lead better lives than their brothers and sisters who have stayed at home.

Building on the notion of children's rights enshrined in the 1989 UN Convention of the Rights of the Child, Duncan Green explores the lives of children through their own eyes, showing them as active protagonists in their own dramas.

Co-published in Autumn 1997 by the Latin America Bureau, Save The Children Fund UK and Cassell

Silent Revolution
The Rise of Market Economics in Latin America

Since 1982 Latin America has embarked on a profound, but almost unnoticed, economic revolution. Formerly protectionist economies from Argentina to Mexico are turning to the free market, privatization, foreign investment and exports to provide growth and prosperity.

Silent Revolution traces the roots of this transformation to the changing global economy, and the growing influence of the IMF and World Bank in the aftermath of the 1980s debt crisis.

Duncan Green contrasts the modest macro-economic successes of the new free-market model with the devastating impact on the poor, and follows the search for new popular alternatives to an economic model enshrined as 'common sense' by Latin America's ruling élite.

Co-published in October 1995 by the Latin America Bureau and Cassell

For a free copy of the Latin America Bureau's 20-page Books Catalogue write to Latin America Bureau, Dept FLA, 1 Amwell Street, London EC1R 1UL (tel 0171 278 2829, fax 0171 278 0165, e-mail: lab@gn.apc.org)

Other books from the Latin America Bureau

Green Guerrillas
Environmental Conflicts and Initiatives in Latin America and the Caribbean
A Reader – Helen Collinson (ed)

"This remarkable collection is just what we needed. Its diverse viewpoints share a respect for the rich complexity of the social/natural environment and a willingness to challenge received wisdom." Richard Levins, Professor of Population Sciences, Harvard School of Public Health

Compañeras
Voices from the Latin American Women's Movement
Gaby Küppers (ed)

"Of the utmost importance to all those interested in how women build viable movements to change their nations and themselves. A vital guide to Latin American women's activism today." Margaret Randall, author of *Sandino's Daughters Revisited*

Return of the Indian
Conquest and Revival in the Americas
Phillip Wearne

"Brings together for the first time the present condition of the forty million indigenous people of North, Central and South America. It is a long-needed work that shows the cultural diversity of the two continents as well as significant parallel historical courses." Dee Brown, author of *Bury My Heart at Wounded Knee*

Published in the USA by Temple University Press

Last Resorts
The Cost of Tourism in the Caribbean
Polly Pattullo

"Lucidly disposes of one after another of the myths about the benefits of foreign incursions [into the Caribbean]. Well-researched and often horrifying facts are interspersed with first-hand evidence." *New Statesman and Society*

Salsa!
Havana Heat, Bronx Beat
Hernando Calvo Ospina

"Ospina's touch is sure, his views salty and uncompromising... his insights into ghetto life in New York, the development of music in Colombia and the attitude of the intelligentsia are compelling." *Q Magazine*

For further information about these and other LAB books, contact Latin America Bureau, Dept FLA, 1 Amwell Street, London EC1R 1UL tel 0171 278 2829, fax 0171 278 0165, e-mail lab@gn.apc.org.
In the USA, contact Monthly Review Press, 122 West 27 Street, New York NY 10001 tel 212 691 2555, fax 212 727 3676, e-mail mreview@igc.apc.org.